T0279612

Tir

By the same author

Welsh Food Stories

Tir

The Story of the Welsh Landscape

Carwyn Graves

2024

© Carwyn Graves, 2024
Reprinted 2024

www.uwp.co.uk

British Library Cataloguing-in-Publication Data
A catalogue record for this book is available from the British Library.

ISBN: 978-1-915279-66-8

The right of Carwyn Graves to be identified as author of this work
has been asserted in accordance with sections 77 and 79 of the
Copyright, Designs and Patents Act 1988.

Cover artwork by David Wardle
Typeset by Agnes Graves
Printed and bound by CPI (UK) Ltd, Croydon CR0 4YY

The publisher acknowledges the financial support of the Books
Council of Wales.

I Sarah, gyda chariad

Contents

Foreword

Before reading this extraordinary book, I thought I knew every square yard of our eighteen acres of Ceredigion. *Tir*, as the study of our landscape through geography, history and language, is unique. Its subject, how to 'read' a landscape through the names of fields, farms, settlements and wilderness, in Welsh and in English, is exemplified by the story of our small patch of Ceredigion, and, more widely, of Cymru, and further, of any land long worked by its inhabitants. It shows how the landscape has been gradually formed over thousands of years, evolving through centuries of farming practice. The secret of its making, its fields, farms, forests and settlements, is preserved in place-names, in the terminology and the naming of our land in both our languages. In researching and writing this fascinating book, Carwyn Graves travelled the length and breadth of Wales, recording detailed local knowledge shared with him in conversations with those who live on and farm the land.

I write in the corner of a glazed oak-frame extension to our old longhouse (house and *beudy* under one long roof). *Tir* has transformed my understanding of what I see from here, the garden and long views beyond the *clawdd* – the bank between garden and field – and even more when I cross the fields. Immediately before me is the terrace we had laid, beyond it the 'lawn' (an old farmyard long grassed-over) now dotted with five fresh molehills. In the corner of the garden, beside the south *clawdd* – the hedgebank which divides our land from that of our neighbour – a small stream rises: the *llymru*, a froth on milk or water, which in Shakespearean English becomes flummery or nonsense. The *llymru* follows our border hedge downhill to become the *clettwr* – 'rough water' – thence to join the river Teifi and flow south through the town of Aberteifi/Cardigan, and out into the Irish Sea.

On the far side of the *clawdd* is Cae Blaen Cwrt, the home field. '*Cae*', I learn, is one of fifteen Welsh words for 'field', each denoting its particular purpose. From the far corner of Cae Blaen Cwrt, a gated avenue, or *rhodfa*, leads to Cae Bach. Beyond Cae Bach are the *fronnau* – steep, south-facing slopes that fall from our top fields down to the lane that borders our land. The first, Fron Blaen Cwrt, is fenced top to bottom from the next slope, Fron Felen – the golden slope, yellow with gorse. Above it lies harp-shaped Cae Delyn, and beyond, marking the farthest border of our eighteen acres, is an ancient wood of sessile oaks on a steep *fron* that falls to the public lane on the border of our land.

On the far side of the lane lies Rhos Llawr Cwrt. Looking down to this bogland on the far side of the lane, I see it with greater understanding after reading Chapter 7, *Rhos. Rhos Llawr Cwrt* is a marsh, too wet to farm, unploughed and untouched in many ways since the last Ice Age, yet occasionally grazed by wandering Welsh Black cattle, and home still to a rare butterfly, the Marsh Fritillary.

Each of the chapters – *Coed, Cloddiau, Cae, Ffridd, Mynydd, Rhos, Perllan* – looks at one type of land, its use and management. With this book's guidance, I read the land I see with a new understanding of its history, ecology, poetry, and I understand how Cors Llawr Cwrt, grazed but unploughed, has remained comparatively undisturbed to the present among the surrounding fields and woods of Ceredigion.

What is unique about Carwyn's approach is that *Tir* is not just a natural history book, but a human story told by the scientist, the ecologist and the literary man. In revealing how the landscape was made and recorded in place-name and poetry in Welsh and in English, it shows us how to read our history in every patch of land through the scientific, human and literary language that names it. I see this exemplified in the ordinary-looking scene before me. With the several disciplines Carwyn Graves offers, *Tir* teaches me to look at our land in a new way, deepening my reading of our eighteen acres of Ceredigion, and the view all the way south to Mynydd Llanllwni, and, on a rare, clear, ice-cold day like today, a glimpse to the north-east of the summit of Pumlumon, source of the Severn, the Wye, and of the legend of two of Arthur's knights, Bedwyr and Cai.

Gillian Clarke

Introduction

old mountainous Wales, the bards' paradise

Hen Gymru fynyddig, paradwys y bardd,
Pob dyffryn, pob clogwyn, i'm golwg sydd hardd;
Trwy deimlad gwladgarol, mor swynol yw si
Ei nentydd, afonydd, i fi.

O land of the mountains, the bard's paradise,
Whose precipice valleys are fair to my eyes,
Green murmuring forest, far echoing flood
Fire the fancy and quicken the blood.
From 'Hen Wlad fy nhadau', national anthem of Wales

The golden sun of early autumn is warming our backs as we pick the apples in the old orchard of Cwmyrarian, a stone's throw from the Tywi river in south-west Wales. My daughter munches a sweet one off the floor. These dozen or so straggly trees with their red-and-green bounty are all that's left of orchards on this farm that go back at least 200 years and used to be much more extensive. Kites are circling overhead, and some of the cattle in the next field are bleating impatiently. We're deep in the Welsh countryside and so much about this semi-ruined place that was once a prosperous farm chimes with the complex history of the wider landscape of this country.

On the one hand, this beautiful country of Wales – Cymru – has a landscape as intimately known, cherished and stewarded as any in the Western world, with a unique, native culture that is umbilically connected to the land. Here, deep currents and stories place real value on community and all that is local, from ancient standing stones to farming tradition. This is the home of the National Trust's first property, one of the birthplaces of the Romantic rediscovery of nature and now of the pioneering Future Generations Act. In Wales, as I'm reminded every time the national anthem is sung in a sporting fixture or Eisteddfod meet, we pride ourselves on the beauty of the 'Land' of our fathers. The land around Cwmyrarian is still farmed by a local family with deep roots here, and if I want to hear the tales that have been handed down about this place, the early nonconformists who secretly met near here and the old route across the river at low tide, there are still people in this community who can recount them.

Yet understanding the tale of the Welsh landscape is no easy task. Differing stories about the landscape run deep and, for centuries, have led to controversies of one sort or another. In many ways, the Wales of today is a blasted landscape: industrialised and polluted earlier than any other Western society. Wracked by bad management and corporate power, it is now one of the most nature-depleted countries in the world.[1] The Welsh landscape has also been despoiled in myriad ways by its governing authorities, resulting in everything from zombie conifer plantations to dead rivers and 'sheep-wrecked' hills. The beautiful stone farmhouse at Cwmyrarian now lies ruined, the people gone, while the orchard it once supported has not only been neglected but even the orcharding heritage it represents has almost been wiped from memory and the historical record, a symptom of a wider malaise.

But this small landscape that covers only 8 per cent of the UK's land area is enormously diverse in composition and contains in microcosm almost all the different sorts of habitat and terrain that exist across the British Isles.[2] Astonishingly, with 1,467 out of a total of 1,727 species, Wales has representatives of almost all the plant species present across the island of Great Britain as a whole. Given how much further north Scotland extends, and how much nearer to the Continent much of England lies, the Welsh number is surprisingly high and betrays the range of geologies and microclimates that makes Wales, Wales.[3]

Such biological diversity may also reveal something about Wales's land-use history, reflected also in the at-first-glance surprising fact that Wales has more than twenty times as much ancient woodland as nearby Ireland,

and may have as many as the whole of France.[4] But whatever may be said about this profusion of plants and land-use history, there is clearly also an important riddle to be solved related to what has happened to Wales's landscape over the past century or so of Cwmyrarian's decline. Despite the fact that there were fewer trees, smaller woodlands and a lot more industrial pollution in 1910 than now, overall levels of biodiversity as measured by bird and insect life were substantially higher.[5] Over a quarter of Wales's land area is protected either as national park or area of outstanding natural beauty, and well over 10 per cent of the land is now designated as belonging to SSSIs – sites of special scientific interest.[6] All these have come into existence over the course of the last seventy years, but the decline in wildlife has only accelerated over this period. The countryside now contains substantially less nature and substantially fewer working people than it did a century ago. To everyone I have spoken to in the Welsh countryside, both these things feel like profound failures.

What has happened here? The broad contours of what has gone wrong may well feel familiar thanks to accelerating climate change and the slow death of the natural world, but as one of the first industrialised societies, understanding the specifics of what has happened to the Welsh landscape may well help bring out wider principles. Getting under the skin of both the death of some parts of the Welsh landscape and the reasons why other parts have remained in comparatively good health seems like an important question to ask in the early 2020s.

Musing on this question, it seemed increasingly clear to me as well that there was an important aspect to it that had hardly been touched upon in English; namely the cultural attitude towards the land and landscape contained and expressed within Welsh culture. The second verse of the Welsh national anthem, reproduced above, may well at first glance reflect mid-Victorian Romantic sensibilities, but scratch deeper at both this and the wider corpus of Welsh culture and you find an attitude towards the land that differs in notable ways from that of the dominant European cultures – whether English, French, German or others.[7] This attitude, I think, is an important part of the story of the Welsh landscape as it has developed, and I wanted an account of it to be a central part of the mix as I explored its human and ecological history.

To that end I am going to draw on a broad and perhaps at times eclectic range of disciplines. I have travelled the country, mined libraries, stood in fruit-laden orchards and wet peat bogs and invited myself to farmhouses, historians' offices and conservation sites to do this. I have drawn on everything from ecological science to archaeology, myth and literature to explore the people and trees, the traditions and motivations that have shaped this homely and contested landscape. As a result, this book is about many things, including farming and conservation, literature and ecology, nature and culture. But perhaps above all it is about how Welsh attitudes to nature and place allow us to chart the tale of the Welsh landscape from the inside. There is, of course, no one essential 'Welsh' attitude to nature and the land that all inhabitants of the land share. But the distinct emphases we find in the record that has been deposited within Welsh culture for over a thousand years does contain a set of standpoints that may well have relevance for the future,[8] and that matters.

I'll argue that understanding the landscape without that nuanced cultural archive is next to impossible. Though I won't do it full justice here by any means, language and culture contain the keys to any rounded understanding of the mechanisms by which this landscape has changed – for good and ill.[9] And to that end, I want to start our tale by taking you back in time some seven hundred years.

A sense of place

The woodland has burst into song, the brilliant northern hemisphere light illuminating the green birch grove on the riverbank. Dragonflies are darting back and forth looking for mates accompanied by the song of a brown-backed nightingale:

Nid addawaf, da ddiwedd,
I'm aur ond eos a medd;
Eos gefnllwyd ysgafnllef
A bronfraith ddigrifiaith gref,
Ygus dwf, ac ystafell
O fedw ir; a fu dŷ well?

[I won't promise for this happy
ending
Nought to my golden girl
but a nightingale and mead
A brown-backed nightingale,
fair in song
A mistle-thrush with
her strong tune
And the sheltering growth
of a room
Of verdant birch; was there
ever a better dwelling?][10]

But this is no poetic fancy. The poem is located very concretely in early June in the 1340s or later 1330s in northern Ceredigion; to be more precise, in a meadow called Minafon on the bank of the river Rheidol a mile or so from the church at Llanbadarn Fawr. The poet is Dafydd ap Gwilym, serenading his lover, dark-haired Dyddgu:

Dyddgu â'r gwallt	[Dyddgu with your
lliwddu lleddf /	silky-black hair /
dy wahawdd ... i ddôl	I invite you ... to the
Mynafon ydd wyf	water-meadow at Minafon]

We know a fair amount about the individuals in question, although neither were in any way influential while alive, nor particularly wealthy even by the standards of their day. Recent scholarship has confirmed what oral tradition had in fact long maintained: that Dafydd was indeed from the house known as Brogynin, just outside the modern village of Penrhyn-coch in northern Ceredigion; that his lovers, Morfudd and Dyddgu, were almost certainly real women whom he undoubtedly knew and that the settings for his poems are contemporary reflections of the context in which he wrote.[11] We can trace Dafydd's own lineage back nine generations into the 1100s, and we know that the husband of another of Dafydd's lovers appeared in court in 1344 for a case concerning the theft of a silver cup. In some of his other poems, we can trace not only his journeys around Wales, from Newborough on Anglesey to Bassaleg near Newport, but also the woodlands, hills and homesteads of his stomping ground in the parishes of Elerch and Trefeurig.

So, when we read in this, and in many others of Dafydd's surviving poems, detailed descriptions of landforms, wildlife and countryside life, we are being led into a very concrete world: his world. The thrushes singing in the birch trees at Minafon are very much meant to be those particular thrushes in those particular trees – regardless of whether the scene depicted in the poem ever really happened or not.

Meanwhile, less than 500 miles to the south-east, the poet Guillaume de Machaut (*c.*1300–77) is also performing lyric verse set in verdant nature. One of the finest poets and composers in medieval France, he was the inheritor of the long tradition of troubadour and trouvère poetry, which created the courtly ideal of love in springtime between fair maiden and gallant knight. In line with this, Machaut's poetry is indeed highly idealised:

Rose, liz, printemps, verdure,	[Rose, lily, spring and greenery
Fleur, baume et tres douce odour,	Flower, tree and all sweet smells
Bele, passés en douçour,	Beauty, passed into sweetness,]

Here, we are not even given the names of the types of tree the poet has in mind; the mere idea of being in springtime nature has superseded any pretence of realism.[12] Given that we know Dafydd ap Gwilym and other Welsh poets of his time had been influenced by the norms of Continental love poetry,[13] might their departure from these norms, their insistence on locating their poetry in particular places and addressing them to particular people, reflect a noteworthy, even a deep-rooted cultural attitude?[14]

We encounter hints of this attitude towards land and landscape throughout the literary evidence left behind by the earliest Welsh speakers. Material remains in the form of archaeological evidence will necessarily be interpreted through the cultural lenses of those who are evaluating the finds; it's the written evidence that's the closest we can get to listening to long-gone people. And we need to listen to voices from the past in order to have any real chance of understanding the world they lived in; to assume, as we tend to do, that the present is a good approximation of the past will mean we see things through our own blinkers. Only in recent years have ecologists come to fully appreciate the importance of humility in the face of evidence from our forebears regarding the world they lived in. At times, our own experiences of the world can mis-shape our perceptions to such an extent as to not only obscure the truth but even to blind us to it.

Numerous examples of this phenomenon, called shifting baseline syndrome, have occurred in the scientific and popular literature in recent years. Defined as 'a condition whereby each new generation inherits an environment that has worsened from the generation before, producing lowered expectations for conservation and restoration', we are as Western societies starting collectively to realise just how skewed our modern, Enlightenment perspective is on the natural world.[15]

The disappearance of the passenger pigeon is a classic example of this: a bird once so abundant in North America that flocks of them would blacken the skies for days, but was hunted to such an extent that the last living member of the species, Martha, died in captivity in 1914, leading to its extinction.[16] Now, the notion that such a bird could have literally darkened the skies for days on end, given the vastness of its flocks, seems *surely* exaggerated. And yet, who was around to disprove it? Or take the more recent example of the 'windscreen phenomenon', a term given to the anecdotal observation that people tend to find fewer insects squashed on the windscreens of their cars now, compared to a decade or several decades ago. A 2019 study by Kent Wildlife Trust found that over the fifteen years since a similar study was carried out in south-eastern England by the RSPB, insects splattered on car windscreens in the region had indeed declined by 50 per cent; a precipitous decline within a short period of time but a finding sadly corroborated by an increasing number of other studies carried out in European countries in recent years.[17] If you are in your later teens and reading this, you might justifiably conclude that these accounts of your elders are coloured by rose-tinted glasses. Or are they?

When we take this as our point of departure, and start listening to voices from the past with the reality of shifting baseline syndrome in mind, we evaluate long-dead writers' descriptions of the natural world differently. Claims of massive shoals of herring in Cardigan Bay that extended for miles and miles in length, for instance, would seem mere hyperbole to anyone who has fished there for herring over the last couple of decades. But according to contemporary reports, during a single night in 1745, 1,386,500 herrings were brought into the harbour in Aberystwyth.[18] Similar catches were recorded at other times from fishing ports not just along the coast of Cardigan Bay but in other parts too. This maritime superabundance was commented upon by visitors to Wales. In 1695, one tells us that the bounty even attracted people from further field: 'upon the shore, as upon all the sea-coasts in this country, abundance of Herrings are caught, and are therefore much frequented at the season of the year by people of several nations'.[19]

The herrings attracted attention because they were a keystone part of the coastal economy, providing an important source of protein. But from an ecological point of view we can confidently assume that this herring would have supported significant populations of herring predators; not just seabirds and other fish such as salmon and halibut, but also dolphins, porpoises and seals. All of these higher order species were present in good numbers in Cardigan Bay during the twentieth century. In light of the vastly greater food sources available to them back in the seventeenth century, it is almost inconceivable that there wouldn't have been much larger populations of them in those days.

Where today you can walk all day along the coast between New Quay and Llangrannog, as I have, with eyes peeled for a sight of bottle-nosed dolphins or a harbour porpoise and not catch sight of a single one; or hike along the coastal path near St Davids during September, keeping a look out for seals in the little coves and not see any, we must assume that our forebears would have experienced them as ubiquitous as the sparrows darting past my study windows as I write this today. Recent estimates have it that 10,000–15,000 years ago our planet had 'ten times more whales, twenty times more anadromous fish, twice as many seabirds, and ten times more large herbivores'.[20]

This discipline of listening can be extended further: beyond records of fish-catches to more diffuse evidence captured in throwaway comments by writers and commentators of all sorts, in folk tales, sayings, place-name evidence, songs and poetry. The species of animal, bird, insect, and tree, flower or fern that surrounded these writers formed – as they do for us – an accepted backdrop to life. So when Dafydd ap Gwilym in the corpus of 151 poems he left behind describes a landscape and a setting that is instantly recognisable to us, we should sit up and pay attention. When he names places, almost all of which are easily identifiable houses, farms, streams, bogs or other existing landscape features today, and describes the views, vegetation and wildlife that inhabited those locations, we find ourselves in the enviable position of being able to listen to a voice from 700 years ago.

And as we would expect, though it's a familiar landscape, it's also a different world. Dafydd sings a poem to the roe deer, a familiar and important creature in the Welsh landscape in his day. By the end of the eighteenth century this species had disappeared from the country and has only in recent decades re-established a stronghold along the border with England. Similarly, his evocation of a nightingale singing at Minafon might have been dismissed by twentieth-century literary critics as a flight of poetic fancy influenced by the poetic tropes of his day. But it could just as well be explained by a realisation that the natural world of Dafydd's day was rich with much wildlife that we have since lost.

This realisation – that so much of the living world in the West has been lost within the span of a couple of human lifetimes – has created much of the impetus towards the policy of rewilding in recent years, touted as a broad-based solution. The basic logic of the current ecological crisis is that wherever humans get involved, nature loses out, and the awe and wonder of life on Earth gets trashed. When presented and understood this way, the most obvious solution is therefore to say that humans should get out of the way; we have it in our power to set aside space for nature to flourish, and for it to have any chance of doing so we must do exactly that.

Wales has recently become something of a focal point for rewilding initiatives and debates. It has long been perceived from the outside as a place of unproductive hills and mountains, where poor sheep-farmers eke out a living from barren acres. Much of the country lies within a couple of hours' drive of densely populated parts of England, providing the denizens of Liverpool and the Midlands with their nearest space to get away from it all in the clear mountain air. Widely publicised conservation successes, such as the survival of the Red Kite in mid Wales and the reintroduction of ospreys to the Dyfi estuary, seem to confirm that this sparsely populated swathe of hilly landscape that forms the backbone of Wales is the ready-made locale in the southern half of the UK for an acceleration of nature restoration.

But despite eloquent and high-profile calls for ambitious rewilding projects to transform the 'sheep-wrecked' uplands south of Machynlleth into an oasis of life stretching from shore to sea, most of the local community was nonplussed. In fact, opposition to the project grew to such an extent that, in 2019, the 'Rewilding Britain' charity pulled out and the plans for this flagship venture were shelved. And although there has been some opposition to similar projects in parts of England and Scotland, the toxicity with which rewilding has become associated in Wales is particularly marked. The Welsh response could be dismissed as merely an understandable knee-jerk defensive reaction by sheep-farmers who perceive a material threat to their livelihoods and way of life. But why has the term and the idea become an item of scorn within rural Wales in general and within Welsh-speaking culture, well beyond farming circles?

This is where we return to Machaut and Dafydd ap Gwilym and their contemporaries. Two poets writing at the same time and influenced by the same broad currents of European love poetry, but who had profoundly different cultural relationships with the natural world. To Dafydd, it was second nature to set his amorous scene beside a particular stream, in a meadow he knew and surrounded by species of bird and plant that he was able to name. To Machaut, all this was beside the point. What mattered was the universal; not the local. But what was true for Dafydd was also true of his predecessors and successors: we are dealing here with deep-rooted and differing cultural attitudes, rather than just individual foibles.

Brodorol

So what is this Welsh cultural attitude and why does it matter so much in a book about the history of the landscape? In summary, it is the deeply held conviction that the land and its people are inextricably intertwined. In Welsh, the term *brodorol* (the dictionary equivalent of 'indigenous', but which carries its own connotations in Welsh) is almost universally used for describing our own culture's status on its own territory – *o Fôn i Fynwy* ('from Anglesey to Monmouth', as the common saying goes). Within the Welsh-speaking world, the idea that the Welsh are the native inhabitants of this land has in fact been the cornerstone on which much of the rest of the culture and its self-understanding have been built.[21] This is not an understanding that seeks to exclude others: as has been extensively demonstrated, the primary barriers of inclusion and exclusion within this culture lie with language (rather than, for instance, race or ethnicity), a feature that anyone can learn and therefore be included.[22] And this sense of nativeness manifests itself in a tendency to tie almost all parts of culture to place.

People are traditionally – and still today – known by the name of their house, village or farm (Bob Tynddol – 'Bob of Meadow House' or Olwen Maesberllan – Olwen of Orchard Field), to the point where surnames may not be known or remembered in conversation. Poets, preachers and popstars are known as sons or daughters of their valley or village, even when they have spent most of their lives elsewhere. And more importantly, this identification with place extends to the natural features of that locality even when this often amounts to no more than a grand poetic fallacy. My grandfather, to pick but one example close to home, spent his childhood and teenage years on a self-sufficient smallholding in the hills of north Pembrokeshire, but spent almost all the rest of his long life in urban south Wales. Nevertheless, in his funeral he was eulogised as being 'one of the independent-minded people of that stretch of moorland hilltop stretching from Blaenwaun to Tegryn, where the eye sees for miles'.

We can get further under the skin of this attitude and its relevance to nature (and rewilding) by considering two more key words in Welsh. These are *cynefin* (habitat) and *diwylliant* (culture). *Cynefin* is the normal Welsh word for habitat, used of animals and insects as the word habitat is used in English. But it has a wider semantic range and much greater resonance than the English word. Part of the word's meaning is the stretch of mountain or hillside on which a flock of sheep is settled or to which it is 'hefted' (to use a good English word with similar resonance). It is also commonly used in everyday speech to refer to a person's own native area, where it holds the sense of home town or stomping ground. In other words, the language itself naturally associates wild species' relationship to their ecological niche with domesticated animals' home range and people's own deeply rooted sense of home. And this is no new phenomenon: the fifteenth-century poet Guto'r Glyn talks of 'fy nghartref, fy *nghynefin*' – 'my home and my habitat/stomping ground/native area/happy place [perhaps]'.

Diwylliant, the Welsh term normally translated as 'culture', derives from a common verb, 'diwyllio' – which could be translated as 'to cultivate', 'improve', 'farm' or 'plough', and is used both to refer to human culture and to agricultural practice. In this, it is not dissimilar to the etymology of the English terms (which derive from the Latin), but in Welsh the word quite transparently is formed of 'di' + 'wyllt' + 'io', with the middle element 'wyllt' meaning 'wild', and the 'di-' more or less equivalent to English 'un-'.

Welsh culture is also defined within the language as encompassing all the works of human hands, not merely 'popular' or 'high' culture. The writer, Margaret Davies, in her foreword to a volume of poems by the farmer-poet Isfoel in 1965, offered this inclusive definition:

> an artist is someone who makes things, whether he fash-
> ions a blade for a scythe, carves a wooden spoon, turns a
> pair of horseshoes, works wood to make a beautiful cup-
> board or dresser, or indeed composes verse – *englyn and cy-
> wydd* – or song. Significantly, we speak of 'carving' verse.[23]

Culture is considered as a collective endeavour to which everyone contributes – whether farrier, carpenter, poet, shepherd or farmer.

So, the collective work of culture, in Welsh, is 'un-wilding' and to

till land is to 'unwild' it. By this measure, the idea of turning over vast
tracts of hill country to nature by removing farming and farmers from
the picture, as rewilding has often been presented by the media, is the
very antithesis of all that rural Welsh culture has stood for. For speakers
of a language where the talk is always of defending and upholding
a threatened culture, to talk of 'rewilding' sounds very much like
'killing [a] culture'. Little wonder then that projects set upon buying
land with the stated aim 'of restoring land to a wilder state to create a
functioning ecosystem where natural processes dominate by carrying
out habitat restoration, removing domestic livestock, and introducing
missing native species as far as feasible' have been viewed with little but
antipathy in rural Welsh-speaking Wales.[24]

Restoration?

Although there is no universally accepted, non-technical definition
of rewilding,[25] the above definition captures much of the way it has
been discussed and understood in the UK. Of the three elements listed
– habitat restoration, removing domestic livestock and introducing
missing native species – the first is uncontroversial, and is similar to
conventional nature conservation as practised in the West for decades.
The other two elements are where things get unstuck, as they are seen
as the means by which land can be 'restored' to a wilder state. This is
where a deeper understanding of both natural history and culture is
key to avoiding false choices and fruitless shouting matches.

In Wales, as elsewhere, nature has diminished almost whichever way
you go about counting. Yet as we have seen, this has happened while the
amount of land set aside for nature has increased enormously. In 1950
conservation was a new and marginal discipline; none of the Welsh
national parks or national nature reserves had been established (the
first NNR, Cwm Idwal, was designated in 1954), and the numerous
monitoring projects of insects, birds or marine life that now provide
such a contribution to our understanding of nature had almost all yet
to be started.

Nevertheless, there is no question that nature in Wales – and indeed
across Europe and the world – was in a markedly better place in 1950
than it is now. The reasons for the decline in nature are manifold, but this
truth hints at an important insight: seeking to conserve or restore nature
in pockets of land or sea set aside for it is far too small a thing to make a

real difference. We can understand this better by looking at it from the other side: what was it about the way the land and seas were managed before 1950 that was so good for nature, and that we clearly seem to have lost since then? More than anything else, the answer lies in farming.

It is a truism to say that Wales is a domesticated land; but this also misses an essential point. To claim that the Welsh landscape is *domesticated* implies, as do proponents of rewilding, that the land used to be wild and that people at a certain point – perhaps when they cut down all the trees to start farming – stopped it from being wild any longer. This idea, reflected in the trope of a primeval wildwood in which a squirrel could jump across the country from tree to tree without touching the ground, has become increasingly untenable as our understanding of both ecology and prehistory have improved.

Until around 12,000 years ago, almost the whole of Wales was covered by a blanket of ice with only parts of the south coast from Pembrokeshire to Gwent jutting out from under the ice sheet. Sea levels were significantly lower than today, meaning that what is now the Severn estuary was a broad coastal plain stretching away to the south-west, ultimately connecting Wales and the rest of Britain to both Ireland and the Continent. Over these treeless expanses of tundra, similar to modern-day northern Siberia, roamed woolly mammoths and other species able to survive in Arctic conditions. Humans lived further south in what is now the middle of France, venturing north on seasonal hunting trips.

As the ice receded northwards, vegetation and animal life started recolonising the land that was revealed beneath. People followed, exploiting the new opportunities for food and resources opened up by these virgin lands. The very first sites with evidence of human activity in Wales after the last glacial maximum (often called the last 'Ice Age') are unsurprisingly coastal, including places like Nab Head in Pembrokeshire and Burry Holm in Gower; both date to around 10,500 years ago (8,500 BC). With the lower sea levels at the time, these would have been prominent hills within reach of the shore, dominating the coastal plains.

Inland, as the climate warmed, vegetation would have returned to the land, following a successional pattern with smaller shrubs followed by pioneer tree species such as birch, willows and juniper. These created niches for birds to nest and will have provided some food for them as well. Air-borne insects will also have almost immediately taken advantage of the vast new habitats, and all this will have allowed varied populations of both herbivores and carnivores to follow.

And from the very start, as the land was being colonised by these species, humans followed. These humans affected the ways the different species interacted both with each other and with the land. These early inhabitants of the British Isles were not farmers – farming techniques only arrived a couple of thousand years later – but it is now understood that hunter-gatherer populations always influence the ecosystems in which they live in profound ways, through hunting, poaching and by causing significant fear reactions in their prey.[26] And in the case of the animal and bird species that recolonised the British Isles after the ice, they had all existed alongside hunting humans for millennia in the glacial refuges further south in Europe; these were not native populations that had yet to learn to adapt to the threats – and opportunities – humans offered. The behaviour patterns and population levels of animal species, and in particular large herbivores, also have dramatic effects on the rest of the ecosystem, and raise questions as fundamental as whether a stretch of land is forested or grassland – which is decided to a great extent by the presence and behaviour of grazing and browsing animals. This means that humans were directly and indirectly influencing these new post-glacial ecosystems in the British Isles from the first. There was no period, either of hundreds or thousands of years, of undisturbed nature colonising the land before humans came on the scene to mess everything up; rather, humans were not only part of the picture, but were shaping it from the very beginning.

Here it may be helpful to consider recent transformations in the way we understand native people's effects on other parts of the world often considered 'wild' or 'untouched' by westerners, such as the Amazon. Whereas Western colonial explorers heralded their discoveries of the Americas, Australia or inland Africa as the opening up of new, virgin frontiers for human exploitation, the reality was that these places were nothing of the sort. Indeed, humans are probably responsible for much of the vegetation currently seen in central Africa, even in seemingly virgin areas.[27] At base, this is down to human ingenuity: over countless generations, decision by decision – to hunt this species or forage that one, to burn this patch or avoid that spot, to favour these eggs and ignore those – we shape our environments in our favour. And this is before we even consider the impact of farming, where we deliberately clear patches of land to grow plants we deem useful and domesticate certain animals for the benefits they bring us, allowing their needs to further shape our relationship to the land. As a result, even in areas such as Australia or Amazonia, where indigenous people have never chosen to adopt a farming way of life, even apparently wild forests are marked by extensive human occupation and alteration that are now imprinted on their ecology.[28] This is not to belittle the utterly extraordinary abundance of wildlife of every sort in these rainforests; only to underline that to call them 'wild' is in many ways entirely beside the point: they are human landscapes.

Cultural landscape

The idea of a human landscape is nothing new, but it has been strangely slow in catching on in the English-speaking world. The term 'cultural landscape' is in fact a translation of the German *Kulturlandschaft*, which originated with a former professor of geography at the University of Halle, Otto Schlüter (1872–1959). He proposed in 1908 that geography as a discipline ought to be framed as 'landscape science', and that its major task was to understand and trace the changes in landscapes as either human landscapes or natural landscapes.[29] A widely quoted summary of this by American Carl Sauer has it that in a Kulturlandschaft (a now common term in central Europe for the landscapes of Germany and the Alps) 'culture is the agent, the natural area is the medium and the cultural landscape is the result'.[30] In other words, we need to appreciate that a great many landscapes (in fact, the majority of the world) are cultural creations, where human ways of life and decisions work through the medium of nature to create what we see and know as the landscape.

Beyond their creation, ecologists have recently come to appreciate just how essential people, and in particular local, native people, also are for the preservation of these landscapes – from the Amazon to central Africa and beyond. Despite major efforts by conservation organisations and governments to protect nature by setting aside land for reserves and national parks free from human influence over the last half century, we are now learning with the benefit of hindsight that the areas best protected from deforestation are those where native populations have remained on the land and have been given title to it. Although it runs counter to the policy orthodoxy of recent decades, this is hardly surprising.[31] It seems that to protect biodiversity, the single best thing we can do is protect the ways of life (or cultures) of those people who have lived alongside and within this biodiversity for centuries or millennia.

We see the same phenomenon partly at play if we compare Welsh nature pre-1950 with 2020. And older cultural evidence, coupled with an appreciation of shifting baseline syndrome, tells us that nature was in an even more bounteous state if we shift the dial back to 1850, even though more of the country was farmed then than is farmed now. Farming itself is clearly not the problem, and government protection of nature is clearly far from a sufficient solution.

Just as in the biodiversity hotspots of the global south today, the key to understanding the abundance of Welsh nature up to the mid-twentieth century lies in the ways of life and culture of the people who created the Welsh landscape, alongside a nuanced reading of the influence of power dynamics and state policy. The landscape that had evolved in Wales over millennia since the last glacial maximum was a cultural landscape. The species that were present in abundance – from insects through to birds, mammals, trees, flowers and marine life – were all in a state of dynamic equilibrium with humanity and people's ways of managing the land. And it was ultimately the shifts that took place in our ways of life, which affected the ways we related to and managed land from the early twentieth century onwards, that upset this equilibrium.

I will unpack this large claim throughout the rest of this book, as I look in turn at the major features of the Welsh landscape, past and present: *cae* fields, *clawdd* hedgerows, *coed* woodland, *ffridd* hillside, *rhos* scrubland, *mynydd* rough grazing and *perllan* orchard. These then open the door to other associated terms (maes, gwaun, allt, gwern, etc.), explored in the relevant chapters, that give texture and nuance to our understanding of these key features of our land. There are of course other important elements in the Welsh landscape, from rivers and lakes through to coal tips and motorways, but these seven and the many other associated landscape terms we will encounter contain between them most of the history of how humans have primarily shaped this landscape through their food needs over the last 10,000 years or so.[32]

We will see that each element bears a double mark: on the one hand, a human creation, put in place for human reasons and for our benefit within a distinct culture; and on the other hand, parts of nature, native to this part of the world and harbouring incredible, abundant life. And in almost every one of these landscape features we will see that one of the prime influences was grazing animals – domesticated grazing animals. These, managed in traditional ways, were sufficient to create the conditions that allowed all the other species – wildflowers, butterflies, birds and so much else – to thrive in the numbers they did into living memory.

This way of life – an ancient farming culture that was for the most part discarded by government diktat and ignorance – contains within it an enormous amount of knowledge that shows how people can inhabit this part of the world right in the middle of flourishing nature. This knowledge is the intimate knowledge of place and all its inhabitants – human and non-human – that had built up and evolved over the generations that have lived here from the time the ice retreated to the twentieth century. It is knowledge encoded in names and sayings, place-names, values and stories that may contain echoes of ecological events that took place millennia ago.[33] Interest is growing in the role indigenous knowledge has to play in counteracting shifting baseline syndrome, and in giving all of us a stable baseline of ecological abundance for particular places, even in the face of undoubted losses over coming decades due to climate change.[34] For North American First Nations as for Nigerian tribes, the knowledge of their land encoded in their cultures and languages should be the first place to consider for an understanding of what it looks like to live sustainably in those places. In Wales, some of that knowledge lies in the old, rooted and highly literary Welsh language and culture.

So, in this book, I want to present the human and natural ecology of Wales through the lens of that culture – its sayings, its myths, its references and resonances, and its understanding of places and place.[35] This also means that I have picked the landscape elements I explore through the lens of that culture – which means human land use, a farmer's and forager's eye – rather than purely through the lens of ecology; I will look at the land by means of its native names and their significance. I am not claiming that each of these words is in some sense untranslatable – though *ffridd* and *rhos* to all intents and purposes are into English. But even *coed*, *mynydd* and *perllan* (woodland, mountain and orchard according to a standard Welsh–English dictionary) as words refer to places in a slightly but significantly different way to the English terms, the understood meaning and connotations being broader, narrower or simply divergent.

If I were writing in Welsh, there would of course be nothing more natural in the world than to refer to these assumed understandings, and I would be in good company in exploring the land in this way. Since I am writing in English, there will be times when I will be trying to fit square pegs into round holes; as the Italians put it, *traduttore traditore* – translation is treason. But the time is now overdue for an exploration of Welsh nature and landscape from within the culture.[36] I am standing in the company of two wonderful adopted Welsh people as I do so – Jan Morris's *The Matter of Wales* went to the heart of the culture in a way that perhaps only she could do, and William Condry's *Natural History of Wales* is a classic of the genre, in no small part due to that Birmingham lad's deep sympathy for the people as well as the wildlife of this country. But both these books were the products of the early 1980s and much has changed since then. In ecology, so much of what is crystal clear now about the damage Western civilisation has done to the natural world was only starting to impinge on nature writing then. In terms of Welsh culture, in a time before Wales's political institutions had even been born, before battles for linguistic rights, S4C and much else had been won, Morris may well have been supposing she was writing an elegy to something that was fast falling away, rather than mutating.

This is a book about how the Welsh landscape in all its beautiful variety is at base just as much a human cultural creation as a natural phenomenon. In an era of climate grief and polarising debates on land use, diet and more, it matters that we understand the world we are in and can evaluate intelligently the roads we travelled to get here. A deep dive into Welsh history and ecology will show us that there really can be stunningly beautiful, richly biodiverse landscapes in these latitudes, that are both ten times richer in wildlife than they currently are but are still full of humans working the land. We know this is possible for the simple reason that this is how most of Wales always was throughout human history.

2

Coed

Native woodland/timber, food, shelter, rough grazing

According to the stories we all tell ourselves, the verdant, rich, majestic woodland surrounding me simply shouldn't exist. I am on a mountainside at nearly 500m above sea level, in the heart of a post-industrial landscape that was despoiled by slag, smoke and coke earlier than almost any other. Locals were already bemoaning deforestation here five centuries ago, and over the birdsong the sounds of a tip blare out loud and clear. But I am standing among the sinuous trunks of an ancient, natural beechwood, the highest occurring beechwood anywhere in the British Isles, and only one valley over from the highest native ancient woodlands of all in these islands.[37] Around me wheatears' chirping is accompanied by the cuckoos' eager welcome of a warm May day, and bluebells still carpet the dappled glades.

This is Coed Tynygelli in Cwm Merddog, a high-lying valley that opens out into the valley of the Ebbw, home to the ex-mining communities of Ebbw Vale, Beaufort and Waun-lwyd. We're near the heads of the valleys, now some of the most deprived communities in the whole of Wales, with joblessness in many cases running into the third generation. Heavy industry in the form of iron started in these upper eastern valleys decades earlier than the coal-mining boom that made the Welsh valleys famous; industry had time to delve deeper here. But these beechwoods, and the neighbouring high-altitude oakwood of Coed Cefn-y-crug a couple of miles away survived all that.[38] Both these unknown but singularly important woodlands are also grazed by livestock, now often regarded in the popular imagination as being fundamentally inimical to woodland flourishing. It looks like the native woodlands of the post-industrial south Wales valleys have a story or two to tell.

A tale of trees

Apart from humans, trees are without doubt the central living creatures in the Welsh landscape. Their presence or absence from particular sites has always been a matter of prime importance for people and nature, reflected in our day in intense debates about the pros and cons of afforestation and deforestation. Today, 15 per cent of Wales lies under tree cover,[39] including important stands of the globally rare temperate rainforests.[40] But a large proportion of these modern woodlands is twentieth-century conifer plantations, the proportion of ancient woodland standing at 4.5 per cent of the country's total area. These two figures cut to the heart of the matter, because not all woods are created equal.

The importance of trees to the well-being of both people and the rest of the living world can hardly be overstated, and in both cases the older those trees and the ecological community that depends on them, the better. Large mature trees standing by themselves, whether oak, ash or chestnut, can create habitat and food for a bewildering array of species. On their trunks in the moist, damp Welsh climate grow some of the richest communities of lichen in the world, sporting a bright range of colours from electric yellow through burgundy to fifty-odd shades of grey.[41] Below the tree lies a community of fungi, some microscopic and others covering an area of many metres; if this mature tree (let's call it an oak) has neighbours further down the hillside, we now know that some of these fungi will have created a communication route for the trees to share both information and nutrients with each other. And then the branches and leaves provide home and sustenance to perhaps five hundred or so species of insect: mites, thrips, springtails, woodlice, centipedes, beetles, butterflies and moths of every description.[42]

Feeding on these and nesting in the branches or nearby will be an entire chorus of birds: pied flycatchers, treecreepers, nuthatches, wood warblers, chiffchaff, whitethroats, and so many more. The massive shedding of acorns in a mast year then gives food for squirrels, voles, woodpigeons, pigs and a community of predators dependent on these smaller birds and mammals. And above and beyond this, our old oak on its Welsh hillside also acts as a carbon sink and oxygen generator, drawing down carbon dioxide from the atmosphere and locking it in its body as it releases oxygen. None of this is unique to Wales, but the concentration of ancient and veteran trees here, and the mild Atlantic climate, mean that the particular year-round pattern of tree-dependent life here and in adjacent parts of the British Isles is incredibly rich.[43]

This intense abundance of life is also true – though with some important differences – of an intact, ancient woodland comprised of oaks alongside perhaps ash, hazel, holly and a range of other species. It is not, however, true of a young oak tree newly planted, or indeed of an entire plantation of young oak trees. However you measure it – biomass, number of species, number of rare species – the abundance of life supported by newly planted woodland is orders of magnitude less than that of an established woodland or tree, and even after decades of growth is still significantly less than in older, naturally occurring woods.[44] Not only are planted trees and woodlands – of whatever species – usually protected by plastic tree-guards that are frequently forgotten about and left on the tree to eventually become just one more piece of plastic pollution in the countryside, they are also highly vulnerable to browsing by deer, sheep or other animals, meaning the failure rate can easily be as high as 30 per cent or more. There is something about naturally occurring, native woodlands that is qualitatively different to plantations – whether those plantations are of native or alien species, such as the conifers that now form almost half the woodland in Wales.

Conifer trees in their massive plantations are by historical standards complete newcomers on the Welsh scene (although there is some evidence that Scots pine may have been present in Wales in ancient times at altitude). Planted from before the First World War onwards on moorlands and hillsides across Wales, with the Sitka spruce (named after the town of Sitka, Alaska) leading the charge, these forests provide shelter and food for very few members of the natural community in this part of the world. They are also able to give you the bizarre and slightly unsettling sensation of being in a silent woodland in spring – quite without the help of pesticides.[45] Taking the perspective of the last 10,000 years, the sixty or so years that have seen large numbers of fairly mature conifer plantations cover swathes of Wales are little more than the blink of an eye that may not have much longer to run. Even now, as some areas of former conifer wood are being abandoned and allowed to succeed naturally, the pines are losing ground to older moorland species such as heather and bilberry. As the climate heats up over the coming decades, rendering most of Wales too warm for these cold-loving trees, they may fade out of the picture almost as fast as they arrived. Or, as we shall see later, they may further colonise the landscape to the detriment of both wild species and local people.

The current conifer blip aside, *coed* in Wales on the whole means and has meant broadleaf woodland. There are some long-present evergreens – juniper, yew and holly – but these find their place in and amongst the larger broadleaf trees, which have long called the tune. But did these native trees formerly blanket the landscape with woodland? This is a key question that has moved from being an academic argument of interest to landscape historians, to being at the centre of the current high-stakes debate about land use and climate change. If, as has long been supposed, Wales and the rest of the British Isles were covered for thousands of years by continuous, unbroken expanses of deciduous woodland with perhaps only the highest peaks and moorlands emerging from this primeval treescape, then that must be the natural state of the country. And, if this was the state of nature, whatever came to change it is guilty of disturbing the 'natural' ecosystem. We have here a fall from natural grace narrative: undisturbed natural woodland – perhaps dominated by oaks – thriving for thousands of years before people came and started chopping all the trees down so as to farm the land.[46]

The truth about historic tree cover in Wales, as best we can ascertain it, is much more nuanced than this. Tree cover is and has always been an essential component of the post-glacial Welsh ecosystem. But it has fluctuated significantly over the last 12,000 years since the ice receded, in complex and varying ways. Archaeology and paleoenvironmental evidence from pollen samples coupled with a better understanding of how ecosystems work have moved us away from this model of a stable primeval wildwood rapidly cleared during the Iron Age after the advent of agriculture and metal tools. In its place they have given us a much more textured understanding of what unfolded, and the key role that humans played not just in clearing woodland, but also in maintaining it; the dovetailing of Wales's natural and cultural history.

Let us return to the fading centuries of the last Ice Age, some 10,000 years ago. We are among the crags of Eryri (Snowdonia), standing on a rocky slope, later to be called Moel Meirch near Snowdon itself. It is mid-spring and the sun is now riding high in the sky, but it is still biting cold as a cruel easterly wind tears down the valley. Around us the high mountain cwms still have vestige glaciers; shadows of their former selves, they are reminders of the 120,000 years that this landscape has been crushed on and off by ice. The past 2,000 years have seen a rapid thaw, century by century, and there are now established communities of alpine and arctic plants including mosses, willow herb and flowers such as purple saxifrage. Increasingly, these are being joined by intrepid shrubs and hardy pioneer trees such as juniper and sea buckthorn that are establishing a foothold in this newly ice-free land. Pollen records from this period in Snowdonia – the ecological history of which has been well studied – suggest that these shrubs and dwarf trees managed to form woodland communities quite quickly in the more sheltered valleys, while grassland and moorland plants were establishing themselves on some of the higher slopes. These supported mountain hares, arctic foxes, voles and other small land mammals, in the company of birds such as ptarmigan, partridges, mute swans and ravens.[47] Several hundred years of unsteady warming later,[48] and birches are starting to appear for the first time thanks to their light, wind-borne seeds: the first true trees. They rapidly proliferate in the landscape, alongside willows, mountain ash (brought north by birds flocking to these new woodlands) and a variety of ferns. Where these trees form communities they throw too much shade for juniper, meaning it clings on only on higher ground and steeper slopes.

And in the wake of these early trees comes hazel. But though hazel trees are very much able to colonise new territory by recruiting mice, squirrels and other animals to spread their chunky nuts, their sheer abundance in the post-glacial British Isles may have much more to do with their recruitment of – and usefulness to – humans. We have seen how humans were already present on what is now the Welsh coastline before this period, and although the earliest archaeological records of human presence in the mountains themselves date from a few thousand years later, known hunting sites from this early period encircle Snowdonia. This era of human history is known as the Mesolithic, and is usually considered to last from around 10,000 BC to around 4,000 BC in the British Isles. Some of these north Walian sites include post holes, used without doubt to hang meat for butchery of animals and perhaps skin drying. These early inhabitants of the land were clearly familiar with its contours and the resources it offered and made good use of it. One of the most important relationships they had was with red deer, which provided meat, fur, bone and, in all likelihood, ritual significance. To understand the full significance of the arrival of hazel and what it tells us about humans and the landscape, we need to think about deer.

Already during the preceding millennia of recolonisation, humans seem to have formed habits around spring and autumn hunting when the large mammals present in this thawing Wales – prime among them deer – formed large herds. Exploiting animals in a herd is a complex logistical challenge, but as herds tend to follow predictable patterns in their migrations, weaker or more vulnerable members can be targeted by a hunter and an even easier and more lucrative target can be formed from grouping together a large number of animals.[49] So hunting groups developed interception sites between two hills or cliffs where herds could be funnelled through, targets identified and a good kill would be fairly certain. Some of these sites in Wales are likely to have included the places now known as Breiddin and Gwernvale in the Powys uplands.[50]

As deer move in herds, graze, browse trees and respond to threats such as humans, they adapt the ecosystem in which they live even as their numbers and behaviours are also shaped by their environment. They prefer some shrubs more than others, and although they eat and enjoy a wide variety of deciduous leaves and shoots, as soon as these become woody, the deer switch their diet to other plants or fruits and seeds. Browsing by any livestock can seriously retard or prevent woodland regeneration, so the very fact of deer presence would have been sufficient to cause further loss of woodland.[51] And knowing the deer's browsing habits, humans encouraged the development of open areas with those young shoots and leaves by burning the forest edges to increase the area of land suitable for browsers such as deer.

Pollen samples from this period at several sites around Wales confirm this pattern, such as Waun Fignen Felen on the Black Mountain at the head of the Swansea valley. On this high plain situated around 450m above sea level, Mesolithic tree cover seems to have been patchy, with tracts of open ground. Without the presence of humans and grazing animals, the climate was warm enough by this period to ensure continuous tree cover. But this place seems to have been the site of a favoured hunting ground for the early inhabitants of this region, with human artefact finds dating to around 10,500 years before present followed by other finds from the following couple of millennia. Analysis of the pollen deposits here show that, from as early as 8,000 years ago, local heathland and open birch woodland were being burnt to encourage large game.[52] This would have been a canny strategy to adopt, born out of the hunters' close observation of the vegetation's response to fire – rapid regeneration bringing fresh growth – and large game's preference for more open spaces and the forage brought about by fire and regeneration. This was early landscape engineering that depended on an intimate knowledge of the ecological dynamics of these early inhabitants' home.

Hazelnuts were found on the same site in associated deposits, because both hazel and heather are resistant to burning in a way that birch and other species are not.[53] In other words, people had a particular preference both for deer and for hazel and seem to have worked out that there was a fortuitous approach to managing sites – namely the use of fire – that favoured both the animal and the tree species, with heather appearing as a tell-tale side-effect. And we can be fairly confident that the evidence for burning that turns up time and again in the paleoenvironmental record for this era is down to direct human involvement. As the eminent landscape historian Oliver Rackham put it, the native woods of Britain will not catch fire in any other way – 'broadleaved woodland burns like wet asbestos'.[54] So this human intervention is probably in no small part why hazel spread north through the British Isles when it did.[55] Their rapid spread and clear appearance in the pollen record from around this time (9,000–8,000 years before present) couldn't have happened without the influence of humans and the grazing and browsing herbivores they hunted; the stands of closed elm and lime woodland would have outcompeted the smaller hazel trees.

Hazels – *coed cyll* – are in many ways a uniquely useful tree in mild temperate climates like Wales. Whereas the tropics are blessed with an abundance of nut-bearing trees that provide people and animals with a rich and dependable source of protein and fat, very few trees in northern temperate climates do this. Almonds need a Mediterranean climate to thrive, while chestnut and walnut trees spread with the help of the

Romans. Acorns and beech mast, though a key part of the human food chain via pigs, are inedible to humans without very substantial processing. Hazelnuts on the other hand are a good source of energy, being rich in unsaturated fats, trace elements including the antioxidant manganese, and protein – all of which made them uniquely valuable to Mesolithic people and their descendants. And beyond the significant benefits of the nuts, hazel is a fast-growing wood that can be easily coppiced and put to all sorts of uses – tent poles, rods, fences, walking sticks, staves. Fossils and stools made of hazel found at Mesolithic sites across the British Isles show clear evidence of coppicing to encourage regrowth.[56] Far from the older image of prehistoric hunters moving through untouched, virgin woodland, these early inhabitants were manipulating the landscape down to something that we could almost call an early form of forest management. It is much more than coincidence that many of the Mesolithic sites known in Wales have produced remains either of hazelnuts or of hazel pollen, from Trwyn Du on Anglesey, at a coastal site near the mouth of the River Ffraw, where hazelnut shells were found and associated with a camp fire and pits packed with flint, to the site at Nab Head in Pembrokeshire, dated to c.8400 before present, where charcoal from wood of hazel and apple was found.[57]

So as we come to the middle of the Mesolithic period, around 8,000 years ago (6,000 BC) how would the Welsh landscape have looked? Trees were able to grow – and in many locations did so – up to 500m above sea level and perhaps beyond.[58] A good number of new tree species have come north as the climate has entered a more sustained warm phase, and woodland communities of the earlier pioneer species have provided the shelter necessary for them to spread. We have widespread evidence of oak, elm and lime in the pollen record.

Most of Wales would have been too mild and damp for lime to dominate, leading to many areas of oak-dominated woodland, which would have created more scope for understorey species (which can't tolerate the dense shade thrown by lime trees) to flourish, possibly allowing a greater density of browsing animals than in areas further east into England and the near Continent.[59] The dominance of oak in some locations during this period is also important evidence that the landscape in Wales was not unbroken forest during this period: oaks require a substantial amount of light during their early growth stage or they are outcompeted by other species long before they reach maturity and have a chance to generate all the pollen we find in the sediment cores. Again, burning and the impact of large herbivores are the only realistic mechanisms of maintaining this sort of semi-open landscape.[60]

People have helped the hazel tree to spread, and it now forms an important part of the woodland assemblages throughout Wales, ranging from around 10 per cent of the pollen record to near 60 per cent at some sites. And people have also helped another species to quickly establish itself in locations favourable for it, namely the alder or *gwernen*. 'Gwern' place-names crop up all over modern Wales in valley bottoms or wetter dips in the land, and some of these sites may well have been dominated by alder – a moisture-loving tree – for many thousands of years. Evidence from a couple of Welsh sites link the rise in alder to continued burning of the local environment, as alder took advantage of the forest damage to establish itself.[61]

Although this is undoubtedly a well-wooded landscape, it is by no means continuous forest, and it is far from untouched by human influence. The higher hills and mountains are mostly free of trees, while the hills, valleys and lowland are characterised by a shifting mosaic of tree cover, openings and perhaps scrub.[62] At some sites oak dominates, at others hazel, elm, alder or grassland species, and these site compositions keep changing during this period. This pattern of fluctuation is ubiquitous enough in the pollen record that we cannot suppose that lowland or upland Wales as a whole was dominated by one particular type of tree species or woodland community; on a historic timescale, all was change.[63]

This early human population, though influential, was low, numbering no more than a few thousand individuals and was probably transient, moving from site to site with the seasons. But this would not have been aimless wandering in the hope of finding food or pastures new: even on foot, a traverse of Wales from the known Goldcliff Mesolithic camp on the banks of the Severn in the far south-east to the shores of the Menai in the north-west is only a six-day walk for fit adults, covering 170 miles. By this point, around 6,000 BC, the landscape would already have been storied, with particular places having emotional resonance as ancestral sites, eerie places, good hunting grounds or the location of childhood memories. Something similar would have been true too of wolves, where different packs respect each others' territories and establish lookouts and hunting grounds that they keep to. The early

human populations would have been keenly aware of the wolves' habits
and favoured spots, passing on the information down the generations;
part of a long-lived equilibrium between humans, wolves, herbivores
and trees that continued to effect Wales for millennia. Wolf place-
names throughout Wales remain in use to this day, reflecting the fact
that the 400 years or so since wolves became extinct here is little more
than the blink of an eye in landscape history terms.[64]

There remains some academic debate as to exactly how open the
European landscape was during this period and what the main factors
responsible were.[65] But as Fred Pearce, environment consultant for
the *New Scientist* puts it, 'what evidence there is suggests that the
patchwork people are right. Pollen analysis indicates that lowland
Europe's ancient forests always contained oak and hazel trees, which
need a sunny habitat.'[66] A close reading of the published findings seems
to lead to the conclusion that, in Wales at least, it is hard to make sense
of things as varied as the mixed nature of the landscape, the evidence
of burning, the preponderance of oak and hazel, and the bones of large
mammals at human sites without acknowledging that humans were
both directly and indirectly shaping the landscape. For Wales during
this period there seems to be:

> growing acceptance of the fact that Mesolithic people
> used burning/firing episodes either as an aid to hunting,
> to promote the growth of a new range of plant species,
> or as a means of controlling vegetation. The fact that this
> form of deliberate manipulation is effectively a form of
> land management, more often attributed to later farming
> populations, is an important observation in this context[67]

As we come to the end of the Mesolithic period around 4,000 BC, this
is a landscape that has already been shaped by the complex interactions
of humans, large mammals and trees for a good 6,000 years. The precise
location and make-up of the woodlands and the more open ground has
varied over time and from place to place, but the key tree species such
as hazel, alder and oak that were present during historic times have
all been here for several thousand years, and as we have seen, humans
have had an important part to play in that. As Professor David Austin,
one of the foremost authorities on landscape history in Wales puts it,

'in our world, for a few thousand years, vegetation has grown where we decide it should and we live only where the elements permit'.[68] And this is also a known landscape, with special spots that were clearly significant – probably even spiritually significant – to the inhabitants of the land. The living world and the particular plants, animals and birds that formed this world in prehistoric Wales would have been vested with deep significance. Although the stories themselves are now long lost to us, their echoes live on.

Wood is one of the most useful natural resources of all for humans. Not only does it provide heating and integrity to any built structure, but its versatility also makes it indispensable for utensils and equipment of all kinds, from looms to spoons. To make full use of wood as a resource you need to be intimately familiar with it: to know how different trees grow and how and when to fell or cut them, how different types of wood fare in wet or damp conditions, how well they bend or bear weight or how hot they burn in a fire. You also need to take the long view when dealing with wood: the hazels you coppice for poles this year won't be ready for the next cut in the cycle for another decade – and hazel is a fast-growing species compared to some. For timber trees you are dealing with decades from the time a slope is felled to it being ready to harvest again.

Trees require knowledge, and there is perhaps no better prehistoric proof of that in a Welsh context than roundhouses. The first roundhouses built in the British Isles so far discovered come from Ireland and date to the early Neolithic period around 3,500 BC.[69] From the Bronze Age (starting *c.*2,500 BC) onwards, roundhouses had become widespread and were the most common form of habitation, becoming a regional building style that developed and evolved into the pre-Roman Iron Age and indeed beyond. For a period of almost 4,000 years, most people in this part of the world lived in structures that depended on the skilful manipulation and use of wood and woodlands.[70]

The Iron Age roundhouses at Castell Henllys, Pembrokeshire that have been the subject of thorough excavation and investigation for several decades now, demonstrate the point. These were large structures that took massive quantities of both wood and thatch to put up, as those responsible for erecting the modern recreations know. As many as '30 oak trees, 90 coppiced hazel bushes, 2,000 bundles of water reed and two miles of hemp rope and twine went into [the] rafters, posts, ring-beams and wattle-and-daub walls [of just one of them]'.[71] According to archaeologist Toby Driver, 'one cannot simply walk into a nearby wood and gather these materials. Woodland must be managed for generations to produce the correct products for roundhouse building.'[72] And this woodland management was absolutely necessary, as roundhouse structures can only survive for a couple of generations at most before they need rebuilding due to the wood rotting.[73] What was true of Iron Age roundhouses and the woods that produced them had also been true millennia earlier as there is now strong evidence that prehistoric woods were being carefully managed as early as 4,000 BC, with the arrival of farming in the Neolithic period.[74] These people built compostable structures from the resources of the landscape for thousands of years; whereas a modern identikit house contains tonnes of decaying concrete that can only be recycled at great cost.[75]

So, although the archaeological and paleoenvironmental records both show a clear reduction in tree cover in Wales during the Neolithic and Bronze Age periods (from about 4,000 BC to roughly 800 BC), this was not wanton destruction of woodland by new arrivals in the landscape, hellbent on destroying it. On the contrary and as evidenced by the increasing numbers of monuments and shrines that dotted almost every prominent part of the landscape, the inhabitants of this land were clearly intimately familiar with it, its wildlife, its trees and its natural rhythms. It is probably closer to the mark to think of woods being harvested rather than cleared by these folk, whose cultural roots in the land by now stretched back over millennia.[76]

When new populations, technologies and ideas – most prominently among them agriculture – came into Wales during the Neolithic and Bronze ages, they did indeed make an impact on the landscape that we can trace in the archaeological record. But they also inherited a landscape that was already named, known and divided. As archaeologist Francis Pryor puts it, whatever the actual detail of tree clearance, some sort of permanent markers were always needed in the landscape – be they trackways, standing stones, barrows, single trees or hedges – to fix the agreed boundaries. The landscape had already been organised over the millennia prior to the newcomers' arrival, and their new ways of working the land would only have accelerated practices of land

and woodland management already present. These early farmers who took over were not *just* farmers: like the Mesolithic inhabitants of the preceding millennia and like their descendants into modern times, they continued to hunt game, to harvest the bounty of the woods from timber to berries, and to decide ultimately where they would let trees grow and where they would be harvested and felled. There was continuity in the midst of profound change.

One of the prime instigators for these farmers' growing impact on the landscape was through their domesticated herds of animals, foremost among them cattle. Recent DNA analysis of ancient aurochs bones from a site in England shows that, despite long-held views to the contrary, herders across the British Isles seem to have successfully incorporated wild aurochs variation into their livestock.[77] There was thus a significant degree of continuity between the older wild cattle species – hunted and perhaps corralled by earlier inhabitants – and the newer breeds, which despite including DNA from domesticated near-eastern cattle, kept significant amounts of the native aurochs' DNA and thus their traits. But these were nevertheless now domesticated herds, and that meant the need for enclosures and fields. It's no coincidence, as we shall see in the next chapter, that the earliest extant field systems identified in the British Isles date from this early Bronze Age period. Paleoenvironmental evidence from Ceredigion shows that from the late Bronze Age onward the amount of woodland cover in Wales steadily decreased and by the time we get to the late Iron Age around 0 BC, the ratio of tree pollen to non-tree pollen in the records falls to levels resembling those of the present day.[78]

Once again, this was not mindless clearance of woodland or wood pasture: areas with better soils for agriculture were strategically chosen for arable fields, while wetter and steeper areas that would make poor pasture were kept under greater tree cover. Climatic effects, tribal warfare and disease all had their effects too, and the pollen record for the first 1,000 AD indicates a cycle in some places of woodland clearance followed by extensive regeneration of trees. Folk memories of this period may well be captured in the oldest of all the Welsh myths, the tale of Culhwch and Olwen, when the hero visits Tylluan Cwm Cowlyd – *the owl of Cwm Cowlyd, in the mountains near Llanrwst.*[79] The owl tells him:

> Pan ddeuthum i yma gyntaf
> yr oedd y cwm mawr a welwch
> yn ddyffryn coed. Ac fe ddaeth
> cenhedlaeth o ddynion iddo ac
> fe'i difawyd. Ac fe dyfodd ynddo
> ail dyfiant coed, a hwn yw'r
> trydydd tyfiant.[80]

> [When first I came hither, the
> wide valley you see was a wooded
> glen. And a race of men came
> and rooted it up. And there grew
> there a second wood; and this
> wood is the third.[81]]

There is no doubt that there was an awareness of past patterns of woodland clearance and growth within the culture this story grew up in. And it is worth noting that, although there are majestic ancient oak woodlands on some of the hillsides within a couple of miles of modern-day Cwm Cowlyd, this is not the case in the valley itself, which given the owl's words at the very latest was presumably wooded at the time the tale was committed to writing in the eleventh century. For now, these mountainsides are bare of trees.

This then is the long prehistoric backdrop to woodlands in Wales, and it shows us that humans have been intentionally influencing where and under what conditions trees have grown here since soon after the ice receded. We can also see that the historic tapestry that emerges with the Roman and Celtic periods some 2,000 years ago inherits a landscape that had already seen millennia of cultural evolution.

No self-respecting historian will vouch for any specific present-day woodland in Wales being older than a few hundred years for some very good reasons. The oldest map of Wales we have dates to 1205, and we have to wait till the sixteenth and seventeenth centuries to find county- or estate-level maps that show landscape features to a degree that gives us confidence in the precise detail. Partly because of this, the standard definition for 'ancient woodland' for both Wales and England is 'semi-natural woodland that has been in existence since at least 1600'. However, in reality, we can trace many native Welsh woods back a fair bit further than this relatively late date.

To really get under the skin of the story of Wales's ancient woodlands, we need to travel back to the country's built-up south-east. Today the old port town of Newport is Wales's third city, a proud place draped over several low hills arranged around the estuary of the Usk into the Severn

Sea (as the Bristol Channel is known in Welsh). It's a post-industrial city that is just a stone's throw down the river from the major Roman legionary fortress at Caerleon. This was the seat of King Arthur according to the Welsh tales, and regardless of the historical accuracy of such myths, the patterns of the landscape in this part of Wales take us back to those first centuries AD. The other 'Caer' (or Roman town) in the area, Caerwent, was the tribal centre for the Silures tribe that successfully resisted the first Roman invasion of this part of the world for many decades, as described rather ruefully by the Latin historian, Tacitus.

The historical significance of this area for Wales's landscape history can be appreciated when we put a few things together. First, the fact that the pre-Roman capital of the Silurian kingdom was probably the hillfort,[82] which directly overlooks Caerwent. During the Roman period Caerwent (or in Latin, Venta Silurum – the market-town of the Silures) acted as the regional capital, combining native hierarchy with Roman architecture and ways of life. Caerwent remained the capital of the post-Roman kingdom of Gwent, which to all appearances was a direct successor to the pre-Roman tribal kingdom. Some of the early kings of this period even used the name 'Caradog' for themselves, hearkening back hundreds of years to the successful first-century military leader Caratacus who had resisted the Roman incursion for so long. The place also became a regional ecclesiastical centre in the post-Roman era, providing another link between the early Christian importance of the area as the location of the first British martyrs, Julius and Aaron, and the medieval prominence of the church across the European landscape.

It is in this heroic landscape of early kingdoms and saints that we find two of the oldest references of all to identifiable woodlands in Wales. The first comes in the Life of St Cadoc, preserved in the eleventh-century book of Llandaff. This tells the tale of Cadoc, who was born in the fifth century in this kingdom of Gwent and went on to found churches all over modern-day Wales, Cornwall, Brittany and Scotland. According to the Life, the saint's birthplace was a spot called 'Allt Gwynllyw', now known as Stow Hill in modern-day Newport. This is the earliest recorded use of the Welsh word *allt* for a place in Wales, an element that appears in place-names all over the country.[83]

In all these cases, there is little doubt that *allt* essentially means a wooded slope, and in likelihood an ancient wooded one at that. We are slightly into the realm of historical detective work here, as the point could only be conclusively demonstrated if we had more detailed maps of Wales from this early medieval period. The standard dictionary definition of *allt* in modern Welsh is hill(side), (steep) gradient or slope, steep road or path, (steep) ascent, cliff, woods, wooded slope, so encompassing a range of landscape forms.[84] But of all these options, very many of these places called Allt are wooded slopes – as opposed to bare hillsides. Many of the oldest uses of the word in poetry and literature also refer clearly to woods, including one passage in the Mabinogi that appears in one manuscript with the word *allt* and in another with the word *coed*; they were clearly seen as at least partially synonyms.[85] And beyond this, there are several other widely used words in Welsh that go back just as far as *allt* which clearly refer to bare rather than wooded hillsides – including *rhiw* and *llechwedd*. Given this and what we know of the recorded history of land use in Wales, it seems clear that originally *allt* only referred to wooded hillsides, with other words used for bare hillsides, and that the slight ambiguity in the modern word came about because of deforestation in historic times.[86]

Allt Gwynllyw (of which Stow Hill is not a translation, but a later naming of the same spot) seems to be part of that same trajectory: the name itself disappears from the record, and by the time the earliest maps of Newport are being drawn, there is no indication that this particular hillside is wooded. There is, however, a counterpoint only a mile or so away: Allt-yr-yn, now the name of a Newport suburb, takes its name from a wooded hillside which has survived right down to the present day and is a nature reserve sandwiched between the M4 motorway and the growing city. This pattern is in fact indicative of a much broader phenomenon in Wales: an astonishingly large proportion of Wales's surviving ancient woodlands are on sloping ground. This is true in every part of the country with very few exceptions and has nothing to do with where trees will grow in Wales; as we have seen, given space, time and protection from animals and ourselves they will happily cover the entire country other than the highest peaks. No: the distribution of ancient woodland in Wales is a direct outcome of human shaping of the landscape.

To find out why this might be, let us return to south-eastern Wales in the centuries before and after Roman occupation. The ancient kingdom that emerged during the first centuries after the Romans left bore the name 'Gwent', as previously stated. This kingdom was divided in turn into two major administrative divisions: Gwent Is-Coed and Gwent Uwch-Coed (literally Gwent Over-wood and Under-wood). The kingdom of Gwent fell to the Normans in 1091, although Welsh law retained legal force here as elsewhere for centuries after this date, including the division of the territory into the two parts known by these names. There is every reason to suppose then that this division was already well established by the time the kingdom was overrun, and it may have been many centuries old by this time. And the key landmark referred to in this division of Gwent into two parts still exists today: the large tract of ancient hillside woodland known as the 'Wentwood'.

Now part of one of the largest blocks of ancient woodland in Wales, the wood dominates most of the surrounding landscape on a ridge of hills that can be seen for dozens of miles, from the Black Mountains to the north to the Cotswolds and Somerset across the Severn to the south. It may have been of symbolic importance – perhaps even as a boundary – as early as Bronze Age times, given the known importance of this wider area within the ritual landscape of Britain then, and the number of Bronze Age tumuli (funerary barrows) on the ridge tops. The area probably furnished much of the timber used by the Romans in their building work in the region, and is mentioned in medieval texts including the Book of Llandaff and a 1271 survey for the lord of Chepstow, which lists twenty-one tenants with rights to timber and firewood. The woodland law regulating harvesting was effective enough that the area was clearly still wooded enough to become the haunt of outlaws following the Welsh revolt against English rule led by Owain Glyndŵr in the early 1400s.

And it is no coincidence that this significant stretch of woodland is found on the largest expanse of steep land in southern Gwent. In other words, the existence of the Wentwood as far back as records will take us and its survival into modern times is the landscape-scale product of decisions made over generations by an agricultural people about how to use the land to best effect. In a hilly, windy country with abundant rainfall, the best land for agriculture is generally found either on valley bottoms or on gently sloping hillsides. Steep hillsides, however, suffer from multiple disadvantages for ploughing and stock-keeping: as well as the practical difficulty, the high rainfall levels in most of Wales would lead to landslips and the leaching away of nutrients downhill, reducing denuded soil to almost nothing. The economically sensible course of action from the point of view of a farming community in this part of the world in need of building timber, kindling and good farmland for livestock and crops would be to keep any steeply sloping land nearby under trees.

This is in fact the pattern we find replicated over the whole of Wales, where almost all the ancient woodlands are steep hillside *elltydd*.[87] These woods are found all over the country, and when viewed on a map are almost a visualisation of the upper reaches of the country's watercourses, fanning out of the hilly interior. If their location is a function of people's land-use choices, their existence and survival is entirely down to their utility within the economy, and the local and national laws and customs that put a brake on their overexploitation. This is by no means a trivial point: in neighbouring Ireland, which suffered under significantly worse Westminster governance post-conquest, by the 1830s only 0.2 per cent of the country was covered by woodland that pre-dated 1660, and much of this is likely to have been lost since to agricultural clearance and modern plantations.[88]

Within Wales, these woodlands had won their place within culture as a familiar, unquestioned part of the landscape. And legal protections had been put in place to preserve some areas of woodland specifically for pannage and harvesting of other forest products, using the designation *coed cadw*, or 'reserved woods'. This became fossilised in some places into the name of a particular woodland – there are Coed Cadw woods in both Glamorgan and Anglesey today. Other designations included *fforest* (royal forests, as per Norman usage also), general woodland and common land on which trees might also be present.[89] These laws encouraged woodland conservation for the sake of game and forest products, and as contemporaneous descriptions of the Welsh countryside testify, they were effective in keeping many parts of the country well wooded.[90] One of the ways they did this was to regulate particular practices that applied to everyday needs for wood: the Peniarth 28 manuscript copy of the Welsh laws contains a memorable illustration of the growth pattern of a tree when either coppiced or lopped.

Eleven species of tree are specifically mentioned in the Welsh laws, with different parts of the tree assigned financial values. But of them all the most valuable and the one treated in most detail is the oak: *derwen*.[91] The tree's cultural roots as the primary timber tree go back at least to the Iron Age and further significant uses developed later in church building, shipbuilding and barrel-making. By the period of medieval

Welsh law-writing, long-established regulation called *mesfraint* was in place, dictating (with regional variation that may well reflect the different growing-season length in different regions[92]) when pigs could be turned out into woodland areas to fatten up on its acorns and on beechmast. And by the sixteenth century, leather tanning using oak bark had become an important rural industry in Wales, with regular shipments of bark going out from ports around the west coast to be used in tanneries in Bristol and elsewhere by the eighteenth century.[93] This led to the widespread practice of women and children spending time in the woods throughout spring and summer to collect the bark to be sent away using a special implement (called a *bilpren*). Given this wide range of economic uses, it is far from fanciful to suppose, along with Welsh woodland expert Linnard, that people at times planted acorns to encourage oak growth, as a traditional Welsh proverb implies: 'Rhaid I'r dderwen wrth gysgod yn ieuanc', 'an oak needs shelter when young' – practical advice for people raising oak saplings.

These woodlands and their trees were a familiar part of people's *bro* – their habitat – and as well as meeting all sorts of indispensable needs, they formed a core part of their mental world. An 'oak needs shelter when young' is both a forester's maxim in a country with plenty of grazing animals and more than enough wind, but also a truism about people when viewed through the connotations Welsh culture has about oaks. 'O fesen, derwen a dyf' ('from an acorn an oak will grow') goes the familiar saying still current in Welsh, coupled with the phrase 'cryf fel derwen' ('strong as an oak'): both phrases used commonly to describe people. Like an oak sapling, a young child needs sheltering from the worst of the world when young; then, he or she can grow to become the full-grown tree that will withstand many a strong storm. This economically indispensable tree furnishes both myriad ecological and economic services, and gives us part of our mental furniture.

Similar connotations and lore could be traced for other trees, but it is notable in this context that the word *allt* is also commonplace in Welsh literature as early as medieval times, appearing in the works of poets from Dafydd ap Gwilym onwards. It always carries a positive connotation, as in this fifteenth-century eulogy to a fallen prince:

Ceidwad allt lwyswallt laswerdd,   [The guardian of a bright verdant
/ Cywrain gyrch, coron y gerdd   *allt* / Skilful blade, crown of song][94]

A sense of the depth of this identification with the living world of the woodland can be seen in more detail in a remarkable sixteenth-century poem from north-east Wales. 'Coed Marchan' tells of a group of squirrels that went to London to file an affidavit for the destruction of a woodland – Coed Marchan – near Ruthin:

> Odious and hard is the law
> and painful to little squirrels ...
>
> Then on her oath [the squirrel] said,
> 'All Rhuthyn's woods are ravaged;
> my house and barn were taken
> one dark night, and all my nuts.'
> The squirrels are all calling
> for the trees; they fear the dog.
> Up there remains of the hill wood
> only grey ash of oak trees;
> there's not a stump unstolen
> nor a crow's nest left in our land.
> The owls are always hooting
> for trees; they send the children mad.
> The poor owl catches cold,
> left cold without her hollow trunk.
> Woe to the goats, without trees or hazels,
> and to the sow-keeper and piglets!⁹⁵

The tenor of this poem, from an era well before modern environmental consciousness, is striking for a number of reasons. For one thing, the (red) squirrels who went to London to take the tree-fellers to court are clearly given agency and voice and are themselves put front and centre as the damaged party from this woodland clearance, as are other wild animals, including owls, crows and hedgehogs later in the poem. But alongside them, domesticated animals – goats, pigs and piglets – suffer from the deforestation, and throughout, this animal suffering is interwoven with the detriment to humans from the felling. So the owls' suffering drives the children mad, and the pigs' plight brings woe to the sow-keeper. Later we learn that 'Cold will exhaust the housemaid / with cold feet and a dripping nose' because she will have to go out to the mountain for bracken or peat to cook with, rather than being able to fetch kindling from the woods. And the economic consequences extend to the fact that there will no longer be cow-collars or pig troughs coming from the woodland harvest now that the trees have been cut down. The consequences of unbridled woodland clearance – as opposed to locally owned harvest – are seen as detrimental to wild animals, domestic animals and people alike, with knock-on effects on people's welfare from the absence of trees.

Coed Marchan had been a reserved woodland under native law, and so its destruction, in the poet's view, is an act that the new law of the land (after the 1536 Acts of Union) must address in light of the egregious consequences for people and nature alike. In other words, the poem insists that any law has a clear environmental duty that extends to the entire living community that depends on the woods: wild birds, domesticated animals and humans alike. But this is most emphatically *not* a modern poem ahead of its time: it's a poem of its time and place, that views nature not as something removed from people to be protected for its own sake, but rather as being part of the home of both people and other living creatures. There is an affinity here with the worldview we glimpsed in Dafydd ap Gwilym's work, and the prevalence of such a view is hinted at in the fact that 'Coed Marchan' was written not by a professional court poet but by a travelling folk poet, who performed his poems at fairs and taverns. It is not surprising, given people's lives in the Wales of the period, that this clever little piece struck a chord with his audience.

We don't know exactly why the wood was felled, though securing timber for the navy during the wars of the sixteenth century is likely. The pressures that led to wholesale woodland destruction in this case came outside the community of local stakeholders, who had both economic and clear sentimental attachment to the woodlands as woods. Although there is no doubt that traditional farming communities in Wales put enormous pressures on woodlands, hunting the wildlife, harvesting everything from wild birds' eggs to mosses and ultimately influencing their entire composition, the historical and cultural record is clear: they maintained them in the landscape. There is, of course, a parallel to the lived experience of all too many twenty-first-century woodland communities in the global south, who maintained semi-natural, harvested woodlands into the present, only to see it cleared for timber or soy by outside entities with a greater say in the 'law'. But in Wales of all places, there is a related final episode that needs to be told in the story of woods and people, as the forces of industry became just as much a shaper of landforms and vegetation as agriculture or the law.

Industry is a cultural force, and the fossil-fuel-powered dynamics that led to the rapid and early industrialisation of Wales are the same ones that, writ large, transformed our entire world over the last 200 years. The south Wales valleys lie on top of one of the richest coalfields in the world and became by the mid-nineteenth century one of the most important centres for steel-working, coal mining and copper production in the British Empire. Capital and people flowed into the area, the valley side terraces housing a melting-pot community where Protestant nonconformity, the burgeoning Labour movement and Welsh-language culture all flourished for a time. This was a frontier society, part of a global network of furnaces where homo economicus was being birthed; and around him, a new kind of denatured landscape.

By the early twentieth century, the hilltops that rise several hundred meters above the valley floors were dominated by slag heaps. These were where the children of this new, modern type of human played, rather than in streams and woods. The air was thick not with pollen but the smoke of the coal fires that warmed the houses and the chapels, drove the enormous smelting works and fired the ubiquitous steam trains. Pit whistles and sirens replaced bird song in the sky. The Glamorgan and Gwent valleys, home to well over 1 million people, had become ultra-modern.

But before they were an industrial powerhouse, these were Blaenau Morgannwg, an upland region of quiet, well-wooded river valleys of small, pastoral farms and a handful of tiny market towns. The English antiquarian Leland describes how the 'water of Taphe cummith so down from woddy hilles' as he traversed the landscape in the 1530s, creating a local woodland culture that included customs like red squirrel hunting.[96] We know from a 1570 estate survey that the woodlands of the Cynon valley (i.e. Coed Glyn Cynon, as they were known), a few miles west of Cwm Merddog, were 'for the most part beech and some oak'. But an anonymous poem from ten years later after this survey, 'Coed Glyn Cynon', captures the anguish of the inhabitants of the region as they saw the first major incursions of industry changing their landscape:[97]

Aberdâr, Llanwynno i gyd,
Plwy' Merthyr hyd Lanfabon,
Mwyaf adfyd a fu erioed
Pan dorred Coed Glyn Cynon;

Torri llawer parlwr pur
Lle cyrchfa gwŷr a meibion;
Yn oes dyddiau seren syw,
Mor araul yw Glyn Cynon!

O bai ŵr ar drafael dro
Ac arno ffo rhag estron,
Fo gâi gan eos lety erioed
Yn fforest Coed Glyn Cynon.

Llawer bedwen las ei chlog
(Ynghrog y bytho'r Saeson!)
Sydd yn danllwyth mawr o dân
Gan wŷr yr haearn duon.

Os am dorri a dwyn y bâr
Llety'r adar gwylltion,
Boed yr anras yn eu plith
Holl blant Alis ffeilsion ...

Clywais ddwedyd ar fy llw
Fod haid o'r ceirw cochion
Yn oer eu lle, yn ymado â'u plwy',
I ddugoed Mawddwy'r aethon'.[98]

[Aberdare, all of Llanwonno
And Merthyr parish to Llanfabon;
The greatest distress that ever was
When were felled the woods of
Glyn Cynon

Breaking many a pleasant parlour
The hunting-ground of men and
sons
In this smart and splendid age,
How quiet now Glyn Cynon

Were a man by turns in trouble
And needing to flee from a foe
He could always receive from the
nightingale
A refuge in the forest of Glyn
Cynon

Many a green-decked birch tree
(May the English hang for this!)
Is now so much firewood
Thanks to the iron-masters' decree

If they wish to break and steal
away
The wild birds' abode
May misfortune them all assay
All Alice's false children...

I heard say, on my oath
That the herd of red deer
Forlorn, have left for fear
And gone to the dark wood of
Mawddwy]

The bitterness in this poem is unmistakable, expressed multiple times in the desire to see those responsible for felling the trees to fire charcoal furnaces hung and cursed. Again, as in 'Coed Marchan', we find the poet – an unknown folk poet, clearly familiar with the territory

– identifying with the wildlife of the woodlands in the shape of red deer, roe deer, badgers, owls and nightingales. The knowledge that the woods are the birds' home and that they have a right to that home, as part of the rightful order of things, is forcefully stated in verse 5, where the accused are called 'Alice's children' – a reference to heinous events in the sixth century, retained in Welsh folk memory.[99]

But again, this despoliation of the natural world is only part of what has enraged the poet: it is the destruction of a core part of his *bro*, his native stomping ground that he views as an unallayed evil. And so as with Robin Clidro in north-eastern Wales, so here in the south-east; the loss of deer is also the loss of deer to hunt, and the loss of verdant birch trees (verse 4) is also the loss of the green rooms the trees provided in summer for meeting up or making love (verse 2). If this is an environmental poem, it is very much of its place and its time: of its culture.

This sixteenth-century clear-felling was only the beginning: industry continued to develop and spread across Glamorgan and Gwent over the ensuing centuries, becoming enormous in scale in some areas from the late eighteenth century onwards. The small furnaces of the sixteenth and seventeenth centuries, which burnt local oak, willow and poplar (as modern analyses of samples have shown), supported in time a rural economy of seasonal charcoal burners, like those described by Revd John Skinner at Baglan in 1800:

> We here discovered a large family inhabiting a mud cabin in the form of a sugar loaf. In the midst of this retirement they seemed perfectly happy, tho' almost all the children were in the state of their first parents, without covering, and seemed not ashamed. These people continue here all summer for the purpose of making charcoal.

But this was nothing compared to the massive furnaces for smelting powered by the coal mined deep under the valley sides. The change of fuel didn't, however, do much to change industry's demand for trees, which needed them for pit props, coal trucks and much else. And so many of the steeply sloping hillsides of the Glamorgan and Gwent valleys became denuded of trees – and some ended up instead as the location of coal tips.

Intact woodlands – whether covering half an acre of steep valley side or many hectares of lowland – provide all sorts of benefits for soil structure and prevention of natural disasters. They improve air quality, slow down wind speeds, create soil through the annual shedding of leaves, act as a soak at times of heavy rain and bind in soil and rocks by their formidable root systems; they are, as current inhabitants of the Alps and doubtless inhabitants of Wales during colder centuries past know, the single most effective barrier against avalanches.

It is therefore bitterly ironic that within the area covered in 'Coed Glyn Cynon' lies the now notorious village of Aberfan, where 116 children and 28 adults were killed by a landslide that happened during heavy rain in October 1966. The blame for the man-made disaster lies squarely with the Coal Board for its lax standards in managing slag heap and tips; but the fact remains that if the bare hillside above Aberfan had been covered in woodland, the tip would have had to be located elsewhere – and the disaster wouldn't have taken place.

This puts into perspective the highest surviving native beechwood in the British Isles where we opened this chapter, at Coed Tynygelli (extending up to 490m above sea level), as well as its near neighbour highest oakwood, Cefn-y-crug. Tynygelli is an ancient, coppiced beechwood that sits on wet slopes – presumably part of the reason it was left under tree cover in ancient times. Importantly, it is a survivor not of unbroken woodland but of a farmed landscape that preceded industry: medieval records imply a landscape of tiny arable and pasture fields, with extensive tracts both of moorland and woodland. The form of the still clear boundary banks around and throughout the Cwm Merddog woods imply that different parcels of the wood belonged to four adjoining farms.[100] In the eighteenth century, with the ironworks growing rapidly, the woods were valued for both charcoal and pit-props and surviving records from the late nineteenth and early twentieth century imply that the woods only started to deteriorate when the need for the wood's produce had dwindled to nothing.[101] Cefn-y-crug, high up on the moorland, also has clear signs of historic coppicing and, with the advent of industry, also of cutting for charcoal.[102] It was only when these uses disappeared that the woodlands started to deteriorate; primarily due to the neglect of boundaries which allowed excessive grazing. Tynygelli is now owned and managed by the Wildlife Trust and is an important sanctuary for the inhabitants of Cwm, just down the road.

There is, then, a happy postscript to this tale of trees: today, these valleys are greening again with growing woods and the towns that

still fill them have outlasted the industry that birthed them. In early
April, the oaks that generally dominate here are bursting into yellow-
green leaf between the stands of conifer that cover broad swathes of
the hilltops. It is wonderful to drive down the valley past some of the
elltydd that have so far survived everything thrown at them. Many of
them bear names that we can trace back to the oldest maps and to the
period when Mr Anonymous sung 'Coed Glyn Cynon'. I stand and
stare at Coed Fforest Ucha on a Cynon valley hillside above a modern-
day business park, which is there on the oldest maps we have of the
area and is still oak woodland today. It is named after a farm – Fforest
Ucha – which has also stood the test of time, and like many of the
surviving ancient woodlands in these post-industrial valleys, the name
betrays a key aspect of its history: the wood was traditionally part of
the farm.[103] Local ownership and manipulation of the natural resource
coincides again with the retention of woodland.

I am finishing my visit to this past by calling in at Pwll Waun Cynon,
a tiny nature reserve just outside Mountain Ash town centre in the
middle of the Cynon valley. We are emphatically not in the countryside
here: though the hills and *elltydd* that close in the valley dominate the
skyline, down here on the valley floor a busy road runs right past and
a railway line bisects the site. This nature reserve borders a housing
estate, hospital and sports ground and is in fact by one measure a post-
industrial wasteland, heavily polluted as the site of a former Phurnacite
coal plant. The plant closed in the early 1980s and in 1986 the site was
given to the local Wildlife Trust, which has managed it ever since.

The sun breaks through the dappled young leaves as I make my way
between the celandines, catching a glimpse of what I think is a rare reed
bunting. I am trying to take in this new, old patch of Coed Glyn Cynon,
and am musing on this place and the hillside woods above. I had earlier
met with a cultural stalwart from the valley, Gwyn, who was born and
raised in the area in the 1950s. In his rich *Cymraeg* he had reminisced
on the traditions of the valley, of which many have barely survived the
linguistic transition in the twentieth century from Welsh to English;
one shared was the saying that there had been a time when a squirrel
could make its way from Penderyn at the head of the valley to its bottom
without leaving the tree canopy. That again takes the memory of local
culture – sustained by poems such as 'Coed Glyn Cynon' – back to the
sixteenth century.

But the real narrative here is not one of loss: it is of ownership and memory, and how both factors seem able to have such marked real-world effects as the retention of old woodlands on precisely those stretches of land that most need them. Lack of local, community ownership led to lamentable consequences for woods and people alike in the eyes of both Robin Clidro and the poet of 'Coed Glyn Cynon', and in later eras led to the despoliation represented both by Aberfan and faceless conifer plantations. And it is of course local volunteers who are now caring for Pwll Waun Cynon, where cattle graze beneath the trees.

3
Cloddiau

Hedgerows-on-earthen banks/
animal enclosures and food source

The sun is glinting off scudding, white-crested waves half a mile away over the greening fields I am surveying. These fields are split into small, regular parcels by low hedges of hawthorn, but I am more interested in the sprawling hedgerow to my right. This runs along the edge of what is now a green lane, a *feidyr* in local parlance, towards the village of Dinas Cross, and it is truly ancient. Just how old is a question we can't currently answer, but this *clawdd* has its origins in the medieval *gorclawdd* that separated the intensely cropped lands at the heart of this ancient parish from the open grazing lands beyond it. This green, living structure has probably been here in some form for the best part of 1,000 years, and quite possibly longer.[104] And it is beautiful: on this fresh May afternoon garlanded with a shower of hawthorn blossom and elder, but also with red campion, white wild garlic flowers and ferns running along its feet. The growth is dense, thick and lush, a tangle of woody and herbaceous greenery providing shelter from the stiff breeze for people and birds alike, all growing out of and holding in a bank perhaps a metre in height made of soil and boulders.

Not all of Wales's trees are found in woods; in fact, the flower and fungi community that I have been enjoying in this *feidyr* today is composed to a great extent of ancient woodland indicator species, though we are a kilometre away from the nearest woodland. The majority of the hedgerows in Wales are over 200 years old; many are 300 or 400 years old, and some are significantly older. All are here because of their function in the farmed landscape. I have come for a walk through this west Wales coastal landscape with Rhiannon Comeau, a landscape historian and archaeologist who knows this place intimately, and I am here to understand this farmed landscape and the place of *cloddiau* within it through the shifting tides of history.

'My father was one of the last Welsh speakers in this little village', Rhiannon explains over coffee in her family's eighteenth-century whitewashed cottage. Rhiannon (née Lewis) grew up here in Cwm-yr-eglwys, the beautiful hamlet with its ruined church and cove of golden sand now frequented by thousands of holidaymakers all summer and lying mostly empty all winter. It is a core part of the ancient parish of Dinas, an intimate stretch of coastal countryside extending from the peninsula of Dinas Island over an undulating coastal plain up to the craggy outcrops of Mynydd Dinas a mile and a half inland. This is a land of vistas and glimpses – moorland rising above you, the sparkle of the blue sea through a field gate – which manages to encompass both a sense of homely nestling and of wide horizons and elementality. Driving down the deep lanes between honey-coloured houses and slate-roofed cottages under rocky outcrops of igneous dolerite, it isn't hard to understand the area's modern popularity, or indeed what attracted people to settle here thousands of years ago.

Rhiannon has spent fifteen years investigating this one parish as part of a wider enquiry into the medieval Welsh landscape and has drawn on every source available – oral memories, field names, medieval charters, archaeological reports and geomorphology – to build a time-lapse picture of this patch of land scarcely more than 3 miles across. The thing about Dinas, as Rhiannon tells me, is that despite its beauty it isn't particularly famous for anything. There aren't any prominent prehistoric monuments here, or medieval abbeys or grand hillforts to get historians excited. But it has been inhabited for an awfully long time: Neolithic stone axes have been discovered in the parish, and the pollen record shows large amounts of farming activity by the early fourth millennium BC, followed by the erection of standing stones in the Bronze Age and the establishment of the first field systems.[105]

Most strikingly of all, the prehistoric habitation sites that remain in the landscape, including small Iron Age enclosures, are adjacent to

areas of known medieval settlement amid the best soils. At Cwm-yr-
eglwys itself, a late prehistoric settlement developed into what became
the medieval hamlet with its church and court-house without evidence
of abandonment at any point.[106] This sort of pattern seems to hold true
for other areas in north Pembrokeshire and Ceredigion, and work in
coastal Snowdonia suggests that many of these patterns can also be seen
there.[107] This is, as far as anywhere can be, a fairly representative Welsh
coastal parish, stretching from hilltop to seashore. And that means its
history is above all the history of farming folk.[108]

This, then, is a good place for me to visit as I try to understand how
farming in Wales worked before the modern period. The fieldscapes of
Wales are clearly enormously significant from both an agricultural and
an ecological point of view. The fields they contain are the basic building
block of almost all farming in the country, while the hedgerows that
surround them are of unparalleled importance for biodiversity. These
hedgerows now form a criss-cross grid of linear forest that join up over
half of the country into passageways and habitat for species of all kinds,
from the soft-shield-fern to the fox, and from whitethroats to wild
angelica. At least 80 per cent of native woodland birds are supported
by hedges, and the thicker, taller and better maintained the hedge, the
more bird species it supports.[109] All tree species native to the British Isles
can be found in hedges. And their importance for insects can hardly
be overestimated: a 2015 study of a mere 90m of hedgerow in Devon,
almost identical in form to this *clawdd* I am admiring in Pembrokeshire
(which has a very similar climate and flora to Devon), showed 1,718
species present – which the study author believes to be an undercount.[110]

But the fields of today are not the fields of yesterday, even if many
are their direct descendants and in some cases are called by the same
names as those recorded in medieval land records. And the hedges of
today are not always the hedges of yesterday, even if in Wales we can
be fairly certain that some of them have been present in the landscape
for hundreds, if not thousands, of years. We need to look a bit closer
at a *clawdd*.

※

The Welsh word *clawdd*, used for the hedgerow surrounding this
Pembrokeshire field, can also be used of stone walls in those parts of
Wales where they form field boundaries. In other parts, *clawdd* can

mean a simple hedgerow, with no stone-and-earth bank underneath, or a dyke, or even a mound. But for Welsh speakers these are not different meanings for the same word; rather, they reflect the fact that the term refers to an obvious, physical field boundary. The prime example of this is the famous Offa's Dyke, built in the eighth century and called *Clawdd Offa* in Welsh since the thirteenth century at least. Is this long structure that runs the length of the Wales–England border a dyke or a ditch? It is of course both – an earthwork with both a fosse and an earthen embankment. So, the form of this sort of boundary may vary from place to place, but the range of functions is much the same. These are man-made creations, established and maintained for purposes to do with farming, herding and marking out territory and relationships. And despite their unparalleled importance for nature, hedgerows were created for very human reasons. We could go so far as to say that hedgerows and dry-stone walls are the clearest statement in the landscape that it is farmed, and inhabited. They are statements of intent.

But this distinctive mosaic pattern of fields, hedges and walls which rural Wales shares with much of England, Ireland and western France is, in fact, a rarity among the agricultural landscapes of the world. Looks can be deceiving; even areas of landscape in these countries now structured by hedgerows as far as the eye can see were in many cases only enclosed by such field boundaries between the seventeenth and early nineteenth centuries, most of central England being a case in point. Previous to this, the countryside in these parts was almost entirely 'open', with villages surrounded by enormous, open 'common' fields, interrupted for the most part only by woodlands, ditches and roads.[111] This may seem improbable for readers who have grown up in and only ever known hedgerow countryside, but to see such wide, open landscapes today one need only visit almost any part of the countryside between Paris and Munich, or Oklahoma City and Calgary.

So, much of the world's agricultural land is 'open' today, with no hedgerows or walls dividing it up; and even much of what is now enclosed by hedgerows was also 'open' until only a couple of hundred years ago. But is this true everywhere? In fact, there is an important counterpoint to the open landscapes, in what are often termed 'ancient' landscapes, that survive in some parts of the British Isles and whose form is thought to long pre-date seventeenth- and eighteenth-century parliamentary enclosures. They include most of Wales from clifftop plains to weather-beaten Snowdonian slopes and sheltered inland *cwms*.[112] Here, the land was not reorganised in as fundamental a fashion as in other areas, and some – but by no means all – of the hedgebanks and stone walls have been a functional part of the farmed landscape for millennia rather than centuries.[113] Although there has been change over time here too, these boundaries hold the key to understanding why the Welsh landscape looks as it does, and the deep agricultural logic behind that. So how old, in reality, are these boundaries that festoon Welsh landscapes? Why were they erected at such cost in labour and time, and what was their intended function? And why does the hedged and walled Welsh landscape look the way it does? In order to really understand the significance of this hedgerow mosaic, I needed to understand the ways of thinking of the countless generations that constructed and used it.

Guides to the British landscape are now easy to find in bookshops, betraying a lively interest in the history of place. They build upon a tradition of studying the landscape and its history that has generally radiated out from England, a varied country with a fascinating history of land use. But these books usually fall silent when it comes to describing Wales, despite often similar patterns of farming and land use and much shared history. There seem to be several reasons for this: different and more obscure historical evidence for medieval Wales compared to England;[114] less academic work on place-name evidence; a fascination with the Anglo-Saxons (not relevant in Wales) and a different legal system that was supplanted only over a period of several hundred years. The particular and complex political and economic dynamics that shaped Wales from the end of the Roman era until the early modern period (and arguably beyond) mean these authors' comparative silence on the history of the Welsh landscape is perhaps wise. But it reflects a sizeable blank in our historical understanding, which has left space for unfounded myths to develop.

David Austin is the (semi-)retired professor of archaeology at Lampeter, who has spent forty-five years since arriving in Ceredigion puzzling over the landscape of his adopted home patch. 'I'm a topographer, really,' he says, with a brandish out the window towards the hills of the upper Teifi valley extending above us, 'but the ways I had been trained to read the landscape just didn't quite translate here.'

What I am trying to get at, it turns out, is a sense of what landscape historians call the 'time-depth' of the landscape. To what extent do the structural features of any given landscape – trackways, monuments and of course boundaries – go back in time? And in this part of the world, the farms hold the first key. 'I have done many digs on Dark Age houses up in the Pennines of England or on Dartmoor – all areas that have a lot in common in terms of the soils, the topography, the climate and so on with these uplands. But when I came here, I was befuddled; there just weren't any remains of such farmsteads.' It took him years of puzzling to arrive at the explanation, one that is emblematic of so much of rural Welsh culture with its rootedness in place.

The reason, as David explains, is that the remains of these Welsh Dark Age farms turned out to be underneath the modern ones. Not all modern Welsh farms, of course – but an important subset of them, whose lineage can be traced as far back as written records go, and which by the sheer logic of their locations on the best soils probably go back much further.[115] Appropriately, one of the very earliest pieces of writing in Old Welsh, dating to the ninth century AD and found in the margins of the Llandeilo Gospels, happens to record field and farm names. The names in question include that of a field, in modern Welsh 'Gwaun Henllan', and that of the farm on which it is found, *Med diminih*, still there and known by the same name (though now spelt as Meddyfnych) and lying just outside the modern town of Ammanford.[116] Assuming that this example is not unique, and that it is only the absence of early documents that stops us from being able to identify such ancient farms across the country, this survival gives us an initial glimpse into the antiquity of core elements in the Welsh landscape.

David has himself done this documentary detective work in the case of a cluster of twenty farms that were inherited by the monks of Ystrad Fflur when their abbey was established in this valley a few centuries later in the mid-twelfth century.[117] Bron-y-berllan, Dol-ebolion, Dol-yr-ychain: these farms, in operation to the present day, bear ancient names that all evoke 'fields' in some way (Orchard brow, Mares' meadow, Oxens' meadow). And as the Cistercian documents themselves suggest in the way they call them 'excellentiores loci' (the superior places), they all occupy the best farming land within this landscape. This is clear from a walk up to the nearest summit with a map in hand: in a landscape dominated by high, exposed moorland on the one hand and wet bog on the other, these farms occupy the well-drained but sheltered slopes best suited for cropping – and indeed for habitation.

That will have been the case here for thousands of years. As David explains, we now know that by the Middle Bronze Age, around 1,500 BC, the Welsh landscape was fully inhabited, with enclosures, farmsteads and monumental structures of social and religious significance dominating the skylines. With the gap in Welsh landscape history finally being filled by historians and archaeologists, evidence is now accumulating for this in many parts of the country, with research published in 2020 showing that many of Snowdonia's long-overlooked prehistoric fieldscapes were first laid out during this early period.[118] An archaeological report from the same year on Skomer Island suggests that the first stage of cultivation on the island's field systems date to the Middle to Late Bronze Age (*c.*1,500 BC +/-190 years).[119] The question is just how far these settled landscapes survived into historical times – or, to put it differently, to what extent this landscape of known and named farms that emerged onto our oldest documents and maps was an evolution of what had come before, stretching back into these prehistoric times. To understand this, and to get at the age and function of the boundaries, we need to build a picture of how the landscape as a whole was used by pre-modern farmers, an understanding that will stand us in good stead as we come to the landscapes featured throughout the rest of this book.

∼⁄⁄∼

The eighteenth-century agricultural revolution that led to planting such a great proportion of the British Isles with the hedgerows and walls that are there today didn't leave Wales untouched. The oldest farms were already present in the landscape, and thanks to people's intimate knowledge of place extending back into prehistory, were based on or near the areas with the very best soils. We know that before the seventeenth and eighteenth centuries, the Welsh countryside didn't have the great open fields and nucleated villages of northern France or central England, but neither did we have all the hedges and walls that are there now. So how did the landscape look?

'Well, we need to talk more about farming first!' Rhiannon laughs. 'You do need to understand the farming systems as best as you can in order to get at that question of what it looked like. And there are two big things to get your head around here. The first is the fact that we are talking about mixed farming – livestock and arable. Almost all of Welsh agriculture today is livestock farming, with very few farms growing corn; but historically, most farms would have been self-sufficient and practising mixed farming. And the second is that this was an infield-outfield system. And those two things really do go together in this part of the world.'

In an infield-outfield system, you use the fertility from your animals' manure to produce the crops of grain your family or community depend on. In a trick of nature that humans learned to harness to their own ends when they domesticated animals, many – like cows and sheep – are able to digest grass and leaves, and so people found a way to tap into the fertility in plants that we are unable to use ourselves by using the animals' manure. Grains are hungry crops, and even on the most fertile soils, a few years growing a grain crop without fertiliser will exhaust the nutrients the soil can provide. The modern solution to this problem – one that has fed billions of people but depends almost entirely on fossil fuels – is to manufacture fertilisers that contain these nutrients. And the medieval and earlier modern solution (fossil-fuel free) that came in first with the 'Midlands'-type common fields systems and then, in refined form, with the eighteenth-century agricultural revolution, which was to rotate crops extensively around different fields, leaving some fallow and sowing others with plants like clover or beans that can fix nitrogen in the soil from the air. But older farming communities in Wales (and other parts of the British Isles with similar climate and landforms) had a different solution to maintaining fertility: the infield-outfield system.[120]

In this ancient system, a small settlement or hamlet (many of which have survived into the present as a single farm) is located on the best land in the locality. Around this farm there are 'infields', which are usually enclosed with a boundary of some sort.[121] This is where animals might spend the winter, fertilising the land with their manure, and there may be a small, hedged field next to this kept as meadow land or night pasture. But this infield is the crucial area that is intensively cropped for oats or barley or wheat, typically in intermixed strips cultivated by different members of the hamlet. Then beyond this you have the outfield,[122] which is much larger, entirely open with no hedges, banks or walls. This is where any extra cropping happens – an area of it may be ploughed up, animals 'folded' overnight on it for a while using wooden hurdles and then put to oats or another grain for a few years until it is exhausted – but generally it serves as pasture for livestock. But the infields and outfields by themselves could never produce enough fodder for all the animals needed to manure the crop fields that supported a community, and this is where the third part of the Welsh system comes in: *tir mynydd*, or literally 'mountain land'.

This is the area – found as far as we can tell in every part of the country, even where there is no hill or mountain present – which lies outside the boundary of the outfield, and where the animals are turned out for the summer. In historical documents in English it is sometimes called 'wild' land or even 'waste' land, but in Welsh the term is *tir mynydd* (see chapter 6), with no suggestion at all that it is viewed as either wild or waste. It is, however, generally uncultivated land covered with heather, gorse, young trees, brambles and rough grass, and it lies on the worst quality land in the locality. These are the poor, thin soils, often on windswept hilltops or hillside; all in all, the kind of area that today might be called either 'moor' or 'scrub'. And the livestock, by spending the summer half of the year on this land, feeding off its growth, become a means of bringing the nutrients present there via their dung down to the in- and outfields.

'Of course,' Rhiannon emphasises, 'this is very much an idealised model! The reality differs in all sorts of ways from place to place, depending on local circumstances and custom. But that basic logic of ensuring the fertility you need for successful mixed farming by dividing up the land roughly into three parts, radiating out from the settlement or farm – that holds.'

It's a model reflected in medieval Welsh law codes, archaeological evidence for cereal cultivation, sixteenth-century descriptions of Welsh farming and place-name evidence. And this model of farming seems to have governed how much of the land was used over an enormously long period of time. In the 1970s, the Llandaff charters of south Wales were found to contain grants of both permanent lowland hamlets with arable infields and of several large upland areas starting as early as the seventh century and using the terminology of late Roman estates – which implies that elements of this way of farming emerged in the early medieval period in direct continuity to how things had been run

during the Roman period, and quite plausibly well before that.[123] This
model held right up to the creation in the eighteenth century of estate
maps that have survived from areas when the enclosures of that period
were just starting, when the infield, outfield and *tir mynydd* were finally
hedged and parcelled up. This three-fold division seems, therefore, to
be fundamental to how the whole landscape was used and viewed in
Wales right through to the enclosure period around 250 years ago.[124]
As Rhiannon puts it, 'the mode of farming that we see in Welsh areas
in the medieval period is there in the fifth–sixth centuries, and very
possibly goes back much earlier'.[125]

So what does this mean for *cloddiau* – hedges, banks and walls – I ask?

'Well, at a minimum we're talking about the boundaries between
the three different parts of the farm system. There is plentiful evidence
for something called a *penclawdd* – a head dyke – dividing the outfield
from the *tir mynydd*. Which makes sense; the two areas have different
functions in the system and keeping that demarcation clear is highly
functional.'

And then the infields – including small paddocks, meadows and
cropped fields right by the homestead – were also usually separated in
some way from the outfield areas. Sometimes this happened by means
of ditches, which have now mostly disappeared from the land, but
sometimes a hedgebank called a *gorclawdd* was used, as archaeologists
and landscape historians are increasingly revealing. The historic Welsh
term for hay meadow – *gweirglodd* (literally *gwair* + *clawdd* = hay +
bank) – that turns up widely in Old Welsh texts from the tenth century
onwards – gives a further indication that a bank or ditch of some sort
was a key and fairly ubiquitous part of the infield part of the settlement.

The exact age of these oldest hedgebanks and stone walls has been a
focus of historical debate for decades, with arguments being put forth
that even the very oldest still in existence could hardly be more than
1,000 years old, while others pointed at evidence that suggested they
might be much older. But until recently, it was nigh-on impossible to
date solid features in a landscape like hedgebanks with any accuracy. Then
a sophisticated new dating technique called OSL (optically stimulated
luminescence) was developed, which has recently been used in Cornwall,
an area of England with all sorts of similarities to Wales, to date the
creation of a hedgebank with a high degree of confidence.[126] The way
OSL works is by measuring how long it is since a patch of soil last saw

sunlight. And as Rhiannon tells me, time and again technical advances in archaeology seem to confirm the sheer antiquity of agricultural features in the landscape, pushing back our best estimates for their age. 'Again, it makes sense. Of course people reused and repaired older field enclosures, century after century, if they were still useful for their way of farming.' In the case of this Cornish hedgebank, OSL sampling at the site confirmed that it had been there since some time between the twelfth and seventeenth centuries BC: the middle Bronze Age.

Recent research using different techniques has also revealed that some of the stone walls draped across the hillsides of Snowdonia are among the best preserved and most complex examples of early land division in Europe, dating from roughly the same era.[127] There is a pattern here: along the western fringe of the British Isles, there are field boundaries associated with mixed farming systems that have survived for a good 3,000 years.

Part of the point here is that even if the boundaries were not in continuous use from the Bronze Age up to the present, as large, solid structures that usually followed a sensible farmer's division of the landscape, they were always there, available for use.[128] And more often than not, the sheer weight of environmental and documentary evidence would suggest that they were indeed utilised. We now know that during every historic period from the Bronze Age onward, most of the population lived by mixed arable and livestock farming. And when you are raising crops and rearing cattle, you need to keep the cattle off the crops one way or another.[129]

On top of this, anyone who has spent any amount of time, as I have, contemplating a thick Welsh *clawdd* on a summer's day or shovelling soil and moving stones, knows that building one of these structures is not undertaken lightly. In other words, if you are a farmer at any time in history – including times that later historians will look back on as times of turmoil and change – you are unlikely to invest time in building a new *clawdd* if an old one will – with a few repairs – work perfectly well. There are records and recollections of the construction of new *cloddiau* in Ceredigion during the eighteenth century, and they emphasise how enormous an undertaking it was.[130] In fact, whether in times of plenty or dearth, the easiest option for farmers is always to use existing boundaries – just as the easiest option for travellers is usually to use existing tracks and pathways.

And this is indeed what we find littered across the landscape. For example, at a farm called Cefngwrthafarn Uchaf in Ceredigion, a very large (18 hectare) cattle enclosure or stockade has been preserved in the shape of modern fields.[131] A few miles to the south-west, a pair of gold-plated spoons linked to British druidical practices of divination were found on a farm called 'Castell Nadolig' (Christmas Castle). There are no obvious remains of a castle nearby, until one sees the pattern of the hedgerows from the air (see colour plate section). It turns out that this was previously a high-status Iron Age hillfort, dominating the landscape and within easy reach of the coast for trade.[132] A combination of ploughing and natural processes have levelled the site, leaving only the hillfort banks in existence as hedgerows; but this shows also that those banks were sufficiently well maintained to survive in useable form from the last few centuries BC up to the present.[133] And to pick another example from the same county, in countryside north of the hamlet of Bronnant a known Roman road bisects a block of fields. The road, being Roman, is completely straight, and cuts several of the fields – which follow the lie of the land – in half. No farmer would lay fields out in this way around a pre-existing road, suggesting strongly that the fields pre-date the road; which would put the creation of these nondescript Ceredigion fields into the pre-Roman period over 2,000 years ago.[134]

Back in Dinas, Rhiannon and I walk along the *clawdd* dividing farmed fields on the hillside from the open mountain of Mynydd Dinas. We can see most of the parish of Dinas laid out below us, from the rich soils of Dinas island, the woodland along the steep stream-valleys, the fields on the coastal plain and then the hillside below us rising to this moorland edge.

I am trying to visualise how this area would have looked during those long centuries when the infield-outfield system was used. Clearly, *cloddiau* were present, but they didn't envelop the entire lowland landscape as now. In fact, thanks to Rhiannon's painstaking work, we can reconstruct with a greater degree of confidence here than almost anywhere else in the country what would have lain before us 600 or 700 years ago.

'So that's the line of the old *gorclawdd* down there, just behind and to the left of the school playing field. And beyond that is the old infield, extending away towards the cliffs,' she indicates. Later, she shows me how even on modern OS maps you can clearly see the curve of the ploughed strips on this ancient infield in the line of the current hedgerows.

'Those hedges date to the eighteenth-century enclosures here, but they respect the lines of the much older strips that lay within the infield and that were held by different families and passed down. One of the tell-tale signs of that is the way the fields often have random-seeming dog-legs in their layout, which don't have any function now that they are used as pasture. But they came about through the ploughlines and quillets – strips of cultivated land – with the grass baulks that separated those strips from each other.'

I ask Rhiannon how typical she thinks this fossilisation of land-forms is across the country, given that similar patterns have been identified in north-west Wales near Harlech in an area that in medieval times had quite a different history to here.[135] It turns out that the key factor is ownership. In Bayvil, less than 10 miles away to the north-east, one large landowner owned much of the area and was able to completely reorganise the landscape under his control in the name of agricultural improvement in the seventeenth century. As a result, although archaeological digs can uncover traces of how people lived and used the land before then, the visible landscape sometimes carries very little indication of this. Improvement came and wiped away what had come before. 'By contrast,' says Rhiannon, 'here at Dinas, as in many other places, it's the fact that the infield had multiple owners or long-established tenancies that meant there was no-one able to do what Owen did at Bayvil. So we have this continuity not just in the settlements, but in the names of the pre-modern fields and in their locations and forms.'

But then what of the land to the south of the infield, this side of the old *gorclawdd*? As we had crossed that area on our way up here, Rhiannon had pointed out to me a beautiful, solid Victorian dwelling by the name of Ty Rhos, and had mentioned in a passing aside that some of the lands here were horribly wet in winter. She'd been giving me clues, I venture.

'Yes, that is the old outfield – here a *rhos*. It's markedly worse land in pretty much every way for agriculture, which explains why the *gorclawdd* dividing it from the infield runs where it does. We know from old descriptions of this area that the line of the main coast road – which has become the A487 – used to run through open common land. The clue is in the name, of course: Ty Rhos (which is 'Rhos

House') is a corruption of Tir y Rhos, or 'land on the common / moor', and that name is first recorded in 1640. So it's clear what happened – as enclosure happens generally in the landscape, someone here parcels off a bit of the open land,[136] and that becomes the basis of a smallholding; over time, the same thing happens across almost the entirety of the *rhos*. Now, to the untrained eye there is no difference between the fields along the A487 and those beyond the *gorclawdd*. But in reality, this is worse, wetter land, and you can in fact see a hint of the different histories in the square or rectangular field shapes here as compared to the long, slightly curved strip shapes within the old infield.'

I am entranced by the agricultural information embedded in the very shape of the landscape below me. We walk further, skylarks singing on the open moorland to our left and sheep grazing in small fields between stone banks to our right. Up here feels like a very different place to Cwm-yr-eglwys just a mile and a half downhill: we're over 200 metres above sea level and what had been a fresh breeze down below is blowing in stiff gusts up here. We can see for miles along the Pembrokeshire coast, down towards Carn Llidi above St Davids. The differences are shown in the field boundaries: what look like stone walls from a distance and turn out from up close to be stone-earth banks. I wonder how this fits into the landscape picture Rhiannon has been painting of Dinas? Are these fields also fairly recent enclosures of the common land?

'That's why I brought you here', Rhiannon smiles. 'Models can be helpful, but you've got to pay attention to the facts on the ground, and reality is always more complex than any talk of models or systems will allow.' It turns out that although there are plenty of farms and fields on these slopes that date from enclosures over the last couple of centuries, there are also places where something much older is going on.

This is Penmynydd. We are on the mountainside here, the other side of the *rhos* from the central part of the parish and the good infield land and church down there. It turns out that this place is first recorded as far back as the 1580s, but everything about it in terms of size, field systems and location is consistent with it being much older. That is confirmed by an archaeological survey of this hill which identifies ancient or prehistoric enclosures up on the hillside beyond the fields we are standing in.

In other words, this was a medieval hamlet in its own right, at the nucleus of its own farming system. Some of the circular enclosures up here are probably remnants of old infields that operated on a drastically smaller scale than those downhill. This is a place reminiscent of the Cornish landscape where the OSL dating recently took place down to the detail of climate and stoniness; it's more exposed areas like this that particularly benefit from the environmental niches created by hedgebanks, making crop cultivation possible.

'You see down there, the dog-legs in the walls? And the clearly curving lines of the field boundaries all along here, compared with the straight Victorian lines back there?' Rhiannon is in her element here, bringing to life texture and meaning in this landscape of sheep, grass and stone. 'This landscape has changed a lot over time; the moor was here in the eighteenth century, and the fields, but we know that at that time some of these fields were cropped. But there's a lot we still don't understand!' She walks over to a particularly tall line of boulders amidst the hillside scrub that turns out to have a regular square form, with another pile of boulders in the middle.

'I mean, what on earth is this? It puzzled the archaeologists who spotted it in a field survey here, and nobody knows what this was, or what period it comes from. Is it related to this line of stones here that you can make out on the hillside? At the end of the day, we just don't know enough about these landscapes.'

Be that as it may, I feel like I am starting to understand how this landscape works, and how the different parts hung together historically. The picture that Rhiannon has built of this parish and its surrounding areas over the last 1,000 years and more, drawing on the widest range of sources could be replicated elsewhere, and what we know suggests that for the most part, many of her conclusions apply to other parts of Wales. Detailed estate maps from north Wales in the 1630s and from mid Wales in the 1740s,[137] at a time when the infield-outfield system was still in use but gradually morphing into the patchwork we have inherited today, both support the general picture. Above all, when it comes to the *clawdd*, this tells us one very important thing: that when we come to seventeenth-/eighteenth-century enclosures, what's happening in Wales is a case of drastically expanding structures that were already familiar parts of the landscape. The dense mesh of hedges ribboned across the valleys of Wales are a legacy of the eighteenth century more than any other period, but the enclosed fields and the banks, hedges and walls that divided up the outfields and the *tir mynydd* were not innovations; rather, they were an expansion of a part of the farming landscape that had already been present to some extent for millennia over a much greater proportion of it.

But whereas the *clawdd* had been one of several key boundary features in the landscape, existing alongside lines of stones, ditches, grass verges and crosses, changing patterns of agriculture meant that their use drastically expanded while the other features' usefulness declined somewhat. Ecologically, this entailed the creation of an almost uninterrupted network of linear forests, that have now blanketed the countryside for a few centuries.

The older hedgebanks probably had hedges growing on top, at least for many of the long centuries in which they were in use; pollen evidence simply isn't specific enough to allow us to be certain of this, but at a Snowdonia site there is evidence for a possible hazel hedge growing along a field boundary tentatively dated to the fifth to second century BC.[138] In areas of high rainfall and fast tree growth where hedges grow even more readily than in wind-battered Snowdonia, and in a pre-1800s era when everything from house-building to the moveable fences to pound in cattle on the right part of the 'mountain' depended on wood to the need for kindling and firewood, it seems likely that this older generation of hedgebanks, then as now, had hedges growing on top.

The dramatic expansion in the number of fields in old documents bearing the name *cae* after 1500 supports this idea. The word *cae* in modern Welsh means 'field' but the etymology of the word lies in the idea of a hedge; a thing that encloses. From there, the meaning shifted to 'field within hedges' and thence to field in general. The spread of the word coincides exactly with the period when we know many more enclosed fields were created within the landscape; but the oldest incidences of the word occur in thirteenth-century documents, and the earliest field in Wales called *cae* dates to 1375.[139] Even before 1500 and the forward march of the hedge, linguistic evidence also suggests firmly that there were hedged fields in the Welsh landscape. If the skill and desire thus existed to maintain hedges, then it is far from fanciful to suppose that *cloddiau* were also often topped with hedges in medieval times, as they certainly were by the time of our oldest landscape paintings.[140]

The newer *cloddiau* laid out from the sixteenth to the nineteenth centuries, other than in areas where they were constructed as stone walls (in Welsh sometimes called *cloddiau carreg* or 'stone hedgebanks'), were certainly planted with hedgerow species, leading to the biodiverse linear forests of today. These require skill and knowledge both to lay and maintain, encoded often in sayings. 'Perth hyd fogel, perth ddiogel' goes a classic piece of countryside lore advising that a hedge should be laid thick to ensure stockproofing. Similarly, the Welsh border hedging style is distinguished by stakes being driven in at a 35° angle 30 inches apart (further than in most regional English styles), and the use of dead wood to protect both sides from browsing by stock.[141] Good farming sense in a Welsh context dictated that hedges be thick to be of value. And, as we have already seen, thick hedges are precisely what most species need in order to make good use of them as habitats and corridors. Dutch hedgehogs demonstrate this well: in the Netherlands, a country with significantly fewer miles of hedgerow than Wales, hedgehogs spend 87 per cent of their lives within just 5m of a hedge.[142]

Other pieces of folk wisdom reveal the place of hedgerows in the known landscape. 'Cynt y cwymp dâr na miaren o flaen gwynt' translates to 'an oak will fall before the briar in a gale', reflecting a landscape where most of the exposed, lone oak trees that may fall in strong winds stand in hedgerows alongside brambles. There is an entire vocabulary here; in English, that of stakes and pleachers, and in Welsh too of the *plygwr gwrych* or literally 'hedge-bender', reflecting the way hedgelaying traditionally involves cutting woody growth in winter and bending it forward to create a dense mat of growth, woven around central stakes.

But the value of *cloddiau* in particular – and here I am thinking of the archetypal pattern of a hedgebank with hedgerow on top – lies also in the oft-overlooked stone-and-earth bank. In a country with plentiful rainfall, the elevated and often sheltered environment this provides creates a crucial microclimate for plants that would struggle in fields or woodland and might otherwise have a more limited distribution – an example of this being the wild strawberry. In spring this drier, warmer soil, sometimes with small gaps between boulders or stones, also provides perfect burrowing grounds for solitary bees and bumblebees. Any semi-exposed stones will warm quickly in the sun, radiating gentle heat out and providing a cosy habitat for young bee larvae, safe and hidden from predators such as the Great Tit.

All this makes me see the hedges of the country in a new light; their presence in the landscape is one of its most ancient features, and they also remain of the utmost importance to both wildlife and farming. Some of the oldest hedgebanks, like the *gorclawdd* in Dinas and some of the ancient *cloddiau* in Snowdonia, are unsung functional monuments of real antiquity in the landscape, rivalling castles, standing stones and, in some cases, Stonehenge. And the newer hedges have provided here, as elsewhere in the British Isles, a lifeline to an innumerable number of species, from declining species of bee to some of our most crucial birds – all of it as a side-effect of trying to keep livestock in the right field.

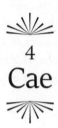

4
Cae

Biodiverse mini-prairies/fodder

The mid-June sun is beating down and this bright-flecked field is alive with the drone and buzz of countless insects, the chirping and twittering of contented chiffchaffs and chaffinches in the overgrown hedgerows forming a happy accompaniment. Around me in the swath is a rich array of grassland flowers and herbs: hawkbit, betony, lesser stitchwort, bird's foot trefoil, buttercups, knapweed and orchids, all flaunting their summertime wares to the invertebrate crowds of this place. We're in a lowland hay meadow, Caeau Llety Cybi, on the edge of the upper Teifi valley in Ceredigion. Within living memory, there were meadows of this kind all over Wales and beyond; but as a result of the chemical revolution in farming, they have declined by a precipitous 95–98 per cent in the past sixty years and now make up only 3 per cent of the Welsh countryside.[143] So this place is now a rare survival, an oasis of biodiversity within a farmed landscape where many of the green fields themselves are, in the words of the international plant charity Plantlife, a 'factory floor – ploughed, re-seeded, fertilised and sprayed with herbicide to maximise productivity'.[144] This particular 7-acre site is the way it is – and is in fact registered as a site of special scientific interest – because it is managed for biodiversity as a lowland hay meadow by the Wildlife Trust of South and West Wales.

Fields make up something in the region of two-thirds of the Welsh countryside by area,[145] and although these meadows for a range of reasons are emblematic of what fields can be in this part of the world, they are only one of many different types. As is true of fields of all sorts, hay meadows as a habitat in the British Isles are overwhelmingly human creations, maintained by people and their farming practices. Just as the diversity of wild species, of livestock breeds or of fruit varieties has declined because of fossil-fuelled agriculture, so too has the diversity of field types. But these human creations that can now be dismissed as industrial artifices inimical to nature were within living memory much more varied and interesting places, reflecting not only local flora and geology but also cultural practices and farming knowledge. The diversity of field types matters. And as we shall see, despite everything, a certain type of traditionalism within parts of farming culture has allowed some of this diversity to survive into the present day.

'The Wildlife Trust took over this place in the early 80s', Doug, one of the Trust's conservation officers, tells me, 'but it had been part of a small farm before then, Llety Cybi. The farmhouse building dates to something like the 1790s, but of course it could have been rebuilt on top of an older dwelling, so the farm itself may be several centuries old.' Although the four fields that make up the site are all marked on the 1905 Ordnance Survey map for this area, the 1840s tithe map show the three upper fields all as one large field, with only the steepest one in the corner separated by a hedge – which, as expected, shows the slightly collapsed remains of the old *clawdd* bank underneath the now outgrown ash and hazel. Frustratingly, the tithe maps for this area give neither field names nor land use, but basic agricultural knowledge dictates that they wouldn't all have been hay meadow.

'What we're doing here to a great extent is trying to *mimic* how lowland hay meadows in this area would have functioned', Doug tells me as we perch in the shade of an ash, overlooking the swaying grasses and flowers that fill the slope below us. 'A hay meadow would of course have been harvested for its hay; vital winter fodder for livestock over winter, where they can benefit from the summer growth and all those nutrients through the dark days.' Since the Trust took over, however, economic realities in both farming and conservation have meant that the only viable way for them to manage the land has been by grazing. Cattle held by a neighbouring farmer come onto the meadows between late July and mid-September, their grazing an approximation of the mowing that would traditionally have taken place here. Of course, their presence on the land during this period also means that this poor, acid soil typical of Ceredigion gets fertilised by two months' worth of manure. And that has an important effect on the growth of the meadow plants.

'It's a really delicate balancing act, trying to keep a place like this as a species-rich hay meadow', Doug explains to me as we circle and loop our way around the fields. 'Without grazing at all, in a place like this the land would become woodland quite quickly – it would definitely become scrubby young woodland within a decade or so. And even with light grazing, which really is what we have here, you can see how blackthorn, hazel, dog rose and bracken are all moving onto the fields from the hedgerows.'

He gestures towards the field edge to our right, where bracken and blackthorn are both encroaching, and are clearly already dominant on an area a good 30m in from the hedgerows. So is the land just too lightly grazed? Could they not put a few more cows on or leave them on for slightly longer and allow the livestock to just keep the growth down? It turns out of course to be a lot more complicated than that.

'The thing is cows have a mind of their own! They'll sooner overgraze the meadow than start on most of this woody stuff that's encroaching! And we actually also seem to have the opposite problem here at the same time. Because none of the plant matter is actually being taken off this land in the form of hay, but fertility is being brought to the site through the cows' muck, the nutrient levels here are being built up. And that means that the site is actually becoming more favourable to grasses than to these herbs and wildflower species that we actually want to see here!'

Keeping a species-rich hay meadow as a species-rich hay meadow turns out to be quite a challenge. And it is of course the flowering species that lead to these habitats being so valuable not only for plants but also for insects and the birds that live off them. Although, ominously, we don't see any on the warm June day I am there, Caeau Llety Cybi is home to and known for a large number of moths, dragonflies and butterflies, including the Small Tortoiseshell, Ringlet, Common blue, Meadow brown, Small skipper, Speckled wood, Gatekeeper, Red Admiral, Small heath, Green veined white, Large skipper, Painted lady, Peacock, Small copper, Wall and Small pearl-bordered fritillary.[146] For the chaffinches and swallows here, the moths and dragonflies are, respectively, important parts of their diet, and for the buzzard I see circling overhead, a healthy population of songbirds gives meal options beyond the fluctuating rabbit populations. Beyond this, in autumn the fields are splayed with the internationally endangered pink waxcap fungi, of which many of the most important populations are in mid Wales and which only grow on grassland not affected by modern chemical agriculture. As we lean back onto this warm hillside after a zig-zag traverse of the four fields and Doug waxes lyrical on the dynamics of this place, I reflect on that reassuring nature truism: the more you look, the more you see. And the more you understand, the more you wonder – and the more questions you have.

Almost all the natural treasures that are present on this site are here because of the way it is managed – as the nature-starved fields around testify. The orchids – *tegeiriannau* – are the star of the show here for people, and hundreds of greater butterfly orchids have been counted in this one field alone. But we know that orchids, as well as relying on a particular sort of land management for their habitat, also depend on a soil rich in fungi. I'm trying to understand exactly what it is that keeps this place so rich in species, so I ask Doug what it would take to kill off the waxcap fungi population living here under our feet? 'Oh, just plough it up and spray it with artificial fertilisers. Easy enough!' That is precisely what has happened to create the bright green fields I can see on many of the hills around. But how about older ways of ploughing and fertilising land with muck? What would that do to the fungi – and the orchids? Doug looks away pensively. 'Well, the ploughing would probably damage the fungi a bit. But as long as it wasn't, you know, heavy ploughing year on year but maybe happening in some kind of rotation system with muck and fallow years, I'd be very surprised if the fungi didn't survive that.' That, of course, is within a traditional system. It's telling, Doug points out, that it wouldn't necessarily work today.

'When you give the cattle ivermectin [a commonly used dewormer], the back of the pack specifically tells you not to put cattle out onto biodiverse or species-rich grassland for many weeks afterwards, because the chemicals are carried out in their dung. We did an investigation into that once where we cut into the dung every few days after application and over weeks and weeks you could see the bacterial life slowly returning to the cowpats.'

The devil, as always, is in the detail. But there's an important point underlying this: the Wildlife Trust, with very good reason given the alarming declines in this field, has been managing this site as a lowland hay meadow for several decades, but that is not necessarily a good reflection of how the fields were used historically. Abundant evidence for field use in nearby parts of Wales until the middle decades of the twentieth century demonstrates the way the landscape worked before the chemical revolution. In any given year, a farm's fields were broadly divided into arable, pasture and hay meadow, each of which had a crucial role to play in the farm's system. But this is where farming knowledge and skill come in: because these categories were – and are – far from set in stone.

Fifteen words for field

The Welsh language has fifteen to twenty different words for field – depending on how you define 'field' – each of which carries a particular nuance. The point is not that there are more shades of meaning in Welsh than in English (on the contrary, English also has a great many terms) but that they express the full range of functions and forms that a 'field' has fulfilled in the rugged Welsh landscape, as well as the ways of managing the land that have given rise to them. Today, most of lowland Wales is composed of the monotonous green of improved grassland; one or two types of field repeated ad nauseam. But the cultural record kept very much alive within the Welsh language belies this apparently timeless verdancy and reveals instead the diversity that had characterised the fieldscape until the mid-twentieth century.

Many of these terms for different fields remain in common usage in Welsh, even though the field types they refer to have been drastically rarer over the past several decades. They all embody a detailed understanding of how the land works and how it can be husbanded:

Maes. This word originally denoted the old arable infields that David Austin and Rhiannon Comeau had been telling me about. As their work has demonstrated, many of these fields had been cropped since time immemorial once our oldest written records appear, and we can surmise that every major farmholding would have been associated with one. At base a single large[147] field, a *maes* was subdivided into strips and parts, each of which had its own name and logic, e.g. the headland or *talar*, left unploughed to give space for the plough to turn around or the *grwn*, a ridge of ploughed land between two furrows, the breadth of which according to Welsh law was 27 feet.

During the early-modern enclosure period almost all the *meysydd* were split up with hedgerows into a number of smaller fields.[148] But the word lives on and is reflected in the modern Welsh word used specifically for a large field, whatever its purpose, such as a sports field, festival field or indeed field of study. And both *maes* and the associated terms for strips and divisions within it (such as *llain, slang* or *erw)* live on in place-names across Wales: the town of Maesteg ('fair Maes'), the Bangor suburb of Maesgeirchen (from an old farm name 'Maes of the oat') or Llain-goch in Anglesey ('red strip of ploughed land'), and in literary and poetic language. The retention of their connotation reflects the depth to which the farming landscape has penetrated the linguistic subconscious.

Dôl. A common word, evocative of summer days, this ancient word related to the Welsh verb 'to worship' (*addoli*) primarily denotes water-meadows. This is low-lying land in a valley bottom on the banks of a river or a lake, suitable for grazing during the growing season – and by extension can also mean other meadows that are not hay meadows.[149] The word appears in some of the oldest Welsh manuscripts – the Black Book of Carmarthen, the Book of Aneirin – from the thirteenth century, and as we saw in the introduction, provides the setting for one of Dafydd ap Gwilym's poems. From Dolbadarn to Dolfor, this element also occurs in place-names throughout the country, most of which are quite transparent in their meaning to a Welsh speaker.

Gwaun. The definition offered for this word in the standard Welsh reference dictionary, *Geiriadur Prifysgol Cymru*, encapsulates the agricultural sense of this term, as a *gwaun* is given as both '*high and wet level ground, moorland, heath*' and as '*low-lying marshy ground, meadow*'. For anyone familiar with the Welsh landscape, this term makes perfect sense from an agricultural point of view, as similar rough grazing composed of many of the same plant species and fitting much the same niche within a farming system can be found in many parts of the country either on low-lying marshy ground or on high, wet and flat hilltops.[150] Reflecting the difficulty of translation even between Welsh and English, and the relevance of contextual knowledge, Lhuyd in 1707 gives the English translation for *gwaun* as 'meadow', while his 1722 manuscript offers 'a plain on the top of a mountain' as the appropriate English definition.

Parc. A word with an interesting history, borrowed into both Middle English and Middle Welsh from the Old French *parc*. It referred originally to an enclosed tract of land kept for animals to be hunted, as in royal or noble parks in the Middle Ages. That sense of the area being enclosed led to it being widely used in Welsh for enclosed fields more broadly within an agricultural setting.[151] Although used in Pembrokeshire for any field, the primary meaning retained the key link with animals, and several early modern dictionaries give 'paddock' as a gloss for 'parc'.[152] This term also appears in place-names all over the country, and often indicates an area (usually a field) where livestock were kept.[153]

Arddlas. An old farmer near Harlech defined this as 'an old parcel of land that has been well looked after' or kept in good heart. The word itself – *ardd* + *glas* (green + cropland) – implies the function these fields had, the origins of which are probably reflected in native Welsh law. The modern Welsh word for 'garden' is related to the *ardd* element here, and it is far from fanciful to surmise that these quite small fields may have been commonly used for vegetable production: leeks, cabbages and the like require high levels of fertility. An analysis of the occurrence of the term in field names in one region of Snowdonia shows that places called *arddlas* have clearly been situated carefully within the landscape to take advantage of shelter from prevailing winds, exposure to sunshine and with access both to water and to a nearby cottage.[154] They also never occur above 300m, where temperatures are consistently lower throughout the growing season. So the distribution of this term within the landscape reflects both historical use and propitious sites. Although the word itself is in common use now only by a declining number of rural dwellers, it demonstrates again the depth of the local agricultural knowledge encoded in the language.

Cae. Although this word now serves as the general term for 'field' in Welsh, it nevertheless has a narrower range of meanings than the English 'field' (cf. *maes* above). We tracked in the previous chapter how the word became increasingly common as hedgerows and walls divided the landscape up to a much greater extent from the sixteenth century onwards, as its meaning shifted from the original sense of hedge or fence to the parcel of land closed in by such a hedge or fence. But the word also demonstrates well the extent to which the logic of an agricultural landscape permeates the Welsh language; the everyday verb *cau* in Welsh (pronounced identically to *cae* in south Walian dialects), meaning 'to close' (a door or a window), is itself derived from the noun *cae*. The first Welsh–English dictionary, published in 1547, gives us a peek of this happening in the entry 'kae cae – to hedge [in]'.

Those are just a fraction of the Welsh 'field' words; there are many others, including *gwndwn, ysfa, ffwyneg, gogor, clun, lledrog, cadlas, braenar, lluarth, cyfer, tonglas, rhandir, twmpath* and *grwn* – all of which are used to describe fields from a range of different viewpoints. Some originate in measures of arable land as defined in ancient Welsh law and custom; others in the way the field is used within a farming system, or its shape or size. These terms all come into their own, though, when it comes to old field names. As we have already seen, the oldest of these can be truly ancient, speaking to us across well over 1,000 years of history of land use. More commonly, we have countless examples that are many hundreds of years old – some of which have shifted slightly in meaning over those centuries while others, remarkably, have kept both their meaning and their form.

The sale of two acres of arable land near Harlech called Cefn y Filltir is recorded in a document dating back to 1390. This block reappears in an estate document from 1574 and so on throughout the early modern period until the fields show up in Victorian tithe maps and still exist sporting the same name in the modern day.[155] Or the field Gafael Crwm in the same area, first noted in the 1420 Record of Caernarvon. *Gafael* was a technical term relating to bond land, and many of the field names that included this element lost it when Welsh law gradually lost its relevance after the 1536 Acts of Union. This name remained in use, however, and reappears in the 1840s tithe maps and is still in use orally today among Welsh speakers in the parish to refer to the same location as the 1420s record.[156]

Field names were chosen carefully to describe a field's location, shape or soil quality as well as ownership or, in some cases, historical events.[157] The large diversity in terms used for fields is a reflection of the usefulness of this information within the culture historically. Although there are a wide variety of terms for all sorts of living creatures, as you would expect within an agricultural culture, where differentiating between species had no practical value, it simply didn't happen. As a result, few species of butterfly or bumblebee ever had specific names in Welsh until the advent of conservation during the twentieth century, when many native species were given names for the first time.

Since fields were already an ancient part of the landscape by the time recorded history started 2,000 years ago, they appear in the Welsh cultural record from the very earliest times, rather than the shadow of some primeval wildwood blanketing the land. This is reflected in the oldest mythological tales, both in Wales and in the contemporaneous Irish tradition just over the sea. For instance, the tale of Manawydan in the Mabinogi takes the planting of corn fields as one of its central actions, while the Irish Lir is associated with the 'hill of the white field'. Fields, as a core building-block of the agricultural societies these myths arose in, are given symbolic and ritual significance.

This relationship to the land is also reflected in the earliest surviving literature, all of which is found in poems that were composed for performance in the first millennium AD. In *Gwaith Gwenystrad* ('the battle of Gwenystrad'), a war poem attributed to the sixth-century Taliesin, the Saxon foe is said to be sheltered from the Welsh warlord by 'neither woodland nor field [*maes*]'. This warlord, Urien Rheged, is called both 'battle-winner', and 'cattle-raiser'. In a very different poem, *Aduvyneu Taliesin* or 'The pleasant things of Taliesin', the wartime poet brings before his audience a word-portrait of a world at peace. What sort of world is it? One where seagulls play and blossom comes forth on pear trees; one composed of slow summer days, crackling fires in the hearth and children at play. It is of course a deeply religious, and a deeply agricultural world too, where the background for all these pleasant things is that of cornfields to harvest and farm animals giving birth:

> Pleasant, berries in the time of harvest;
> Also pleasant, wheat upon the stalk ...
> Pleasant, the open field to cuckoos and the nightingale ...
> Also pleasant, the charlock in the springing corn ...
> Pleasant, the time when calves draw milk;
> Also pleasant, foamy horsemanship.[158]

The 'open field' here is of course a translation of *maes*. The 'charlock' is a translation of *cadafarth*, a Welsh term for field mustard, defined in modern botany as a weed of arable ground, which Taliesin knew implicitly from the world in which he lived. He also knew from everyday knowledge of the land that there is a profusion of berries in western Britain at harvest time; we don't need to claim him as a proto-ecologist to note that an intimate familiarity with the agricultural landscape of his day is the stuff of this very earliest of Welsh, and British, nature writing. He is, of course, also writing at a time of mass destruction and war, his poems replete with references to mangled flesh, bloodstained men and grief as the order in which he lives is threatened by outside, pagan forces. His poetry is the product of this terrible pressure on British (i.e. Old Welsh) culture, and the evocative references he makes to a peacetime setting are therefore all the more significant.[159] It is noteworthy that the cultural landscape it reflects is a farming one, and that much of it also comes to us through a time of deep trauma.[160]

Jumping forward a few centuries, we come to an array of Middle Welsh poems praising the natural world, one of which will suffice to give us a flavour of twelfth-century sentiment:

> Month of May, loveliest season
> The birds loud, the growth green
> Plough in furrow, ox in yoke,
> Green sea, land cut dapple.[161]

Six long centuries after Taliesin's singing we find a remarkably similar image of how the world looks when all is well. It is striking how once again the *maes* and its activity comes above all to symbolise peace and life; springtime birdsong finds its place alongside the oxen yoked to the plough. Although an image that resonates with the broad thrust of Western culture, it is worth noting that this is not a reflection or imitation of the *pastoral* idyll inherited into modern European languages from Greek and Latin; this is a Welsh *arable* scene. A final poem illustrates the extent to which this image of the ploughed *maes* penetrated medieval Welsh literary culture:

Cnwd a gyrch mewn cnodig âr,	[It [the plough] fetches crops
Cnyw diwael yn cnoi daear.	from the rich earth,
E fynn ei gyllell a'i fwyd	It's a good beast biting the ground.
A'i fwrdd dan fôn ei forddwd.	It must have its knife and its food
Gŵr a'i anfodd ar grynfaen,	And its board right under its
Gwas a fling a'i goes o'i flaen.	thigh.
	It goes unwillingly through
	stones,
	It skins the earth with leg
	outstretched.][162]

This is a poem – 'Y Llafurwr' (The Ploughman) by Iolo Goch – that is focused entirely on the common ploughman, who occupied one of the lowest rungs within medieval society, and that culminates in the majestically laconic statement 'Aredig, dysgedig yw' – ploughmanship is nothing less than scholarship. Within a culture of praise poetry primarily directed at princes, nobles and God, the inclusion within the corpus of a long and eloquent poem honouring the work of ploughmen in upholding society tells us something of that society's conception of itself and of the key place the ploughed field had within it.

In fact, this poem is one of a significant number of references to ploughmanship that crop up throughout the classical Welsh literary corpus of the fourteenth–sixteenth centuries, where every aspect of arable farming, from furrows to lead oxen and threshing, are used as metaphors for the leaders of society. The sixteenth-century 'chief bard' Simwnt Fychan articulates this in a treatise on poetics where he explicitly states that 'a good way to praise a patron is to call him a good husbandman. And husbandry is to plough. And ploughing is to welcome all and sundry to one's court ... and then to sow. And that sowing is to shower gold and silver on bards and poets.'[163] The Welsh poetic tradition has been at the core of the culture's conception of itself, the land and nationhood; the degree to which the idea of field-work has in turn permeated that tradition can hardly be overstated.

All of this retains real salience in Welsh-speaking culture today. Within a cultural group numbering some half a million speakers, the range of publications and the amount of grassroots interest in the fieldscape as well as the landscape, and its linguistic and cultural history more broadly, is remarkable. The television channel S4C ran a whole season in 2014 of a documentary series exploring specific field names on farms in different parts of the country; it was so popular they returned for a second series. The Welsh Place-Name Society is an active community group, operating primarily in Welsh. Its campaigns to safeguard the names of everything from field names to mountain peaks and slate-quarry terms have gained wide traction – sometimes spilling out from the Welsh-language media into discourse in English, including from London-based newspapers. Similarly, the grassroots Llên Natur (The Literature of Nature) website has a large active community that has collaborated on projects like a historic weather bank localising weather records for very specific locations in Wales, based on diary records from farms and smallholdings extending back to the mid-nineteenth century.

And all this is, of course, reflected within Welsh-language music, poetry and novels, which have spent a significant amount of time and energy dissecting the meaning of place, rootedness and change, and within that the significance of deep knowledge of a small area of land. It comes, for instance, as no surprise within the culture to find families like the farmers on the edge of Dinas Mawddwy near Machynlleth who pride themselves on having kept field names constant in their patch for 1,000 years.[164] It comes under the heading of 'local knowledge' that is viewed within this culture not as a parochial matter but as one intimately related to the meaning of a life lived within a known landscape. For a large number of Welsh speakers, this is not a matter of antiquarian or academic interest; it can be a visceral thing that touches on identity and loss.

Mwnt arable fields

The *maes* has, for the most part disappeared from the Welsh landscape,[165] but the smaller enclosed fields that succeeded the *meysydd* often kept their original names even as they were closed in by *cloddiau*. For centuries these newer, smaller arable fields lay side-by-side with hay meadows, paddocks and pastures in a true patchwork landscape. But this enormous variety of field types, reflected in the broad Welsh terminology we saw earlier, has become a sort of linguistic relict as the diversity of fields in the Welsh landscape has declined dramatically over the second half of the twentieth century.

The arable fields above Mwnt on the Ceredigion coast are designated today as a site of special scientific interest for its now rare arable habitat, of value because of the threatened community of arable weeds found there. Populations of annual knawel, small-flowered catchfly, narrow-fruited cornsalad, corn marigold and weasel's snout make this in all likelihood the single richest complex of arable fields for plants in Wales.[166] Viewed in the light of the last several thousand years of Welsh agriculture, there is something almost pathetic in this need to conserve for its weeds a type of fieldscape that was almost ubiquitous until within living memory, but it's true – there are hardly any arable fields left in Wales, accounting for only 6 per cent of the country's farmland.

As you descend the steep and narrow lanes from inland Ceredigion into this little arable world hugging the clifftops, you feel something shift in the microclimate which partly accounts for the persistence of arable cultivation here. This hunch is borne out by Met Office statistics that show a pocket here of consistently higher annual sunshine hours and lower annual rainfall than areas only a few miles inland.[167] We are at the tail end of a summer drought when I come here with a South African farming friend, and the company allows me to see with fresh eyes the dramatic difference in the landscape between the brown and yellow vistas around us and the still-green hedgerows and pastures we had just passed through, inland.

Caeau Crug Bychan, Tŷ Gwyn, Llwyn Ysgaw; some of these seven fields remain in cultivation by local farmers, while a couple are held by the National Trust. The 1840s tithe maps for the parish of Mwnt reveal contemporary land use in these fields and the names of the farms and cottages, many of which in rural Wales were taken from the patch of land they were raised on. Many of these names reflect the long-established arable landscape here with names like Llain-y-Mwnt or Lleine (simply 'strips'). But we also find a 'parc' – Parc-y-grachen – and an old 'gwaun' in the form of Pen-y-waun. Even this most arable of Welsh landscapes was historically always a mixed farming landscape, and the tithe maps themselves testify abundantly to this, with different fields noted in the record as arable, pasture, meadow, rough grazing, ryegrass and clover, pasture and furze, or indeed pasture-or-meadow. And the state of cultivation of the fields now designated as a prime example of an arable site in an Atlantic context are by no means all marked as 'arable' on the tithe apportionment. The field below Tŷ Gwyn, for instance, directly above the foaming waves and behind Mwnt's iconic whitewashed chapel and now a precious home for the arable weeds corn marigold, corn spurrey and field woundwort, was in 1847 noted as pasture. Within a traditional farming set-up, the categories of different fields are far from set in stone.

This sheds light on the conundrum at Caeau Llety Cybi; although, for good reason, fields had names and often designations based on what they were suited to, within this overall framework farmers have always rotated fields in one way or another. The old patchwork field landscape doesn't just display geographic diversity; it also displays diversity viewed over time, as fields were brought in and out of cultivation, laid fallow, managed as ley or in later centuries sown with clover. Local farmer George Owen describes the practice as carried out in Elizabethan Pembrokeshire, where land was dunged and cropped with oats for seven or eight years before being turned to pasture again 'for eight or ten years'.[168] We can see this patchwork landscape in action in the next parish over from Caeau Llety Cybi, called Cellan, where the tithe maps record field names: here, llain isa (lower ploughed strip) lies next to cae gwenith (wheat field), while cae coch (red field – red denoting ploughing) is next to dôl isa (lower watermeadow) and Wairglodd ucha (upper hay meadow). In some of the tithe maps from this period, the field names directly contradict the stated current uses at that point in the 1840s.[169]

Given all this, the Wildlife Trust's efforts to keep the four fields at Llety Cybi in a state of almost suspended animation as hay meadows turns out to be doubly beset by problems: both by the economic constraints which means they can't actually cut it for hay anyway, and by the fact that these four adjacent fields on a relatively steep slope may never have been kept as hay meadows decade after decade. Some of the fields may well have been alternately ploughed, put down to pasture and managed for hay at different points over time.[170] The best way to maintain a traditionally farmed habitat, it turns out, could be just to farm it traditionally.

Cwm-yr-Alaw

In some special places, the biodiversity of hay meadows has survived even without the Wildlife Trust to deliberately manage the land for the sake of its wildlife. What's more, these places seem to exhibit exactly that equilibrium that conservationists have been trying – to some extent – to restore. These places are all in the care of farmers who decided to resist the 'improvements' pushed on the farming industry by government and agri-corporations throughout the second half of the twentieth century and beyond.

The farm of Cwm-yr-Alaw is one such place.[171] This is fairytale country: almost 10 miles away from the nearest market town of 1,500 souls, lying among steeply diving hills sprayed with oakwoods and crags. Kites, sparrowhawks, peregrines and buzzards circle overhead as we crawl along the narrow lanes up and up to the farm. The farm itself is the very last one before you climb out onto the mountain plateau beyond, and there is something distinctly continental, almost Alpine, about this setting even though we are only 270m above sea level and the peaks nearby – Foel Fadian, Creigiau Esgair Fochnant, Hyddgen – don't even attain 600m in altitude.

I'm with Sam Robinson, a young local shepherd and friend who has worked on many of the farms among these mountains and folds. The road has turned to a dirt track and we leave the pickup to walk on and around this holding nestling beneath the crags, amounting to some 300 or so acres. He's brought me here to show me the land and to see how the landscape and its nature hangs together around the hill farm itself.

'Of course, what's now one farm used to be three separate holdings', he explains as we approach a low-slung stone longhouse. 'Both this farmhouse and the other one we'll come to are holiday cottages – leaving just Cwm-yr-Alaw itself. Gareth farms all this alone, though his brother lives and farms only a couple of miles away.' As we approach the longhouse we can see that they have a fire going in the hearth, even though it's early June, the sun is shining and down in the valley behind us we left people in T-shirts chatting on benches.

'This place is really on the margins,' he tells me. 'You've got to understand that what you see here is only the way it is because of that, and because Gareth, and his father before him, have resisted certain changes on this farm. He'd probably be regarded as old-fashioned by most farmers in the area, despite the fact that he has actually got the farm system here working in a delicate balance. He's kind to the land – he doesn't push it too far.'

We're coming up to a ramshackle wooden barn with a quad bike outside it under the sessile oaks and pop our heads round the door. Three men – Gareth, his brother and a friend – are hard at it, dagging sheep (removing dirty, wet wool from between the beasts' legs). Gareth has a flock of 200 to 300 Welsh mountain sheep, and then a small herd of fifteen cows, a mix of native Welsh blacks and continental breeds.[172] Though it's a Saturday evening, they're clearly going to be working away for a while yet among the warm fetor of the animals. Gareth lives alone and like many hill farmers, the never-ending work of the farm keeps him there most of the time. 'Dech chi'n dod i'r côr nos Lun?' – You coming to choir on Monday? – comes the question in lilting Montgomeryshire Welsh. 'Yes! See you tomorrow!' is the friendly reply; tomorrow being Sunday making little difference in a cycle dominated more by the natural course of the year than society's pattern of weeks.

There's been a suicide in the last few days in this scattered, close community, and the mood is sober. But as we come up to the next field gate my eyes widen. Here in front of us is an upland wildflower meadow of precisely the sort that has become an endangered species. 'Yes,' Sam smiles, 'this is Yr Henfaes – one of the farm's most important fields. It is incredibly productive, but look at this for a wildflower display.'

The place is a pastel profusion of colour on this June evening: purple tufts of self-heal and knapweed peeping out among the sunny hawkbit, pignut, eyebright and yellow-rattle. The latter – arian y gweirwyr (haymakers' money) – is a well-known indicator of a traditional hay meadow in good health, and plays an essential role as a semi-parasitic plant in reducing the vigour of grasses and allowing a wider mix of flowering plants to thrive. The air above is thick with the buzzing of bees and countless flying insects, hoverflies and moths, and as we walk slowly through the field drinking in the abundant life, the piles of crusted cattle-dung from earlier in the year are clear to see. The enthusiasm of nature-loving gardeners aside, establishing a new hay meadow is in fact a difficult feat, almost impossible without judicious use of the right number and sort of grazing animals. This wonderful wildlife haven, so different to many of the fields in the more fertile lowlands a few miles downhill, lives a precarious existence.

And this is all here because of the field's place in the farm system. Unsurprisingly given its name – 'the old *maes*' – until only a matter of decades ago this was the farm's main arable field, and Gareth's father grew traditional varieties of oat here for a year at a time (quite possibly the grey oats native to this area), before giving it a rest in a multi-year grass ley rotation. Who knows just how old this *maes* is, or how long it was used as an arable infield until Gareth's father last sowed oats there. But both the name and the evidence of our eyes show why this particular patch of land, up here among the poor mountain soils, served as the bread-provider for people and livestock alike. And it is also no surprise that since then it has become one of the farm's core hay fields, and so continues to play a crucial role in feeding the livestock through the winter. Gareth has found the sweet spot with this field, getting the most out of it for his animals without exhausting the land. Modern, conventional livestock agriculture is based around reseeding fields and making silage. The aim is to create a high-input, high-output system using the most protein-rich grasses to get the maximum return on investment. Although Cwm-yr-Alaw isn't farmed in the same way now as it was even fifty years ago, much of the underlying logic of low-input agriculture has persisted here. This field receives nothing but cow manure – it's managed completely organically. In a few weeks' time, in July, Gareth will dry cut the hay here and then in August he'll bring the lambs onto this field for the *adlodd* – the aftergrass that comes through vigorously after the haymaking, which will help fatten them up. Then the hay itself will help feed the flock through the winter. That is in fact the main reason he keeps a small herd of cows – for their manure on fields like this. The farm's sales do include heifers and store steers, but this is a sheep farm really, raising organic lamb. How do you feed sheep through the winter in a mountainous area like this where growth stops in autumn and doesn't restart really till mid-spring? You need feed of some sort – silage, or hay. Modern know-how will sell you all sorts of products (most of which depend heavily on fossil fuels) to that end; or older wisdom will tell you, as some of the older farmers around here still say, that without cattle and their manure on a farm, the fields start getting sick.

What impresses me most as I listen to Sam's description of how the farm works is the fact that Gareth has got the whole system to a kind of equilibrium: yields of hay from Henfaes are consistent, meaning that in terms of nutrients year on year about the same amount is returned to the land in the form of manure as is taken off it in the form of hay. The abundant wildflowers are the byproduct of this, along with the beetles that populate the manure pats, the insects that live off the flowers, the small birds providing prey for the peregrines and sparrowhawks here, all the way to the teeming soil life. In other words, a sheer but unsurveyed number of wild species here owe their existence to the fact that Gareth has continued to base his farm system around cattle manure. Take the cattle out, stop making hay from the field and reseed it instead, and you can be pretty sure that the soil life, insect life and, in all likelihood, much of the bird life that this field supports would start declining. Similarly, take the cattle out and don't reseed and it will become scrub and then woodland; a wonderful home for many other birds and insects – but not these particular ones.

There is a fascinating comparison to be made here with the hay meadows at Caeau Llety Cybi and the Wildlife Trust's valiant efforts to keep them as hay meadows using volunteers and techniques from the world of conservation practice. As Doug had told me and the encroaching bracken and blackthorn abundantly testified, getting the balance right has been difficult for them. But of course, theirs is an exercise in conservation, whereas traditional low-input farming is a different exercise, which involves juggling the growth and decay of a system where every component is profoundly alive – the soil, the livestock, the crops, the labourers, the plants, insects and birds that all contribute to its state on any given day. Poor soil, sick labourers, a surfeit of one insect species – all have knock-on effects on every other part of the farm. And so, as Doug points out, where the Wildlife Trust needs to use volunteers is to clear the bracken: any bracken encroachment onto hay meadows before the mid-twentieth century would have been harvested for animal bedding.

What's more, as we've seen, the chances that all four fields were used as hay meadows for decades or centuries on end are small. Any good farmer knows that different fields or areas of land have different capabilities, and much of the skill in farming lies in really knowing the land; knowing which parts of your land are best suited to cropping or pasture, and also how long a piece of land can cope with different management regimes. But once you move out of this system and into a modern, chemical system, the ball game changes entirely. Doug likens it to taking out a mortgage. You buy in the fertilisers, the seed, the machinery and you need money to do that. Then you need those higher yields to finance the loan. Once you're in that kind of system, it's really hard to get out. But the economics of that system, developed ultimately for the benefit of agribusiness corporations and suited only to the most productive lands in the northern hemisphere, have turned out to be a debt trap to farmers in any other context. The neighbouring farmer at Llety Cybi, whose cattle have grazed these fields for years, would love to return his land to the sort of state the reserve is in. 'But I think he feels it's too late for him. The system is against it.'

Hay meadows are defined as semi-natural grassland; from an ecological point of view they are an approximation of what happens when wild grazing herbivores are present in large enough numbers to keep the land open from tree cover, but without overgrazing. But that doesn't explain at all how they came about in this context; here, they are the product of a farming system that has identified one particular state that the land can inhabit if managed in a way that harnesses the naturally occurring grasses and herbs for winter fodder. That, when done in a traditional way, many wild species happily find a niche within it is an entirely unsurprising outcome of a low-intensity, organic system developed over millennia.

5
Ffridd

Lightly wooded mountainside/
seasonal grazing and nutrient source

We trudge up the steep trackway on a mild September afternoon, peak after peak emerging into view as we climb the slope. Eventually we clamber up onto a rocky outcrop, immediately above a ruined dwelling, wrongly marked on the OS map as a sheepfold, and survey the view. This is Snowdonian grandeur of the sort people cross oceans to enjoy. 'Dyma fy hoff le i ddod â phobl iddo ar y fferm,' Alun explains to me. 'Dyma ni'r Arenig, Y Dduallt, Carreg Lusog, Rhobell Fawr ac yna'r Gader lawr fan acw' ('This is my favourite place to bring people on the farm. Here we can see Arenig Fawr, then y Dduallt, Carreg Lusog, Rhobell Fawr and then Cader Idris down over there'). And 50m or so below us down the mountainside is what I have come to see, and to try to understand – the layer of *ffridd* lying lengthways across the hillside on this farm, like so many others in this part of Snowdonia. The *ffridd* is at once one of the most important habitats within these mountain landscapes, and like hay meadows, one of the most unstable: entirely dependent on human management of the landscape.

I am deep within Welsh-speaking Wales, in a place layered with cultural resonance – and for nobody more so than Alun, who now farms this 700-acre hill farm by himself. This is an area renowned within Welsh-language culture for raising generations of poets, musicians and novelists, and keeping the unique musical tradition of *cerdd dant* alive.[173] As I wander through the deep-slung 300-year-old farmhouse, volumes of poetry, novels and literary criticism spanning the last century and more of eisteddfods prop up shelves, and perhaps even the roof, in places. The bonds of community and culture here are tightly knit and, as I am to learn, are intimately bound up in the landscape.

The farm, Cae Coch or 'Red Field', takes its name from the lower hillsides that turn red each autumn from the sea of bracken. There is some bracken on the *ffridd*, though less than there was in Alun's youth when it was still cut to be used as bedding for the sheep during shearing. In total there are five fields at Cae Coch called *ffridd*, all of which retain their key function within the farm's system. The difference between these and the farm's infields on the valley bottom are obvious, even to the untrained eye. Up here, rather than improved grassland there is a feracious mix of hawthorn, willow, ferns and rushy grass, all forming rich hues and shades today as September starts to tip into autumn in the uplands. 'The farms around here that lost their *ffridd* back in the mid-twentieth century to the enforced forestry really got dealt a body blow,' Alun explains, with a gesture over towards some of his neighbours' holdings. 'That's Hywel Dda and you can see how all the middle slopes that were *ffridd* are covered in those conifers. A lot of it was compulsory purchase for government-backed forestry, and it just made many of the farms uneconomical. We have a family story around how Taid, my grandfather, fought to keep our *ffriddoedd* which is how we held onto them – but whatever the truth of the matter, having them on the farm enables the kind of traditional hill-farming I try to do here.'

We wander back down the mountainside, before crossing the highest of the stone walls back onto the *ffriddoedd*, each with its own identity: Wyneb y ffridd, Ffridd ganol, Ffridd 'foty, Ffridd bella, Ffridd hyrddod. Or, roughly translated: Face of the *ffridd*, Middle *ffridd*, Summer-dwelling *ffridd*, Farther *ffridd* and Rams' *ffridd*. All are bounded by impressive and substantial stone walls, with the lowest three backing onto the richer green of the valley bottom fields. Some of them are full of hawthorn and gorse, with large stands of bracken. Others are substantially grassier or have expansive areas of reeds. But the striking thing about this collection is how different they are, not only to the mountain above and the green infields below, but also to each other.

This diversity reflects something of the *ffridd*'s history. Although the term 'ffridd' is now dotted all across the uplands of Wales, it was originally borrowed into the language from an Old English word for woodland or wood pasture, first appearing in writing in Welsh in the early fourteenth century. Ironically, as it was incorporated and moulded into the pastoral farming systems of these hills, it became a term difficult to translate adequately into English, with the standard University of Wales dictionary offering 'moorland, frith, rough mountain pasture, sheep-walk, woodland, forest and park'. Ecologically speaking, the functional gap between moorland or rough mountain pasture on the one hand, and woodland or forest on the other is substantial – and none of those dictionary terms comes near to recognisably denoting what a *ffridd* is. A Welsh–English dictionary from 1783 helpfully offers 'a shrubby place'. And a more native sense of this scrubby place can be deduced from two common Welsh plants: *Ffion y ffridd*, or foxglove, and *ffriddlys*, or anemone, which grows not only in woodland but also in bracken and heathery areas. To expand on this loose definition, what we are dealing with here is a usually enclosed area of slightly scrubby, grazed hillside set between the infields and the open mountain, found anywhere in the mountains of mid and north Wales.[174]

And in a very real sense in an area like this valley the *ffriddoedd* define the landscape, precisely by virtue of their slight amorphousness, neither one thing nor the other. Make your way attentively through the valley bottoms of Meirionnydd trying to interpret the landscape, and you will quickly land on the *ffridd* as a stand-out feature that needs some work to understand – all the more so if you are familiar with other mountain landscapes in Europe. Pure woodland is easy to comprehend on a mountainside – though its survival always merits asking why. The open moorland of much of the Scottish Highlands similarly can be understood as owing its existence to the (forced) absence of (local, farming) people and the preponderance of sheep. Improved pasture, as can be found on mountainsides anywhere from mid Wales to Italy can also be easily explained. A mix of valley-bottom infields and open moorlands above is also a common feature of upland landscapes in the British Isles. The *ffridd* is none of the above, but rather a transition-zone collection of habitats in constant, delicate balance: walled in like greenfield pasture, but scrubby like young stock-free woodland and sometimes extending up to the mountain-tops.[175]

Perhaps for this very reason – this shifting in-between-ness, married with its ubiquity here – it has a strong emotional resonance within this rural community, comparable to the love of the *Alm* in Alpine culture, as immortalised in stories like *Heidi*. The very word *ffridd* evokes to this day among locals in these mountains the very best of a peasant farming tradition rooted in its locality, coupled with good husbandry, ancient royalty and a sense of home-outdoors. One farmer I asked, who grew up on a farm on the slopes of Cader Idris, described it as one of those words that can bring you close to tears if you think too much about it; a place of mystery and discovery, bound up not only with the cycle of the seasons but also with children's play among the reeds and the rowan trees. These are not mere fancies read into childhood memories, however. Places likes Ffridd Pennant on the ramparts of Cader Idris are still bound up within folk memory with the Welsh princes of the thirteenth century, despite the passage of 700 years since their demise. Or Ffridd Gwanas and Ffridd Penantigi, which the local community still associate not only with the ruins of the Welsh royal court at Castell y Bere, in ruined state now for hundreds of years, but also with the fertile lands around the castle; showing a folk memory linking disparate parts of the landscape, even after the elapse of several centuries.[176]

Poetry from that medieval period mentions *ffriddoedd* as 'golden' places belonging to noble families, and a line like 'ffrwythau glyn gwyrdd ffridd Glan Gwy' ('the fruits of the Wye vale's green *ffridd*') encapsulates the place of the *ffridd* within the Welsh medieval imagination as a place of bounty. All this suggests the widespread existence of *ffriddoedd* already by the literary flowering of the high Middle Ages, and it seems likely, based on linguistic evidence and the pollen analyses suggesting slowly declining wood cover from the sixth century to the thirteenth century, that both the word and ecospace gradually emerged during this period. In this reading of the available evidence, the *ffriddoedd* were initially more wooded hillsides used for grazing, which over time, as a result of that grazing, gradually became the more open areas with occasional trees and shrubs we have inherited in modern times.[177] If this reconstruction strikes true, then these older *ffriddoedd* were later joined by another wave created by enclosures from common land and mountain land in the sixteenth century.[178]

Regardless of the exact mechanics of how the *ffriddoedd* were created, that sense of bounty already associated with them in the Middle Ages is echoed and, if anything, intensified in later centuries, with the elderly Iolo Morganwg (1747–1826) making the Maytime *ffridd* into his poetic *locus amoenus*:

Ac adar a'u dysgeidiaeth   [And birds with their wisdom
Acw'n y ffridd â'u cân ffraeth   Over in the *ffridd* singing wit]

And this continues into modern times with life-affirming poetic
statements such as *Yr Oed* by I. D. Hooson (1880–1948) associating
the *ffridd* with the miracle of life itself:

Ond ti gei hefyd beth o'r rhin   [But you may also taste
A rydd y ddaear fyth i'w phlant   some of the gift
Yn si y dail a murmur nant   Given by the earth to her offspring
Yng ngwên blodeuyn ar y ffridd   In the leaves' rustle
Yng ngwyrth yr haul, y glaw a'r   and stream's song
          pridd   The flowers' smile up on the *ffridd*
                                      The miracle of sun, rain and soil][179]

This is a remarkable homage, maintained over so many centuries, paid
to what is ultimately a comparatively small part of the upland farmed
landscape – and one hardly known about outside Welsh farming
and literary culture. Later on, I call by at one of Alun's neighbours, a
farming family of poets and nature lovers deeply involved in the valley's
culture to try and understand this from a local's point of view.

Over the course of a leisurely afternoon talking with them, it turns
out that both poetry and nature are simultaneously unremarkable and
deeply important to them. A conversation about poetry, in an area like
this, turns into a conversation about social gatherings. Rhys, from the
youngest generation, tells me how 120 people had turned up to a folk
gig he'd helped organise in the village hall recently, whereas only half that
number went to a comparable event in the local market town. 'Everyone
is connected, aren't they, here? And most people are linked to farming
in one way or another, so you're supporting each other by coming.' His
grandfather, John Glynmor, who only gave up farming in his eighties, had
won an eisteddfod chair in one of the village's three annual competitions
in the early 1960s and this has pride of place on his mantlepiece still. I read
the poem: it describes in strict alliterative metre the alienation from land
and people that takes place as alien conifers come to the area, set against
machine-age man's ominous nuclear threat. It is a good poem, and I am
told, with pride, by three different family members that at the eisteddfod
in question it beat an entry by the famous poet, Gerallt Lloyd Owen.

But it isn't to be found in any anthology: the bound copy at John Glynmor's home nestled under Aran Fawddwy was made by the younger generation as a gift for their grandfather. In fact, the chances are that something of the sort is true in a great many, if not the majority, of families in these mountain valleys. Each village in his day had its own weekly poetry class teaching strict-metre *cynghanedd*, a form that stretches back in Welsh to the early Middle Ages, and in this community of 250 people (including outlying farms), at any one time a dozen or more would turn up each week – farmers mostly.

When I ask about the *ffridd* the answer comes immediately: 'Cae – ffridd – mynydd. It's the part of the farm between the infields and the high mountain. Better land than the mountain but worse than the inbye; you keep sheep and cattle there on their way up and down from the mountain.' It seems natural to him that farming and poetic culture go hand in hand, and his best guess as to why it has always been so popular in this area is that it brings people together. And though I press for more of his own lines, he is much more interested in sharing with me others' work, a great many of which he has memorised by heart and can recite in the deep lilting tones of this part of southern Snowdonia:

Yn gynnar mae'n y gwanwyn –	Early in spring he goes –
wrthi'n troi	turning, then
Wrthi'n trin ei dyddyn	Tending the holding
Ei ydau a fêd wedyn	His corn then he sows
A bwyd o'i law ddaw i ddyn	And food from his lands he hands to man

Each of these poems, the tip of a great iceberg of centuries of exploration in verse of every aspect of life lived on the land, situates people explicitly within this known and laboured landscape. Both poles matter; people and place. The first line of verse that comes to mind when I ask John's son, Huw, about the *ffridd* and poetry is 'fforest lle bu ffermydd' – a forest [of conifers] where there were farms. And as he puts it with aplomb, 'you can't have a poetic tradition if you don't have people!' The absence of *ffridd* is associated, ultimately, both with the thinning of community and with the presence of non-native plantations.

Ultimately the *ffridd* seems clearly associated in the local poetic imagination with wholeness; a functioning landscape, perhaps slightly romanticised, but deeply respected for all that. The constituent actors, from the oak trees and birds to the harrow, gorse and mountaintop, all feature here – even if in newer verse they are, in reality, no longer all present. And it turns out, unsurprisingly, that the cultural celebration of the *ffridd* in verse reflects its wealth when viewed both from an agricultural and an ecological point of view – which is what I want to understand with Alun at Cae Coch.

Cae Coch

The sun comes out as we stand in *ffridd bella*, chewing over the farm's history and its future. We are on the higher edge of the *ffridd* below a massive, silver-grey stone wall, with the old slate-roofed farm buildings squatting some 70m downhill from us. I know that these unique places are one of the most ecologically rich parts of the Welsh mountains and fêted in verse, but what I am keen to understand is what use they have in Alun's farm business today.

'I need them! It's like I said earlier about the conifers,' he says with gusto. 'This is where the sheep come first when it finally warms up here in spring – that'd be towards the end of May usually. And then they might spend two or three weeks here in these fields before going up onto the mountain in June.' That turns out to be a key period, allowing the lower-lying infields and meadows below the farmhouse to put on a good spurt of growth without any grazing before they are cut for winter feed. But this shoulder season on the *ffridd* also gives the sheep a more protected area to spend time in before going on to the mountain – allowing plant growth up there to advance before they arrive, and giving the sheep the advantage of sheltering walls, shrubs and trees in case of late-spring cold. Having this is also beneficial for the lambs that are still only a matter of weeks old when they come here.

There's a system in operation here: the farm's 70 acres of intensely farmed valley bottom fields need to be given a rest by the 100 acres of *ffridd* in both spring and autumn; which in turn have a rest in summer courtesy of the almost 500 acres of mountain land. And crucially, the *ffridd* needs and receives no outside inputs to provide this grazing or this shelter. But take that middle rung out of this three-step ladder, as happened on so many farms in these uplands with coniferisation, and the bottom falls out of the system; the growing season is simply too short here. In Cae Coch's case, however, all this marginal land supports in turn 500 lambing sheep and a small herd of 18 Welsh black cattle – which, as it turns out, play an important role on the open mountain.

There has been, of course, significant change in all this over the past few decades, with Alun's father keeping significantly more head of sheep and buying in more inputs to try to improve the land than his father before him, who operated a much more traditional system. Alun, over the fifteen years he has run the farm, has found himself slowly reverting to a system more like his grandfather's – and sees that direction of travel only continuing.

'In a place like this, it's just pointless me trying continuously to improve the land,' he says. 'The soil is thin, it's cold, high and very wet. Rather than do what some of us have been trying to do and improve on nature with these inputs, I think we need to go back to focusing on the breeds. Finding the best breeds for the land and the environment we have – and improving those.'

This is not current farming orthodoxy, but it contains a key to that essential and elusive balance between wildlife and farming viability: inputs and improvement are what have driven wildlife out of habitats of all sorts globally over the past fifty or so years. Hardier breeds of cattle or sheep, however, are a fundamentally different proposition.

As we lean back against the sun-warmed stones, a skylark suddenly bursts into song overhead. Alun points out to me the bushy hedges he has been restoring over the past few years, and some of the wildlife that has proliferated as a result. The British Ornithological Trust have visited this place and studied the breeding birds here, the vast majority of which depend on the *ffridd* for their habitat. In fact, in Wales as a whole, by one measure *ffridd* has the highest mean habitat diversity per kilometre square when compared to coastal, lowland and upland landscapes, and it is the sheer variety of vegetation, communities and structural features that make it so.[180]

What this means for birds is that the *ffridd* areas typically contain a little of everything many species need in their lifecycle, due to the presence of trees, shrubs, high bracken, gorse, open grassland and puddles within a comparatively small area. Tree pipits, yellowhammers, linnets, twites and whinchats are all present in higher densities in *ffridd* habitat than in any other part of the Welsh landscape.[181] Indeed such is the importance of these areas that when the RSPB studied fifty *ffridd* sites in 2014 that had previously been looked at thirty years earlier, they found that of 18 key bird species, a full 14 had increased in abundance – against a backdrop of precipitous declines generally.[182] And despite the comparative paucity of studies looking at the *ffridd* in particular – reflected in the lack of any kind of protection or designation for *ffridd* areas nationally – the relatively substantial studies that do exist have found more birds in *ffriddoedd* than in woodland areas.[183] And though birds are one of the major beneficiaries of the existence of the *ffridd*, numerous other species thrive in these romping grounds, like the rare Welsh clearwing moth with its striking yellow tail-fan, known only in parts of Wales and Ireland thanks to the existence of scattered, old birch trees in *ffridd*-like environments.

Alun – along with many other farmers in these parts – has been an enthusiastic adopter of the public funds that have encouraged habitat creation and protection on his farm. And these things are costly: keeping sheep in the right place is not just of practical importance for farmers, but also essential for wildlife so that grazing pressure in particular spots are kept at the right level.

'But I think people in cities and towns just don't realise that I can only do many of the things I have done here for wildlife because of these agri-environmental schemes,' he tells me. 'Much as you'd love to be able to spend thousands on laying a hedge or wetland restoration, it just isn't viable on its own terms.'

Those grants – like on any other upland sheep farm – keep this place afloat. There never was any money to be made in small-scale upland farming, it's a way of life; but the ties that bind in an area like this in many cases go much deeper than money.[184] It turns out that Alun had in fact been a professional actor, making a successful start to his career with a theatre company in Aberystwyth. Taking over the farm had never been the plan, but when his father died leaving his Mam alone here, he was faced with an impossible decision. I don't press him, and although he clearly loves this place, the tears in his eyes as we talk about that fork in his life a decade ago betrays the fact that the labour of love that has kept the farm going these past years has its own fair measure of grief attached to it.

He reckons he won't last another decade of farming alone through the winters here, and will have to sell at some point, bringing the long line of family attachment to this patch of land to an end. Farming economics have changed drastically because of fossil fuels, and this farm, which in his grandfather's day in 1886 supported 14 people, now only supports him. The dearth of people is ultimately what brought an end to the pigs, chickens and ducks that also had their place in the farm's community; the silence is not just from the lack of human voices. Happily it has already been decided that the farm will go to a neighbour's daughter who would never otherwise be able to start up on her own, and it won't go for market value; that was never what this was about.

As we amble back down to the farmhouse, I am still quizzing him on why everything is where it is – and in so doing stumble again on the vein of cultural knowledge embodied in this place. It turns out that the wall separating the *ffridd* from the mountain on this farm – and on many others – lies on what is very often the snowline. Then the wall lying at the bottom of the *ffriddoedd* and dividing them from the farmyard and infields is the line for spring frosts, where cold air descends and is then caught in the hollow just where the wall runs. Most strikingly of all, both this farm and a great many others turn out to have been built right at the spring line, with a fountain supplying fresh water to the humans, and streams running down through the infields below. In other words, the placement not just of the different fields and their functions, but also the very farm buildings, reveals a deep, accumulated knowledge of the landscape and its dynamics throughout the seasons.

There is a reason for everything in this farming system, and the deep logic for this develops from the kind of manipulation of the natural environment that only arises when a place is known and inhabited over a multi-generational timescale. This is evident throughout my time with Alun, who throws in unprompted references to events, people and places across the farm that could form a scatter-graph of the last few hundred years of habitation there. One moment it's the Quakers, who emigrated to America 300 years ago, but who had met to worship on a neighbouring smallholding. The next it's a spot in a mountain stream he points out to me that is called *yr olchfa* (the washing-place), where cleaning happened during shearing time traditionally and which lies near the *llwybr mawn* – a now invisible path that was followed to get to the peat beds for cutting. Later, he muses on how the cattle were kept outdoors throughout the winter a century ago – other than in extreme weather when they were brought into the cowshed (which is a house, not a shed in Welsh). This is knowledge – common in these parts –

passed down over generations of throwaway remarks and conversation, the significance of which always waits to be discovered; who knows when it might come in useful again? As in any craft or profession, the implicit, build-up knowledge is the distinguishing factor. Here, a core part of that has always been the land and its stories.

Both cattle and sheep are an important part of those stories; indeed, without them there would likely be no farm here in the first place. But although the place of sheep on upland farms is well known, and their effect on wildlife and ecosystems bewailed by many ecologists and conservationists, what is less well known is that until within the past century they found their place in many Welsh upland farms was alongside cattle. This is of real significance from an ecological perspective: high stocking rates of sheep can easily lead to an area being overgrazed (or 'sheep-wrecked' in some campaigners' terminology), whereas cattle graze less selectively. As a result, their presence allows a greater diversity of plants to remain in the pasture: sheep will actively avoid species they dislike, allowing those very species (such as the now plague-like Molinia purple moor-grass) to dominate. Cattle, though, will browse those species, including also the more mature forage that is undesirable to sheep and on top of this their heavy trampling can break up the thick tussocks that sheep simply skirt around.[185] And from an ecological point of view, mixed grazing of both species tends to keep moorland pastures in better all-round condition, without encroaching bracken, gorse or Molinia.

On Alun's mountain, the effects of this are clear: the mountain areas on his side of the fence grazed now by Welsh Black cattle as well as sheep are visibly different to those on his neighbour's side grazed only by sheep – and are clearly not dominated by the same old species that can cover thousands of acres in monotony. A visiting ecologist told him that there were species of fungi now appearing on the open mountain that hadn't been there previously, probably because of the cows' manure and grazing patterns. It will take years for the full effects of this reintroduced, more traditional cattle-driven grazing regime to work through the mountain's ecosystem: but change it will.

His Welsh Blacks spend high summer on the mountain's summer pastures, roaming up to 2,000 feet above sea level. They are slowly getting used to it, learning where to find water, where the sheltered spots and the better grazing are to be found. 'The calves are coming down in good shape, which is lovely to see. Really, it's just going back to something my grandfather used to do – though we've lost some things in the meantime.' One of those is the infrastructure – there were old stone walls on the mountain that served a variety of purposes, which have fallen down over the decades and couldn't be rebuilt. Tellingly, Alun has lost two cattle to a fall at the exact spot at the top of a steep slope where one of those walls used to run.

A few hundred metres higher up from that spot is the summit of Aran Fawddwy, the sixteenth highest peak in Wales and the highest in the whole of southern Snowdonia at 905m. The views from here are spectacular, taking in hundreds of miles of countryside from south Wales, through the Welsh Marches, mid Wales, Snowdonia and the sea. In the eyes of almost anyone else in the UK, this is a wild summit in a remote mountain range. For Alun and his community, this is a core part of his farm. There are farms on the other side of the mountain, which by car it would take the best part of an hour to drive to. But there are paths through the mountains, trod by generations, and in Alun's eyes these are his neighbours whom he refers to in passing. The abode of the hiker and the skylark, seen through a different pair of eyes is a farmer's familiar field, summer home to the cattle.

Taking the long view, in certain *ffridd* areas the loss of suitable cattle grazing has led to the loss of structural diversity of scrub. As the RSPB bemoans, through this, over time, the wildlife-friendly upland fringe mosaic is lost.[186] The reintroduction of cattle to the farm brings many things full circle, part of a return to a system more similar to the one that created these landscapes. For the *ffriddoedd*, bereft of cattle for a few decades, their return may well bring a new lease of life. For Alun, the inherited knowledge is still there, allowing him to see the reintroduction of cattle to this whole landscape as something entirely in keeping with its heritage. In some areas of Wales, however, that cultural knowledge has been lost, creating a layer of distance between current land management and the land's past.

The wind is buffeting the car as I turn off the A470 and wind my way along the sinuous hillside track above the Marteg river in mid Wales. We're in the heart of the country, a land in which two ecologically distinct worlds exist side-by-side: the sheltered, wooded valleys below and the open, windy moorlands above. It's mid-May, but up here, even in the valley bottoms, everything is a fortnight behind the areas down country; the buttercups splayed across the fields 10 miles downriver are only just emerging here. Nevertheless, all is frenzied action around me on this blustery day, and a cuckoo is in full song as I round the last steep bends up to Gilfach farmhouse.

I am here to meet Ray and Lara from Radnorshire Wildlife Trust, who bought this 383-acre hill farm in 1988 from the last of the long line of Lewises to farm here. Ray is Wales's foremost expert on lichens and fungi, and I've come to learn from conservationists like him about the dynamics of this place in order to get my head around how a marginal environment of this sort can be so important ecologically. Economically, this is a tough place to farm. With over 2m of annual rainfall, thin soils, slopes everywhere and a long way to go to get to population centres to sell any farmhouse produce, hill-farming in these areas has never been an easy life.

The farm extends from near the summit of Yr Wylorn mountain down to the valley bottom fields where the Marteg flows, encompassing all the variations of altitude and aspect within this valley.[187] Most of the land is steeply sloping, with unwalled *ffridd*-type hillside marking the transition between the moorland and the enclosed valley bottom fields. At the centre of the farm is the longhouse, a beautiful late medieval construction built to provide accommodation for both humans and animals in the same building, providing the humans with welcome warmth and enabling them to tend their beasts easily during long, cold winters.

The Trust was interested in taking over this Radnorshire farm in particular because of the way the last of the Lewises – Hughsie – had resisted new agricultural techniques after the Second World War; although, as Ray is keen to point out, he had overstocked the land with sheep. 'The heather on the Wylorn has been overgrazed, and we're now trying to let it recover… but should we be doing that? The truth of the matter is that though we're managing this place for nature, we just don't know what we're aiming at.'

He explains how there has been a diversity of management here, with complex and changing patterns of ploughing for different crops (oats, rye, clover) with varying rotations and other practices such as 'betting' (beating and burning an area of turf in order to prepare it for a crop of wheat) and liming all, influencing the nutrient levels and biological make-up of the place.[188] 'There is no stable, unshifting baseline in the history of this place that we know we're trying to return to. And there's also a whole lot we just don't know about its history even.'

Language shift took place early here, with the area around Rhayader moving from a Welsh-speaking community to predominantly English-speaking in the later Victorian period. Already by 1931 fewer than 5 per cent of the population of Radnorshire was able to speak Welsh, compared with almost 90 per cent over the mountains in neighbouring Cardiganshire.[189] One of the results of this was that cultural links to the landscape – in place-names, stories, traditions and sayings – were filtered down or forgotten at the same time as its communities were opened up to the world with railways and industrialisation. In Gilfach, even the names of the fields and the hints to past land management that they contained were lost.

The Trust depends on a tenant farmer to manage this land with a small flock of 54 sheep alongside 13 traditional breed cattle, and markets it to visitors as a fantastic place to see dippers and otters and migrating salmon. But in this marginal place, it's also the apparently fringe members of the living community – the lichens, mosses and insects – that show us the importance of a farm like this. Ray and Lara take me on a walk from the old longhouse, and as we come through a gate onto a steep, north-facing scrubby field, he exclaims, 'What if I were to tell you that we're now about to come face-to-face with the blue whale, Bengal Tiger and Snow Leopard all at once?'

I laugh, but I know he's serious. Wales hosts some of the most diverse communities of fungi in the world, in large part because of the high proportion of the country that is covered by unimproved, marginal grassland, not enriched by fertilisers.[190]

'Five of the rarest waxcap fungi in the world can be found in this one field,' Ray says. 'These are fruiting bodies that only appear every twenty years or so, and we still have no idea why or how to predict it. What we do know though is that they are a warmth-loving species that appear in hay meadows. They need to have flowering plants nearby and they need the turf to generally remain short – otherwise, in a climate like this under a long sward it's just too cool and damp, even in summer.'

Whether they fruit or not – and some of these may go sixty years without fruiting – these fungi live in these soils, though they would be killed if the habitat were to change drastically. He tells me how there is an isotope of nitrogen (one of the most common elements on earth) that has slightly more neutrons in it. This so-called 'heavy nitrogen' occurs in grassland with 1 per cent higher frequency than in the air; in humans a little more and in cows with 8 per cent frequency. But in waxcaps the frequency is 15 per cent more and in the earth tongue waxcap measurements are as much as 30 per cent more. 'These are just extraordinary things,' Ray goes on, lying down on the hillside with a broad smile, 'and we just don't know almost anything about them yet. But we do know they feed on mosses – so a regime that weakened the mosses here would probably get rid of them too.'

I ask about the mosses, and we walk a few metres further to a beautiful, spreading oak. Ray explains that the golden moss on the oak is an indicator of base-rich bark. Oak bark is acidic and the soil in all this area is also acid soil – so how is the bark alkaline? As we sidle around the trunk, wonderingly, he indicates all the different clumps of the moss. 'Here's the moss we're talking about – and here, and here.' All these clumps are almost certainly here in this acidic environment because this field was limed in the past.

'You haven't heard yet the best thing about this oak though. It looks just like fly crap.' He takes us around to its north-facing side and gets out a little pocket microscope with a brandish as he explains that the bulk of the entire world's population of this species, *Bacidia circumspecta*, is in Radnorshire. And again, this incredibly rare, nondescript creature is a lichen that needs slightly more basic conditions to thrive than would occur naturally in this part of the world; a relict, therefore, of mixed farming and the use of lime.

The importance of these lichens is starting to become clear to me. We move on to another stand of trees, this time of hazel with oak. The lichen that are now starting to pop out to my previously naive eyes are a rich mix of greens, whites and greys, blanketing swathes of the trunks and branches. These are all lobarian communities of lichen, a whole family of species that are globally rare and for which Wales is of crucial importance. 'The thing with these lichens is that they fix nitrogen – that is, like peas or beans they draw nitrogen from the air and bring it down into the terrestrial ecosystem. And this isn't trivial; it makes a substantial contribution to the ecosystem's annual nitrogen uptake.' As gardeners know, the three most common limiting factors for plant growth are nitrogen, potassium and phosphorus (or NPK, using the symbols for these elements). As the lichens grow, and then decompose, this brings nutrients down to ground level, releasing the element for other plants to take up and in turn feed insects and other parts of the ecosystem.[191] Lichens are well known as good indicators of air quality, and part of the reason why the lichen populations in Wales and Scotland are so important is that most of the time the air here comes straight off the Atlantic, so as well as being moist it's a lot purer. But lichen are also key indicators of age and ecological continuity in a landscape.

This valley, in which every part of the landscape was until within living memory used and managed by humans as an upland farm, accommodates an enormous diversity of living creatures, from the earth-tongue fungi and the lobarian lichen to the redstarts and proud oaks. This ancient farm contains these key signs of ecological continuity that are missing from comparable sites where there has been less farming continuity. That, of course, is why it is a site of special scientific interest and why it was of interest to Radnorshire Wildlife Trust in the first place. If the grazing animals were removed, the fields and the *ffridd* would all – within the space of one human lifetime – become ever denser woodland. And although it would be beautiful, it would contain notably fewer habitats than it currently does.

The RSPB's assessment chimes with this, noting that declines in grazing or tree-planting for carbon capture would threaten much of the priority biodiversity contained on *ffridd* sites.[192] But for all the Wildlife Trust's hard work in managing Gilfach in a way that mimics traditional farming, the farm is still becoming increasingly different to the rest of the landscape in which it resides. As Ray tells me, the number of intact semi-natural grasslands in Radnorshire has declined markedly within the last twenty years, and the difference between Gilfach and its surrounds – particularly when it comes to the *ffridd* areas higher up on the farm – are clearly visible. Unlike Cae Coch, which still shares a common approach to land use with many farming neighbours, Gilfach has become a living museum.

6
Mynydd

Mountain or moor/ drier, rough grazing land

Mynydd Clogau. I am standing on a mountain summit in north Wales, surveying the grandeur below and around me. All is natural splendour; ahead the grey sea glints in the scudding sunshine, and to my right a jagged range of peaks stand as snowy sentinels over the landscape. The contrast between the sea and the dark mountain peaks, the late winter heather and buffeting Atlantic gusts could all place me in the famous Scottish Highlands or Irish west, except that on closer inspection there are significant and instructive differences. Here, stone walls snake up the slopes, and the valley bottoms are dotted with farms, cottages, fields and woodlands. Half an hour previously I had stopped for a conversation in Welsh with Gethin, one of the farmers in this valley, born here and expecting to pass the farm on to his children. In a similar spot near Fort William in Scotland a few years previously, both mountain sides and valley bottoms were bare of all but rough grazing and heather; an open, empty space, with no farmers but wealthy, distant land magnates. The land there has been emptied of almost all that matters: people, trees, wildlife and culture. The evocative Gaelic names for the valleys and summits cling on, but only as vestiges of a language no longer echoing in that vast expanse of mountain land.[193]

You could make a strong case that in these instances, the fate of the landscape and that of the language and culture are not unconnected. What is certain is that it is not the vagaries of climate or geography that account for the marked differences between these places, but rather significantly different cultural histories: in the Scottish and Irish cases, experiences of profound, terrible disruption and uprooting. Despite tensions, struggle and real loss, the fate of life in the Welsh mountains over the past few centuries has been one of survival – of farming culture, woodland and the associated wildlife.[194] That is the tale told by the Snowdonian landscape of Cwm Hirgwm spread below me.

If the last couple of chapters of this book have explored the story of key parts of the farmed landscape in some detail, this is where we venture out into those parts of the Welsh landscape viewed by tourists both past and present as representing 'wilderness'. Sometimes that is qualified in clichéd phrases as 'the closest you can get to wilderness in these crowded isles'. But as we touched on in the introduction, that view of Welsh mountains is a particular cultural view that has arisen relatively recently and is not reflected almost at all within Welsh-language culture.[195] We can gain a fascinating insight into this from a 1765 landscape painting by Richard Wilson of Snowdon from Llyn Nantlle, in the very centre of mountain country. This is an undeniably *mountain* landscape: sheer rock faces, scree, expansive views and a mountain lake in the foreground. But the view is far from empty: there are people crossing the lake by boat, in the background smoke from a fire is curling up, probably from agricultural activity, and in the foreground three boys are fishing. The mountains are an inhabited, working space and had been so for millennia.

These mountains areas are all typically called in Wales *mynydd*, from Mynydd Mawr and Mynydd Drws-y-Coed that frame Wilson's painted scene, to Mynydd Preseli in the south-west and Mynydd y Berwyn in the north-east.[196] But the meaning of *mynydd* within the Welsh language is much broader than this and includes locations like Mynydd Mechell on Anglesey or Mynydd Aberporth on the Ceredigion coast that in no way resemble the expected summited landform.[197] Once again, we need to adopt a different perspective to get under the skin of these landscape terms and their history; one rooted in inhabiting and using the land, that we can understand best through looking at the *mynyddoedd* through the twin lens of sheep and peat.

Buarthau

The Carneddau is the largest open mountain range in Wales, and include the country's second-highest peak, the great lump of Carnedd Llewelyn, summiting at 1,064m above sea level. They are also home to somewhere in the region of 10,000 sheep, spread into flocks owned across a couple of dozen farms organised into three grazing associations. And these sheep, though they may spend half the year on the mountain, need shearing and selling. And for that, in this area, remarkable structures called *buarthau* were developed. These are almost monumental, stone-built multicellular constructions, with sinuous curves and ancient-feeling stone walls that belie their practical function as sheepfolds.[198] Stumble across one standing proud on one of these mountainsides on a bright summer's day and you'd be forgiven for thinking yourself among the ruins of a palace in Minoan Crete or ancient Turkey. And although not restricted to the Carneddau, this particular patch of mountain grazing is extraordinarily rich in these structures, of which there are around a hundred across the mountains of north Wales.

They are here, of course, precisely because these mountains are grazing lands and have been since time immemorial, and a great many – perhaps half – continue to be in a good state of repair solely because of sheep-farming. They act as a sort of signifier that all this land, from the mountain wall up to the high summits, plays a key function in working farms. Today, the 10,000 sheep share the Carneddau grazing with a population of native, semi-wild mountain ponies.[199] Feral goats also occasionally make an appearance, the descendants of domesticated herds that used to be kept for their milking and fleeces and which, according to local tradition, were finally released into the hills as the fashion for wearing wigs faded in the eighteenth century.[200]

A few hundred years ago, these animals would also have shared the land with hardy native cattle (related to today's Welsh Black), with figures from the sixteenth century suggesting that at the time the ratios of sheep to cattle in these mountains stood at around 2.5 to one.[201] A generation earlier, the antiquarian John Leland had commented that this part of Snowdonia also had an 'abundance' of deer – though these were extirpated by the middle of the following century. Going further back, royal records soon after conquest indicate that on some mountain pastures in north Wales as many as 200 heads of cattle were kept out grazing year-round, and not in summer only.[202] And as early as the sixth century AD when the Roman departure from these shores remained a fresh memory, Gildas describes the western half of Britain as possessing 'mountains especially suited to varying the pasture for animals'.[203]

Gildas's comment confirms the witness of all other writers over the past millennium and a half that the uplands in western Britain, including Wales, were generally open and used for grazing. But his reference is also tantalising in what it suggests, not least in the implication that a wide range of domesticated animals made use of mountain grazing land, and that a feature of this pasture was variety.[204] To go further back than Gildas we need to rely on archaeological reconstruction of the environment, but strong indirect evidence for reliance on mountain land for grazing in north Wales – keeping it open – is provided by the evidence for heath burning from as far back as 2,000 BC.[205] This practice is still carried out by farmers today in order to encourage the nutritious young growth of heather that provides particularly good browsing for livestock, and there is no other obvious reason to engage in the practice.

And so these mountains have been grazed by a slowly changing range and mix of animals for the last 4,000 years, and, as we saw in chapter 1, perhaps longer. Sheep have been a part of that mix since the Neolithic, around 6,000 years ago – although in nowhere near the numbers kept for the last couple of centuries. In the Carneddau, the significant shift away from keeping a range of animals on the hills to only sheep and semi-wild ponies took place relatively recently, around the turn of the nineteenth century, when several factors coincided. First, with a rapidly growing human population across the UK, the transhumance *hafota* system which had still been in use half a century earlier in Snowdonia finally collapsed, as summer dwellings were converted into year-round holdings. In parallel with this, and as we will explore in the next chapter, government was pressing for enclosure and 'improvement' of common and shared grazing lands to increase yields. And, thirdly, in the Carneddau in particular, this period saw a boom in the slate quarrying industry, which led to a large number of smallholder quarrying families keeping small flocks of sheep on the mountain in order to supplement their income.[206]

It is towards the beginning of this period of change that we find the first written reference to a sheepfold in the area, in a handwritten book dating to 1779.[207] But intriguingly, a large number of them seem to be located in the middle or even on top of much older settlement remains and some incorporate structures that seem to be the remains of former summer dwellings that never became year-round habitations. The cluster lying underneath Moel Faban at the western end of the area is typical in this, with a large sheepfold with three cells incorporating lower-lying walls from an older enclosure, which in turn is surrounded by a range of noteworthy prehistoric remains including homesteads, huts and enclosures.[208] Though the majority of the large sheepfolds that dot the mountains today probably owe their genesis to the growth in sheep-farming in the late eighteenth century, their organic shape and location on sites with an existing history of use imply that some of them may well be adaptations of pre-existing structures.

In addition to sheepfolds, other structures often linger nearby including wash pens, fox traps, shepherds' shelters and *cytiau myn*, or feral goat enclosures.[209] Some of these may well date back another couple of centuries, and there is strong reason to suppose that in the medieval period they were accompanied by temporary summer dwellings in the mountains.[210] As in the Alps today where *Berghütte* restaurants, cable cars and ski-slope apparel at 2,500m all betray to the romantic hiker that this is a commodified landscape heavily used for tourism, this dense web of stone-built structures in the Carneddau remind the visitor that it too has been shaped as a working landscape.

For all their possible antiquity, the *buarthau* sheepfolds are not relics of a bygone agricultural age, but retain their key function in the farming system today as the stage for the breathtaking practice of *hel y mynydd*: gathering the mountain flocks. Released onto the mountain progressively from April, the sheep need gathering in July for shearing, and then again in September, to separate the lambs from the ewes, and October to clear the mountain and return them to winter pastures. And since this is one open, unfenced mountain area, extending to over 220 sq. km, one of the key elements of this is separating different flocks out from each other in a way that depends on the very structure of the sheepfolds.

Nigel Beidas, a Nottinghamshire lad turned Welsh-speaking local historian for the area who has chronicled the history, architecture and use of the *buarthau* (the local word in this part of north Wales; in other areas they are known as *corlannau*) takes me on a close-hugging May day up to see a cluster of them. We walk up a track past one of the many smaller quarries on the lower slopes of the hills, soon passing a group of Carneddau ponies lazing in a hollow. After half an hour's climbing, we approach a ridge. All of Anglesey had been spread out behind us as we climbed up. Now, as we crossed over the whaleback, a broad valley extends out in front of us towards the peak called Drosgl; away to our left a series of sharp cliffs fall away seawards into the distance while to our right the peaks of high Eryri brood under dark clouds: Elidir Fawr, Y Garn, Carnedd y Filiast and somewhere behind, Snowdon. The overpowering song of the skylark surrounds us; from here there are no signs of what is commonly called 'civilisation' – only a felt elementality.

Nigel points out a shoulder of the ridge opposite, a good mile and a half away. 'This is where I was stood in September when it started,' he explains. His friend Dafydd, a local farmer, had told him they'd be gathering the mountain that day, and Nigel had left early to be in situ in time. 'The farmers had gone over Drosgl – the ridge opposite – before 7 that day, and as I arrived you could just about make out a few sheep coming over the brow of the hill towards us.' The key gathering spot would be Buarthau'r Gyrn, a large multicellular sheepfold just a few hundred yards from where we were now stood.

'Three sheep became six ... then twelve, then forty ... and it just kept doubling!' he continues. 'Within an hour there were easily 2,000+ sheep charging down the mountainside, surrounded by a dozen sheepdogs and the farmers on their quads, driving them towards the *buarthau* right here. It was utterly unforgettable, and it struck me that apart from the quad bikes, every other element of this scene has carried on in this way for centuries, with many of these farmers' own fathers and ancestors.'[211]

Even the grazing areas the different flocks had been rounded from and the ancestry of the flocks themselves can be traced back in an unbroken line over generations. This is the *cynefin* of the flock, an area that often has no obvious distinguishing boundary to the naked eye but which sheep from a particular flock, hefted to it for generations, have learnt to keep to. This knowledge is passed on within the flock from one generation of ewes to the next, with complications only arising when sheep from outside the flock are introduced into it.[212] As we saw in the introduction, the word has wide resonance in Welsh culture, and is readily applied to people to imply a sense of belonging to place.

The sheep are driven as one to enter the *buarth,* which has a large funnel-shaped gathering pen, leading into a central dividing pen. This is the main sheep race, through which the sheep are driven before being separated out through small sheep-gates built into the stone walls into their farm's traditional pen. To have a chance of doing this successfully when each farm is responsible only for a few hundred from among 2,000 sheep, another cultural practice comes into its own, namely the rapid identification of *clustnodau*, or marks cut into the sheep's ear. As Nigel explains, 'Each farm has its own unique mark which is cut when the lamb is young; the cuts are made in the cartilage of the ear so that it is relatively painless. A large number of different sorts of cuts are used in these earmarks and there is a real wealth of Welsh terms to describe them.'

In shepherding friends' houses I have visited, books of earmarks organised by farm often sit comfortably on the mantelpiece; some farms have handwritten logs of these going back 200 years and more. As might be expected, the marks do not change much. In many cases, the same earmarks are used on descendants of the same sheep hefted to the same patch of mountain as the current farmers' great-great-great-grandparents. They are also sorted using the same pen in the same sheepfolds.

This *hel y mynydd* – or 'mountain sheep-gathering' – is a co-operative exercise, only possible because of strong relationships coupled with close, established regulation. In this particular case, all the land in question has been owned for several decades by the National Trust, which acquired it from the estate of Lord Penrhyn, the despised slate magnate in this area. But land management among the commoners is governed not just by the owner but by a grazing association, which in the case of where we are – Llanllechid – happens also to be the community council.[213] They are tasked with ensuring that stock levels are kept to appropriate levels, that licences are adhered to and that any disputes are resolved. They are also responsible for employing a *Setiwr* (English 'escheator'), who as Nigel explains must make sure that stray sheep (*defaid diarth*) picked up in any of the gatherings are reclaimed by their owners in neighbouring farms and also auction off any unclaimed or orphan lambs found at the time of the gatherings in July and September. Usually these are the lambs that have no earmark to identify which farm they belong to.

And then, the flocks being gathered and any stray sheep identified, the *buarth* empties, ready for its next use in a few months' time. As we wander on to another *buarth* lower down the mountain (Buarth

Bwlch Molchi), Nigel muses on the farmers' own attitudes towards this remarkable continuity in farming practice, a topic that he has researched over the course of the last decade.

'There's certainly a lot of family pride involved in this, and they're all quick to explain how everything works to me. And it's worth saying that they all know these mountains intimately – they're up here regularly, at different times of year. You've got to know all the names and distinguishing features in this environment when the sheep are up here and they are your livelihood.'

And though this remains true for farmers and shepherds in areas like the Carneddau today, this need-to-know and name-your-environment according to its natural features and function within the rural economy held much more broadly across pre-industrial Wales. This is particularly true of landforms, where Welsh has a noted wealth of terms for hills, slopes and other features of mountainous country, from *esgair* (a long, prominent ridge) and *cefnen* (a low-lying, less prominent ridge) to *llechwedd, rhiw, bron, goleddf* and *llethr* (all variations on the theme of 'slope'). Why then does the term *mynydd* seem so unspecific in its use, covering everything from Snowdon to what looks like nothing more than low-lying heathland?

The answer, as suggested in chapter 2, lies in setting aside a topographical approach to the landscape and adopting in its stead a pre-modern agricultural view. Here, in a country where much of the land is not particularly fruitful and is, in the presence of grazing animals, primarily useful as rough pasture, the area for the summer grazing of such animals was formerly by necessity quite extensive. The areas that lent themselves to this kind of use were naturally the higher ground in much of the north and centre of the country (what we might call mountains), but in other areas they might well be rolling hills and moors or even flattish heaths.[214]

This is how seeming anomalies arise all over Welsh toponymy in places such as Mynydd Bychan in Cardiff, in its entirety lower-lying than surrounding areas not called 'mynydd' and possessing no prominence whatsoever, or Mynydd Pen-banc in Pembrokeshire, which amounts to no more than a low-lying slope dominated by summits 200m higher all around. *Mynydd* here means that part of the farmed landscape used primarily for rough, summer grazing;[215] also called, as we saw in chapter 2, the 'outfield'. Crucially, this core meaning of *mynydd* is just as true in the mountains as in non-mountainous areas: the open part of the Carneddau governed by the grazing association of farmers who use Buarthau'r Gyrn and others in that area is known collectively as Mynydd Llanllechid. It remains the key summer grazing for most farmers in the parish of Llanllechid, and this is true regardless of the proximity of lofty summits.

As suggested by the presence of burning since the Neolithic period and possibly even earlier (as we saw in chapter 1), these *mynydd* areas have been open places, with tree cover at most comprising wood pasture rather than unbroken high forest. The famous megaliths of Wales, with concentrations both in the mountains and in lower-lying areas like Anglesey and coastal Pembrokeshire, indirectly confirm this. Many of them are located on skylines or in locations where peaks or estuaries can be clearly seen and may well have been at the time viewed as highly symbolic parts of a ritual landscape.[216] These other seemingly 'timeless' parts of the mountain landscape further add to the layers of habitation these apparently wild places have accumulated. The Welsh mountains, in more senses than one, are much more products of human culture and land use than they are even of geology.

Nigel explains that the Carneddau farmers he knows take a keen interest in these remarkable, beautiful structures. For some, their focus is on conserving these old agricultural heirlooms and the layers of history they represent; while for others, their interest lies in the way these extraordinary constructs are used. This doesn't surprise me: just as some fishermen or politicians are fascinated by the history and tradition of their vocation and others warm to a different aspect, so also with farmers, including Welsh mountain sheep farmers. But the persistence of upland sheep-farming in Wales in the face of consistent obstacles speaks of nothing if not a broad cultural regard for place and tradition, and I am keen to learn more about this and how it has shaped the *mynydd* from someone at the heart of the industry and its culture.

Erwyd

'Mae'r dirwedd yn gwneud pobol, on'dyw hi?' ('The land makes people, you see?'), Erwyd explains to me with a sharp glint in his eye. We're meeting in a Presbyterian chapel next to his home in the middle of the Ceredigion hills, just below the snowline on this early December day. 'There are the mountain people and then the flat-land people – and those are flat people. Do you know what I'm saying?' he finishes with a chuckle. 'There's *hwyl* and humour up on the mountain.'

Erwyd should know: he knows the hill-farming community through a broad swathe of Wales like the back of his hand after a lifetime of shepherding. In the few hours I spend talking with him, a string of neighbours calls by for a conversation. He has no e-mail and getting through to him on the landline is a nightmare, simply because the line is always engaged. I quickly realise that here is a man living a markedly different way of life to almost all the 66 million other people on this island; not because he has sought out an alternative, as some do, but because his world of necessity has continued to embody ways of being that are now at profound odds to most of the rest of the late modern political economy.

The way of life that Erwyd inhabits gives the lie – or at least exemplifies the contradictions – implicit in many widely accepted truths in current Western culture when it comes to urgent and contested questions around land use, climate change, biodiversity and energy use. This older-but-still-active shepherd has spent his entire life engaged in an occupation – upland sheep-farming – now castigated as one of the root ills of modern nature depletion. He also maintains the skills of cutting peat for fuel from the mountain – in an age when the harvesting and burning of peat has been shown to be one of the most carbon-intense practices in existence. But the nuance behind these things makes all the difference.

I've come to ask him about the culture of shepherding in the mountains of mid Wales, and it doesn't take long for me to fill pages of my notebook with the reminiscences and observations he shares. He remembers from his early years in the 1960s an elderly generation then living in old mountain farmhouses now abandoned, whose entire world took place in those high places.

'It is sometimes lonely now in these places – I can go to them and remember the people who were there, and the voices and the busyness. They had a hard life, that is true, but yet again – they didn't have the same pressure on them as today, and they had more leisure as well, and certainty, which a lot of people are missing now.'

He enthuses as different farmhouses – Glanhirin, Hengwm Annedd, Eisteddfa Gurig – are conjured up, bringing back memories of mountains gathered, jokes shared and anecdotes remembered. He tells of an older couple whose trouser knees were always brown come spring from long evenings spent a little too close to the fire, and the hilarity that caused. Old photos come out – some black and white – that have been handed down to him.

'On the eastern slopes of Pumlumon [mountain], there had been 25 different flocks, you see, up there in the summer. Each with its *cynefin*, and some of them were scores of sheep and others just ten. Then the shepherd's job was in part to reinforce those boundaries between the flocks, to instil that in the ewes.'

You cooperate with the farmers, and any other shepherds, and of course, your constant companion is the sheepdog:

> Hel a didol diadell
> Yw camp hwn yn y cwm pell

This strict-metre couplet comes out spontaneously, as do so many others during our conversation. This one is part of an *englyn* (strict-metre four-line aphoristic poem, like a more advanced version of a haiku) to the sheepdog. Translated for sense only, it comes out:

> In bold strides, easily led – onto the mountain
> And its remote dell
> Gathering and sorting the flock
> Is this worker's feat on the far fell

You wouldn't trade couplets from poems in a conversation in English. In Welsh, for people with Erwyd's background (and indeed mine), it is utterly unremarkable: nothing to do with romanticism; everything to do with a shared outlook on the world, and this part of it.

The shepherding season in these parts traditionally begins on the second Wednesday of May (or thereabouts), when sheep were walked up to the mountain and handed over to one of the shepherds for the summer until they were returned in early November. 'It gets into your soul, there's no doubt about that. June is the best time on the mountain, and there are spots you can be on a quiet afternoon where it is paradise.' He opens up a time-worn leather case and brings out what looks like a miniature wreath of sorts. Do I know what it is, he asks? I don't.

'Torch sidan bengoch': a ring made of the dense haircap moss, abundant on the mountains. I am intrigued; Erwyd explains that these are no longer made, though he remembers how it was done. 'They were used as fetters around sheeps' necks to keep them from wandering when you brought a new one into the flock. You gathered them from many patches up there.' What about other wildlife, I ask? To this, he puts his hands to his mouth and out comes the most startling imitation of a bird I have ever heard. It's the cry of a curlew (which he calls *chwibanog*, in mid-Ceredigion dialect), clear and piercing. He goes again, fingers to mouth and out comes the distinctive pee-wit song of a golden plover (*cornicyll y waun*). He can see my amazement and bursts into laughter.

'But those are both gone now from the mountains,' he goes on. 'Mae gen i hiraeth am eu clywed' ('I have a longing after them'). 'They were always a sign that the spring was coming – and then, from 1994, they were gone.' We go into it further: he's convinced that higher numbers of badgers are responsible, as they kill these ground-nesting birds. Whether he's right or not, his observations bear out his summary of the situation: 'Mountain people know what goes on in their mountains.'

His words are borne out by the history of the modern 'discovery' of Welsh mountains by outsiders, precipitated by the Cambridge scholar Thomas Gray's 1755 poem 'The Bard', which led to a growing wave of romantic interest in Wales's dramatic scenery and laid the foundations for the modern tourist industry. But from the start, the knowledge on which these visitors depended to 'discover' the peaks and moors, from poets to botanists and early mountaineers, was held by local people who were employed as guides. It's not that all hill farmers, even in the pre-industrial era, had an intimate knowledge of the mountains' plant and bird life and the herbal and animal lore associated with them. But in isolated mountain communities it was necessary for at least some members of the community to know all the habitats of the plants used for medicinal purposes. As modern mountaineer and Snowdonian botanist Jim Perrin puts it, in north-west Wales at least, 'the mountain plants were believed to contain healing qualities equal to, if not stronger than, those of the lowland species. Localities such as Clogwyn Du'r Arddu, Cwmglas Mawr and Cwmglas Bach on Snowdon … were noted for their variety of flowers from the earliest times.'[217]

This knowledge often ran in families and continued to be passed on well into the twentieth century. In Snowdonia alone this botanical pedigree starts with William Salesbury in the 1570s, author not only of the first Welsh dictionary but also of a noted herbal (the *Llysieulyfr*). He was followed, amongst others, by Edward Lhuyd, discoverer of the endemic Snowdon Lily; Hugh Jones, compiler of the first Welsh county flora in 1813; J. Lloyd Williams, the Victorian botanist from Llanrwst, and Evan Roberts, the quarryman and botanist from Capel Curig who died in 1991. These were all experts not only in the flora of the mountains, recognised as such well outside Wales, but they were also people steeped in the language and culture for whom the native Welsh name for plants of all sorts was the first port of call in understanding their significance. A trivial but telling example is the rare purple mountain saxifrage, or *tormaen* ('stone-break'): its meaning in Welsh clearly indicates its high, rocky mountain habitat and which set Evan Roberts off on his botanical career.[218] In contrast to the modern image of the sheep-farming community as one alienated from the natural environment, the witness of both the history of botany and shepherding in these hills points towards an intimate knowledge of it, born of custom and familiarity.

There is no saxifrage on the grassier summits of mid Wales where Erwyd has spent his shepherding life, but there is a good deal of *mawn* – peat. After the summer grazing, this was until the last few decades undoubtedly the most important resource that mountain areas offered, and Erwyd's experience gives us a way into understanding people's relationship with it and the nature of the ecological pressures on upland peat today.

Erwyd learnt the craft of *lladd mawn* – 'killing peat' – from his parents,[219] and ensured that he taught his children the skill. In places and at times where timber for burning was scarce or expensive, peat provided an essential lifeline for heating and cooking year-round. The properties of peat fires were celebrated, with a generation only now finally passing in areas of upland north Wales who grew up with peat fires being the smell of home. Peat remains a source of winter warmth, and on the bone-chilling day I visited, a stove burning with fuel was a welcome sensation. The process is labour-intensive, though efficient enough. 'You need to know where the peat beds are, of course, and then you go up in early summer, say, to cut them.' He shows me the traditional hand implements he continues to use for this purpose (as well as to demonstrate the skills to younger generations), every aspect of which has its own nomenclature and terminology, prime among which is the *haearn mawn* – the 'peat iron'. In the peat-bed itself you need to know what you're doing: you score the face of the earth with the marking knife, before cutting right down into it and bringing one out with the *haearn donni*. There are layers to the peat, each of which has its own name, with different burning qualities belonging to each part. When a suitable depth had been dug in one line, this was pulled out and put to dry in the wind and sun for some weeks before being taken off the mountain. The peat lengths with strands of visible roots were favoured for a brisk fire, to bring a pot or kettle to the boil quickly, while black peat would have more lasting heat.

'Dyma ti – mawnen i chi gael llosgi adre', as he hands me a *mawnen*, a coffee-black length of peat for me to burn at home. It's lightweight, odourless and bone-dry, with the fibres plainly visible along its surfaces; in feel it has a certain resemblance to a lump of coal. We're in the winter sunshine in the backyard now, where his garden and the chapel graveyard border each other. He opens his corrugated iron shed and brings out some of the peat-cutting tools for me to handle. I express interest, and more hand tools come out, including several old scythes, which it turns out he has always used to mow the graveyard grass.

I ask him how he feels about the fact that peat-cutting is seen as highly environmentally destructive. It doesn't surprise me that he seems quite unperturbed, though thoughtful, in answering. 'There is a place up near Nant-y-moch where the face of the peat is near some ancient dwellings from the old people – Bronze Age, I think. You can see there where the peat has grown back.' He is right, of course; people have been harvesting peat for fuel here for thousands of years, and at the rate it has been carried out over that period, driven by human labour for a small population heating small cottages like his, it becomes a renewable energy source. Peat regrows at a rate of 1cm a decade; to regain a metre therefore takes 1,000 years. Since Erwyd's postulated Bronze Age peat cutters were active, 3 to 4 metres of peat have in all likelihood reformed.

As I leave, I reflect that his sanguinity probably stems to a great degree from a clear conscience when it comes to the natural world. This is a man who through a combination of circumstance and choice has spent the past sixty years away from the headlong rush into materialistic intoxication that has overtaken the West and thereby poisoned the earth. Having lost his wife in her twenties, he found solace in lambing, shepherding and raising his own two children – who live nearby. He lives in a single-glazed cottage on a back lane in the mountains of mid Wales. He drives an old banger of a car and keeps his manual hand tools sharp for use. He knows his environment intimately, from weather patterns to mosses and birds, and has noted with keen interest the changes that have taken place over his own lifetime.

Peat-cutting, for him, is simply an inherited life skill; a way of life that he has kept to even as the rest of society has moved away from it at a rapid pace. To point this out is not to suggest that the rest of Welsh society – or even those who live in upland parts of country – should for some reason revert to burning peat for fuel and cooking (and it is by no means Erwyd's primary source of heating – though I am told it remains so for a handful of homes further north). But it is to point out that the ostensible environmental crime turns out, on closer investigation, to be embedded in an outlook and physical relationship with the world that has much to teach us. All the emissions from his negligible peat burning in a year amount to fewer CO_2 emissions than one return flight from the UK to the USA, or the amount emitted simply in manufacturing the battery for one electric car.[220] While most of society around him has spent decades jet-setting to everywhere from the Costa del Sol to Thailand and upgrading houses and cars every few years, this shepherd has contentedly made done with community, sheep and a slower way of life.

Erwyd is not unique in all this in the rural and agricultural community in Wales,[221] even among people of my acquaintance; though the remaining others like him in his generation may well be the last for now. In his own haunting words: 'the land makes the people, doesn't it?'

Mawnog

If hand-harvesting of peat has, in Wales, had a comparatively small environmental footprint,[222] the same cannot be said of the draining and digging of peat using heavy machinery that started on the mountains in the 1950s, and that rapidly transformed these *mawnogydd* for the worse. There are now large-scale initiatives underway to restore such degraded mountain peatlands in the Welsh mountains and to do so in a way that works with and through the mountains' role in local farms. To this end I join Dion from the Snowdonia National Park Authority on a site visit to Waun Lydan on Ffarm Penrhiw on the edge of the Berwyn mountains.[223]

'This site was degraded through mechanical drainage in the 1950s and 60s,' Dion explains as we hike up on a blue morning in early May. 'The idea the government had was to improve the productivity of the grazing up here by digging large ditches that carried the water away and down the mountain.' As the water flowed off the mountains more rapidly, the land would dry out allowing grasses and heathers to replace the sphagnum that is so essential for peatlands – thereby improving grazing.

If any plants deserve to be called keystone species, then sphagnum – *migwyn* – is undoubtedly among them. These unglamorous looking mosses are almost single-handedly responsible for engineering the environments known as blanket bogs in places like Wales, along with all the millions of cubic metres of peat they contain. They are so abundant in some areas that entire moorlands have been named after them, such as the Migneint near rainy Blaenau Ffestiniog. Sphagnum mosses thrive in wet conditions and can quickly colonise pools of standing water. Once in, they will rapidly set to work acidifying their environment by multiple means and can bring the pH of a pool down from above 7 to under 4 (i.e. from neutral to vinegar), making it difficult for competing plants to flourish and thereby starving the environment of oxygen. The moss will also hold within its own cell structure as much as twenty times its own dry weight in water, contributing to the maintenance of the wet environment in which it flourishes. Then, as an individual moss dies and sinks into the water, the acidic and oxygen-poor environment that the sphagnum has helped create is bereft of the microbes that normally decompose dead plants, meaning the only partially rotten sphagnum (along with any other organic material, from wood to dead bodies) is swallowed into the underbelly of the pool, forming over time what we call peat.

Crucially – both for those who depended on it for winter fuel and for those who need to stop emitting it – this peat therefore contains all the CO_2 that would under other circumstances have been released into the environment by the live plants' decomposition. In other words, a square metre of peat that is 3m deep contains within it 3,000 years' worth of plant carbon that otherwise would have been released into the atmosphere but has instead been locked up in the bog. So astonishingly, peatlands globally – which cover only 3 per cent of the world's surface – hold more carbon than all the other vegetation types in the world (including all forests) combined.[224]

Digging those ditches and trenches in the mid-twentieth century, which didn't only happen here but took place on a massive scale across the whole of the Welsh uplands, not only degraded this bog but will have been responsible for untold emissions of CO_2 – for almost no benefit.[225]

As parts of the bog dried out, large, dark tears in its vegetational skin open by erosion, forming scars called peat hags. As we walked up the steep slope, Dion points one out to me that hadn't yet been restored. It looks for all the world like a dark brown gash in the land, a couple of metres tall and a dozen or more metres long. The unique combination of insects and birds that flourish on intact, wet peatlands suffered drastic declines by the added insult of overgrazing, encouraged by governmental subsidy regimes. Ironically, Dion tells me, at some sites in Snowdonia, overgrazing in the latter decades of the twentieth century was so bad that it was the primary cause of degradation. This is, perhaps, what happens when progress-driven policy meets a fragile livelihood operation – upland farming – taking place in a fragile environment.

We make it onto the open *gwaun* where the land is level enough to allow water to collect and a bog to form, and high enough (over 600m) for rainfall to be substantial year-round.[226] A lot of work has taken place here. Among the heather, and clearly spreading, are dark pools with young, growing sphagnum. Dion is visibly pleased at the progress here since his last visit a few months previously. Bending down, the process that has taken place is clear. Low ridges (or 'baffles') made of peat themselves have been positioned at regular intervals across the ditches and gullies to slow the flow of water and encourage the formation of the types of pool amenable to sphagnum growth. These ridges are only a few dozen centimetres in height, but their effectiveness is visible, with languid pools forming in a sequence behind them and slowly filling the gully with a watery cover. This is coupled with large-scale work to re-cover the bare, brown peat 'hags' by stretching out lengths of native vegetation to around 1.5 times its length in such a way that the areas of bare peat are once again reintegrated into the bog, stopping emissions.

In this one location of over 250 hectares, this has clearly been a substantial piece of work, and I am eager to find out who it was that came up with the idea and drove it to become reality. Was it the National Park, government or a conservation agency? 'Actually,' Dion says with a smile, 'It was the farmers at the head of this valley.' The park has spent decades building close relationships with farmers and is used to offering them support to implement schemes that they want to see take place on their own land as part of upland payment conditions. It's a good example of complex, landscape-scale working in the public interest, where Welsh Government disburses grant monies originally supplied as part of green financing carbon credit schemes, that the National Park then implements in the field at sites selected at farmers' own initiative. Here, six farmers had bandied together to have the peat on their mountains restored and to have nature-friendly hedges laid on their valley land; the cost to the green financing purse lying at around £80,000 all told.

The cumulated benefits for what is substantially less than the price of a house astonish me. Restoring the peatland would be an eminently sensible investment for society even if it only resulted in the cessation of CO_2 that they currently emit; but, in reality, their restoration to growing, living ecosystems makes them highly effective carbon sinks. But as well as the 4,500 tonnes of CO_2 this place will now lock in each year (equivalent to the annual emissions of 700 westerners), the recreated pools and growing peat also substantially lessen flood risks downriver. The filtering effects of the bog plant life, coupled with the covering up of the eroding hags (which previously stained streams and rivers brown in heavy rain), also combine to improve water quality, saving large sums of money to water companies and the public purse.

The restoration of the peatlands also leads to habitat for precisely those wetland species – of plants, insects and birds – that have suffered so much under the intensification of agriculture. Here, a native carnivorous plant, the sundew, springs up from the bog in summer, trapping insects in its 'dew' to supplement the sparse fare it can otherwise glean from the bog's nutrient-poor environment. Also endemic to these places is cotton grass – *plu'r gweunydd* – which provides food for the rare large heath butterfly, that can only survive here. Bright yellow bog asphodel, cranberry and bog rosemary grow among the darting Golden ringed and Black Darter dragonflies that thrive in these environments. And the thrumming insect life in a healthy bog provides food for birds that have been declining precipitously in recent decades, including the golden plover, curlew and, higher up the food chain, hen harriers.

It's too early to know which of those species are slowly recolonising this mountain bog, but assuming the rewetting holds, the potential for these species to return is now there. Promisingly, at an upland bog rewetted just a dozen miles away in 2017, curlews and golden plovers had both returned to nest by 2021 after decades of absence.[227] All this would be enough to suggest peatland restoration should be a matter of urgent policy priority, and this becomes an irresistible conclusion when the lack of negative effects on upland livestock farming are factored in.

I ask Dion about grazing on this peatland now that the restoration work has been done. 'Oh, we absolutely want this area to continue to be grazed – there's no question about that.' With large areas of spruce plantation still common over upland Wales, one darkening the horizon barely a mile to our west, the potential for self-seeded spruce to arrive on these bogs and establish themselves, thereby drying out the land again, is real; livestock mitigate that. 'We would be looking at something in the region of 0.2 livestock units per hectare to help keep the bog in a healthy state. But that can be sheep or cattle or, ideally, both.' The key thing, it turns out, is that this is principally summer grazing, between late April and early November – in an echo of the long-established practices mandated, as we have seen, under Welsh law. But having the bogs restored has a real practical benefit for farming with sheep in that it keeps them both safe and clean. When this mountain was full of those hags of bare peat, they would dirty the sheep's fleeces, and then the trenches and ditches were also a real problem because sheep would fall into them. Dion tells me he knows of farmers who have lost dozens of sheep over the years to them.

These bogs are of incalculable value both to wildlife and to human society, and that will be as true over the coming century for carbon sequestration as it has been over the past few millennia of dependence on them for fuel. But even these extraordinary places are at most a semi-natural ecosystem in our context, where human influence from as early as the Mesolithic is likely to have had a substantial influence on their formation and spread; they are, just like our woodlands and pastures, semi-cultural creations.[228] These peatlands have been with us, covering much the same surface area as they currently do, for something in the region of 4,000 years. There is some evidence that in slightly less oceanic parts of Wales more amenable to tree growth, such as the Berwyn mountains, the major spread of peat first took place only around 2,500 years ago,[229] and in the Preseli mountains as recently as the early medieval period.[230] Even after this, upland environments like any other went through cycles of change in response to grazing pressure and other land-use patterns, but studies of pollen and plant fossil data demonstrate that, these normal fluctuations aside, most of the degradation and floral impoverishment in the mountains of mid Wales took place in the twentieth century.[231] Strikingly, the paleoecological data show a greater proportion of sphagnum than currently, with recent declines in sphagnum coinciding with significant increases in invasive Molinia. As with all the other ecospaces in the Welsh landscape, a notable downturn in their vitality and quality has occurred within the lifetime of the oldest generation of people alive today. Thousands of years of human management stretched and squeezed these upland bogs, but the data clearly suggests that it was only with the fossil-fuel driven changes to our farming and land use that their condition drastically worsened.

The inhabited mountain

The great Dafydd ap Gwilym, in his inimitable fashion, gives us a pen-portrait of an upland peat bog in fourteenth-century Wales in his poem 'Y Pwll Mawn'. Describing his crossing of a cold moorland by night to see his lover, he finds himself and his horse sinking into a peat bog:

Pyd ar ros agos eigiawn	[Cursed thing on this
Pwy a eill mwy mewn pwll	brown ocean moor
mawn?	What can you do when
Pysgodlyn i Wyn yw ef	you're stuck in a bog?
Ab Nudd, wb ynn ei oddef	A fishy pool in
	Gwyn ap Nudd's realm
	We're fools to suffer that demagogue]

This Gwyn ap Nudd is the king of the fairies and the underworld, beings and kingdoms that are irreducibly other, and whose interests only occasionally coincide with our own; the watery bog, for Dafydd and his contemporaries, is a portal to this underworld.[232] But this clear supernatural association between the bog and the realm of fairy and magic does not, in this medieval Welsh context, arise out of its pristine 'natural' status. On the contrary, for all Dafydd's cursing of the place as it hinders his route to his lover (as do briars and fog in other poems of his), he notes at the end of the poem that the blame lies on the wretch who dug it 'in hot weather' – a phrase that makes no sense unless it refers to the ubiquitous practice of peat-cutting in summer. The pool might well be supernatural for Dafydd. And regardless of whether the spot he fell was in fact created by human activity, for Dafydd the tradition of human peat-cutting is the ultimate origin of the place. Nature, culture and the supernatural intertwine in his unfortunate incident on a Welsh moor.

Above: A mixed landscape near Tregaron emblematic of many across Wales, with open mountain, wooded slopes, thick hedgerows and different field uses.

Right: The highest naturally occurring beechwood in the British Isles, only a stone's throw from the site of some of its heaviest industry over the past centuries.

Below: This photo was taken on the Llŷn Peninsula as recently as 1960, but shows a now vanished world of hayricks, small poultry flocks and working horses.*

All photographs © Carwyn Graves, unless stated otherwise. *© Geoff Lloyd Collection, National Library of Wales

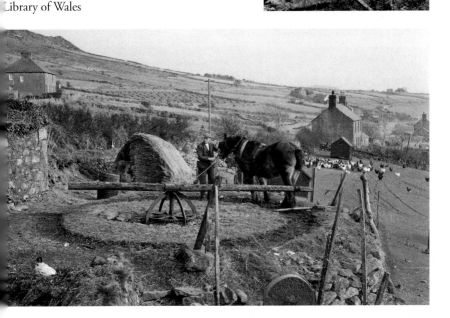

Above: Twisted beech trees at nearly 500 metres above sea level in the eastern south Wales valleys.
Left: Familiar Welsh hedgebank in late spring, with the massive boulders hidden by a profusion of wildflowers.
Below: An exposed *clawdd* showing typical boulder stone construction with hedge growing above.

Above: Early June wildflowers at Caeau Llety Cybi wildlife reserve.
Left: A young farmer taking part in a hedging competition at Pontfadog in 1957.*
Below: A once massive Iron Age hillfort in Ceredigion, whose banks remain clearly to be seen in the hedge and field structures.
© Toby G. Driver/RCAHMW

Right: Carneddau pony, one of a herd of semi-feral horses on these mountains that have been here for millennia.

Below: Classic *ffridd* land in northern Ceredigion, with the mixed scrubby land on the slope giving way to open mountain above.

Bottom: Not only the small-scale grain crop but the number of people involved in harvesting have now disappeared from our countryside within one lifetime.*

Above: Henfaes, a rare surviving upland hay meadow maintained by a local farmer as part of his mixed system, with cattle lightly dunging the thin soils.

Left: Restored '*mawnog*' peat bog near Bwlch-y-groes, showing the re-covered hag and wetness returning with sphagnum.

Below: Buarthau'r Gyrn from the hillside above, showing the cells and runs built into this still-working sheepfold.

Above: The traditional mountain sheep gathering at Glan Meryn, near Machynlleth in the 1950s. Still a key communal activity now, though the practice is threatened.*

Right: All this land was *rhos* till the early twentieth century; the late-summer heather on the surviving land is a tell-tale sign of the poverty of these soils for farming.

Below right: Snowdon from Llyn Nantlle by Richard Wilson; the inhabited mountains. (© Miles Wynn Cato)

Below: Rhos on Mynydd Bach: One of many surviving *rhos* areas on lower Mynydd Bach land, in its distinctive browns.

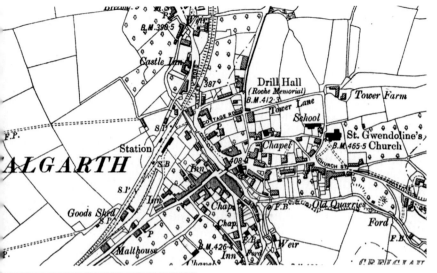

Above: Talgarth as an orchard town in 1888, with fruit trees surrounding the town on three sides.

Left: Evan Jenkins and David Jones, country folk poets, discussing their work at a cobbler's in their village in November 1959.

Below: The bull in the wildlife-rich orchard of Maesydderwen farm on the lower slopes of the Black Mountains, Breconshire.

Above: Mixed farming focussed on horticulture at Troedyrhiw, working within the inherited, biodiverse field structures and hedgerows.

Left: Fruit festooning one of the surviving ancient perry pear trees at Tredomen.

Below: This Ceredigion vineyard in summer 2022 could easily pass as northern Spain; what will fifty years' further warming do to that picture?

What is true of an unnamed peat bog is all the more true of the mountains as a whole. There are layers of tradition around place-names, linking for example giants' abodes in the highest peaks, like one Idris whose chair became 'Cader Idris' or Rhita Gawr, who lies buried under a cairn on Snowdon. Mountain lakes, from Tegid to Rhos-y-cwn in the Glyderau, contain miraculous creatures including one-eyed trouts and *afancod* (lake monsters).[233] Natural features from standing stones and tumuli,[234] to caves, fords and fountains have names and traditions associated with them. The boundary between myth, legend and half-remembered history is often thin in these story collections, with ancient battles connected with place-names,[235] and historical or semi-historical figures such as the Emperor Constantine III and Arthur associated with particular mountain spots.

Enough of this oral folk tradition still existed around Snowdonia for an entirely new collection to be published in Welsh in 2008, drawing on material recorded in the last decades of the twentieth century.[236] These include a particularly rich vein of stories about ghosts and fairies, with certain peaks and valleys universally associated with the fairies. The mountaineer Jim Perrin recalls that when he went to live in Cwm Pennant in the 1970s, 'the farmer at the topmost holding in the cwm, Wil Braich Dinas, was, Mr Morus gave me to believe, descended from the fairies. When I asked around, everyone in the valley of Mr Morus's generation knew this – it was an accepted fact that he was one of the *Belisiaid'* – in other words, descended from fairy folk.[237] These fairies lived both on mountains and in the valleys, with their abodes betrayed by certain stone structures in the landscape, powerful stones and lawns of especially verdant grass. They could be seen, dancing, in the right conditions – at night or in foggy weather.

A local lad, W. J. Jones, was recorded recounting his encounter with the fairies, one summer's night alongside his brother on a mountainside in the Nantlle valley. They were at a spot – 'y Garreg Lefain' – that their grandfather had mentioned was famous for fairies, and just after the sun had set they both saw a circle of fairy folk dancing. 'Odd 'na both math o liwia 'no – fatha bloda i mi' ('There were all sorts of colours there – they looked like flowers to me').[238] Another account, from Capel Curig, recounts how fairies were often seen by entire families on summer peat-cutting days on the mountain, but only in foggy weather: 'There was a sort of music, quite beautiful. And then the fog would open up and you'd see these little people dancing, and then they'd disappear.'[239] Given the antiquity of this sprawling mass of interrelated folk tale and legend, first collected in the Middle Ages by figures such as Gerald of Wales and then expanded upon with each generation of antiquarians from Camden and Lhuyd until the late twentieth century, it is fair to say that these traditions were thick enough to thoroughly shape local attitudes towards the mountains, as storied, known places.

There is another side to this oral tradition, of real importance when viewed from a twenty-first-century vantage point, and that is the accumulated lore around non-supernatural animals and their places in the landscape. This is extensive, and in the mountains bear especial witness to the ubiquity within cultural memory of large herbivores and apex predators no longer present. These include: *carw/ewig* (red deer, m/f), *iwrch/iyrches* (roe deer, m/f), *blaidd* (wolf), *baedd/twrch* (different names for wild boar) and more controversially *arth* (bear), the memory of which lived on in personal names used in the first millennium AD such as Arthur and Arthog.[240] Although both red and roe deer effectively became extinct in the wild in Wales by around 1650, their presence is recorded in countless place-names, from Moel-yr-iwrch (Bald hill of the roe buck) near Llanrwst to Bwlch Ewigod (Hind's pass) in the mountains near Dolwyddelan, both of which betray precisely the locations in the landscape where we might expect to see these deer congregating. Unsurprisingly, the written cultural record shows the same pattern, with the cantref of Buallt around the modern Builth Wells described by a late medieval bard as possessing 'ym mhob plwyf, lwdwn hydd' – a stag in every parish.

This lore is clearest though in the case of the wolf, which is likely to have gone extinct in Wales around 1500, with a number of counties claiming to be the location of the killing of the country's 'last wolf'.[241] There are over 225 unambiguous 'wolf' place-names in Wales, including places named after still-extant wolf-traps (*bleiddbwll*), many crags and hills named after wolves and she-wolves, and numerous wolf caves (*Ogo'r Bleiddiau*). These names reflect the distribution and behaviour we would expect from modern understandings of wolf ecology, if they had been present in a populated and agricultural Welsh economy. Historians writing in English on the subject seem strangely reticent to entertain the notion of wolf survivals in Wales beyond the fourteenth century, but there are plenty of reasons to suppose that the cohabitation of wolf and farmer here may well have continued well into the early modern period.

There are of course local stories and legends about wolves and wolf-packs from Gwent to Snowdonia, reflecting folk memory, but the most haunting echoes of the wolves' presence in the land are those recorded instances that reflect clear lived experience of wolves and their ways. This comes to us frequently in the work of the medieval poets, whose poems of loss and personal tragedy often pull on the howling of wolves as a signifier of grief and longing. Sometimes these reflect a personal encounter with a wolf, as in Tudur Penllyn's (*c*.1420–90) poem about how a wolf bit his father's balls. A cattle drover, he tells how of a morning he was on a hillside and came face to face with a young wolf, which, cornered, jumped on him and snapped at his balls.[242] And the most intense accounts of all such encounters comes down to us in the form of dozens of proverbs in Welsh that bear the mark of a pastoral people living alongside wolves:

'Blaidd er ei ladd, ni lwydd ei abo'
Though the wolf be killed, its prey won't flourish

'Gwaeth un blaidd cloff na dau iach'
Worse is one lame wolf than two healthy

'Cyfeill blaidd bugail diog'
The wolf's friend is the lazy shepherd

'Main fel blaidd Chwefror'
Vicious like February's wolf

'Mwy nag y mae da i'r blaidd, nid da ei isgell'
Even the stock made from a wolf is good for nought

Some of these sayings, such as 'oes yr arth a'r blaidd' ('in the age of the bear and the wolf') remain in common use as idioms in Welsh, including in my own natural use of the language. And these things are, as always, personal: down the road from where my grandfather grew up in north Pembrokeshire is a pub called 'Pant-y-blaidd' – the wolf's hollow. This, according to tradition told to me as a child, is where the last wolf in west Wales was killed during the reign of Henry VIII. Nearby was a standing stone, which according to my great-uncle, was thrown by a giant from the summit of Frenni Fawr mountain nearby, 'maen nhw'n dweud' ('they say'). Surveying all this – my own cultural heritage – it is hard to escape the conclusion that the presence of wolves in the Welsh landscape and in particular their association with the uplands remains a core part of the cultural subconscious, and that as such wolves are also native here. But as all the sayings, proverbs and stories attest, a key element of that cultural memory is a profound wariness of the wolf; a distrust and fear. It may be true that the presence of apex predators in an ecosystem can have startlingly positive knock-on effects on everything from water quality to biodiversity. But it isn't in the least bit surprising that the mere notion of reintroductions awakened an incredulous and fearful response, not just from the farming community in Wales but from Welsh-speaking rural communities in general.

And it was within this wider oral tradition about places and localities and how they should be known and called that the term 'mynydd' always had a wider sense than simply 'mountain'.[243] As touched on above, 'mynydd Llanllechid' is a reference to that part of the Carneddau used for extensive grazing by the farmers and graziers of Llanllechid; 'mynydd y Dyffryn' in Aberporth (where there are no 'mountains' at all) was that part of the farm used for extensive grazing and occasional cropping and some of which was slightly higher up within the farm as a whole, and some of which was lower but all of which was open, unhedged.[244] The key thing here is the close association – right down to the level of naming – between the human dwelling-place and the *mynydd*, whether that be a 'mountain' or not. The *mynydd* sits firmly within the sphere of the farm or community, rather than being in some sense beyond it.

Back on Mynydd Clogau, at all of 288m above sea level, the March sun is gradually waning. There are sheep here on the open mountain, grazing at a low-stocking density which has led to significant bracken incursion. Stone sheepfolds merge into the mountainside a couple of miles further up the ridge, and below me smoke is starting to rise from one or two of the old stone farmhouses and cottages in the valley. None of them are likely to be from peat-fires, though they are coming out of fireplaces that would within living memory have burnt peat. Gethin, the farmer who I had chatted to earlier, was keen to tell me about his family's links with this place, and their farmhouse marks those in black-and-white pictures commemorating not just older ways of farming on the mountains here but even winning a livelihood inside the mountain, from gold-mining. I doubt that he would be able to tell me all that many in the way of old folk tales from here, though he's clearly versed in the wider cultural and poetic traditions of the north Wales mountains. There is a mountain culture here, and it remains alive in a long and self-aware continuity with untold centuries past. It is, though, tinged with a very Welsh melancholy, as a heady mix of pressures – economic and cultural – continue to press on its survival. One other thing Gethin mentions, with a resigned air of regret, is the fact that during his boyhood in this mountain valley there had been a dozen, fifteen working farms. Now that was down to three.

7

Rhos

Heath, moor and bog/
wetter, rough grazing land

Of all the traditional components of the Welsh landscape, the one that we have lost in greatest measure over the last few centuries is also the least known. The *rhos* lands of Wales once covered something in the region of 40 per cent of the land,[245] forming the single most common type of landscape encountered as people travelled the country. Rhos gave its name to entire regions of medieval Wales and to modern-day villages; was an essential part of the farming system across most of the country until the nineteenth century; managed to give rise to localised wars and probably represented the single largest haven for Welsh wildlife for millennia. And although this habitat exists in other parts of the British Isles and Atlantic Europe, Wales may now account for well over half the area of 'rhos wet pasture' in the UK as a whole.[246] Yet no books have been written on the Welsh *rhos,* few studies ever undertaken, and the loss of many *rhosydd* that did survive into the present millennium continues apace in the early 2020s.

The glosses and translations given to the Welsh term *rhos* have contributed to the maligning of this key habitat: variously rendered 'waste', 'wilderness', 'heath' or 'moor', these are large, open and scrubby areas of countryside found in places that by Welsh standards are either lowland or hilly, rather than upland proper. A great many of them, amounting to hundreds of thousands of hectares, were historically held as common land, and confusingly were sometimes referred to in

English as 'mountain' land; as we have already seen, this is a translation of the Welsh *mynydd*, which at base denoted rough, summer-grazing land – sometimes true mountain upland, and sometimes what would in England be called heathland, commons or, in recent times, wet pasture.[247] There isn't necessarily a hard and fast distinction between *rhos* and *mynydd*, with the terms overlapping both in terms of function and use. But at least in the not-too-infrequent places across Wales where both a *rhos* and a *mynydd* are present, the *rhos* is likely to be the lower or the wetter of the two.

Regardless of name, for commentators over the centuries these areas were both ubiquitous and of very little interest. Neither the focus of agricultural activity of the sort to please sixteenth-century antiquarians, nor offering dramatic scenery to please eighteenth- or nineteenth-century romantic travellers, they were places usually passed through as you went from one place of interest to another. And for local countryside dwellers, until they started being parcelled off, *rhos* areas were simply so common as not to merit attention.

But these areas may well be the missing piece of the puzzle as we try to understand what a farmed Welsh landscape looks like that allows wildlife to thrive alongside people with crops and animals. The historical record we have for these areas suggests they must have been rich in wildlife, and current experiments in what some have called 'agricultural rewilding' often ends up recreating exactly the type of habitat we know many Welsh *rhosydd* would have been historically. That, in itself, makes them important to try to understand as we look ahead to the coming century. But when coupled with the long history of contestation and conflict for these ultimately marginal areas of land, these less productive grazing lands turn out to be the lynchpin in our tale.

This is a personal story for me, with the issues at stake in this chapter entwined in my own family history and forming the backdrop to many of my happiest childhood memories. My grandfather and his many brothers and sister grew up in the 1930s and 1940s on a windswept patch of *rhos* in the hills on the Carmarthenshire-Pembrokeshire border. They were at the bottom of the pile economically, owning at any one time just one set of clothes and shoes (clogs). My great-grandmother, Ruth, died in childbirth when Dadcu was only two, and he and most of his siblings were raised by their sister, only a teenager at the time. Their father was in bed, suffering from silicosis after spending stints working in the mines in south Wales.

Money was short, but like many people in that rural community, one of their highest aspirations was to work the land. In the end, they rolled an old railway carriage into the corner of a field surrounded by *rhos* only a stone's throw from a good spring that didn't run dry. There, my grandfather grew up in a life as different from my childhood in 1990s Cardiff as mine was from that of most kids my age in the global south. Three tiny bedrooms made out of carriage compartments, and one kitchen in which to cook, eat and dry clothes by the single stove. All vegetables home-grown on the plot's poor, yellow soil, fed by copious amounts of manure. Fowls for eggs; potatoes and goats in the field. Only flour, sugar and tea were regularly bought. And the radius to which life extended were the 10 miles or so it took to walk to the cobblers' hut in a wood near Gelliwen. The nearest towns were known by name and hearsay only; bananas, chocolate and much else familiar to contemporaries of theirs living in towns, cities or indeed richer rural areas, unknown.

The place was called, ironically, Rhos Mansion; the irony heightened by the use of English in a community which census results show was among the most Welsh-speaking in the country at the time, with most neighbours monolingual Welsh.[248] In the late 1960s, when stewardship of the place passed to my grandfather, our own family name for the place changed to Tyddyn y Rhos (Rhos cottage).[249] Either way, at the time the name was entirely apt: it was surrounded on three sides by scrubby heath extending for the best part of a mile in each direction with just a few other 'real' cottages for neighbours also carved out of the *rhos*-land with their garden and a small infield or two.

This was the home stomping ground; where Dadcu and his brother Martin would get into all sorts of childish mischief, and roam for whinberries in summer, blackberries in September and hazelnuts in October. Many decades later, my brother and I discovered several hollows and hideaways among the gorse and blackthorn perfect for secret dens; of course, it turned out that the very best of them had been known and used by Dadcu and Martin long before.

But none of this changed the fact that this was a hard life on poor ground. Their older brother, Ifor, returned to take over the tenancy in the 1950s, building a lean-to corrugated iron kitchen onto the side of the carriage, and trying to make a living on the smallholding. It didn't work: the land is poor and the growing season short, even compared with areas just a few miles away and a couple of hundred metres downhill. His venture failed and he moved away only a couple of years later.

That, ultimately, is why these areas became *rhos*. As we saw in chapter 3, in every area of Wales until the changes in the late eighteenth and early nineteenth centuries, the basic pattern for farming consisted of arable infields with some permanent pasture or meadowland, complemented by large areas of summer grazing. In most areas outside the true uplands, much of this was *rhos* land and the reason it became such rather than being made into infields or meadow was the knowledge that these areas were the worse parts of any given area. Thinner or sourer soils, sometimes stonier, sometimes wetter and boggier, and always unable to dependably give a crop of hay or grain.[250]

They were, nevertheless, essential. We have already seen that by the beginning of the Iron Age all lowland areas of Wales were densely settled, with farmsteads dotting the landscape with their associated meadows, woods and *maes* arable fields. But pollen and weed seed analysis by archaeologists of sites in Ceredigion have shown that there were also areas of scrub land near settlements with evidence of ample bramble, hazel, heather and bracken.[251] These had multiple uses: as well as the foraged value of nuts and blackberries (*mwyar* in Welsh, descended from the proto-Celtic for 'fruit' in general, betraying their importance), both bracken and heather provided important animal bedding and thatch. These *rhos* areas, far from being neglected wasteland, were in fact indispensable for the entire agrarian economy's function, primarily by virtue of their role as summer pasturage.[252]

And so, like every other part of the landscape, these *rhos* areas called 'waste' or 'wilderness' by later outsiders were in fact closely governed and regulated with many of the records in the oldest surviving Welsh book, the Book of Llandaff, regulating use of outfield pasture. Indeed, much of Welsh law and custom was strongly oriented around the dates of Calan Mai (Mayday on 1 May) when cattle were allowed out onto the summer grazing *rhosydd* and other rough pastures and Calan Gaeaf (Hallowe'en and Irish Samhain on 1 November) when the animals were brought back down to the winter dwelling.[253] The latter date was also associated with feasting, while Calan Mai was also the date on which peasants were due to pay their annual food rent and the arable infields were closed to stock, with strict punishment for infringements.

We don't know exactly how far back these customs go, but their close parallel to the Irish traditions, and what can be pieced together from Classical writers about the customs of the native tribes over 1,000 years earlier suggest that they stretch back into the Iron Age if not further. In any case, they were long-lived and encapsulated a strict regard for the ecological carrying capacity of the land. Even after the Conquest in 1282 and the subsequent abolishment of Welsh law, these regulations survived into traditions, noted in 1552 in the Conwy valley and in Radnorshire as recently as 1844, that folk had the right to keep only as many animals on the commons in summer as they could feed on the home farm through the winter.[254]

In earlier periods at least, the extent of these *rhos* areas was such that when coupled with woodlands and high mountain, they provided open expanses large enough to also permit significant degrees of hunting. Both stag and boar hunts play a prominent role in medieval tales and myths and were clearly a celebrated part of the annual calendar, with Calan Gaeaf also marking the end of the stag season and the beginning of boar-hunting. Boars are creatures not only of closed woodland but are equally happy in scrub and overgrown grassy areas, happily ranging from one habitat to the other as their needs require. Deer – both the red and roe native here – also happily live both in closed and more open areas, and before the establishment of deer parks in the thirteenth century, ranged widely from places such as Cnwc yr hydd (the Hart's hillock) to Afon iwrch (Roe deer river).[255]

Other linguistic evidence corroborates this picture of these seemingly wild areas serving an important functional role in the landscape. The Welsh for 'sheepwalk' is either *hysfa* or *arhosfa*. By some minor sound changes this can easily become *rhosfa* – which sounds like '*rhos*-place' in Welsh. In an indication of the greater prominence that sheep had in the landscape after the Cistercian establishments in the late Middle Ages, by the sixteenth century precisely such a merger had happened between the words, with the 1547 Welsh–English dictionary entry for *rhos* running 'rhos or rhosfa = A heath', and Lhuyd in 1707 describing *rhos* as 'mountain meadow', further cementing its role at the time as pasture.[256]

And despite the subsequent disappearance of much of the *rhos*, it retains its resonance within culture. One of the more successful Welsh bands of recent years is called Cowbois Rhos Botwnnog (the cowboys of Rhos Botwnnog); there are dramas, songs and novels all bearing the name 'rhos' in their titles, as well as Christmas carols that place the shepherds watching their flocks on a middle eastern stretch of *rhos*. The word remains freighted with cultural significance, as captured in a couplet by Geraint Bowen (1915–2011) from the middle of a well-known longer poem entitled 'Cân y Ddaear' (The Song of the Earth), which is spoken in the Earth's voice:

Gwêl ogoniant perarogl
    y gweunydd
A'r myrr a'r aloes a roes
    y rhosydd[257]

[Smell the glory of the
    gwaun's fragrance
The myrr and aloes given
    off by the *rhosydd*]

Enclosure

'Mari Waungron was a distant relative to my late partner', explains Meic to me in his low-slung stone cottage high up on gusty Mynydd Bach. 'She had one acre of land and kept one cow and as far as she was concerned, the *rhos* up there was massively more important than the acre she actually owned.' I have come to this brown, rough part of mid Wales because it strikingly illustrates both the disappearance of most of our *rhos* and the extent to which the tale of the landscape is inseparably interwoven into the fabric of our human cultural economies at every level.

As you drive into this stretch of low hills some 12 miles long and 7 miles wide commonly called 'Mynydd Bach' or 'Little Mountain', you can't help but notice at almost any time of year how much browner this landscape is than the fertilised green that now characterises most of south-western Wales. Scraggly willows and rank grasses continue to hold their own in patches of *rhos* between ranks of plantation conifers and small, square fields. The willow warblers' song on a bright day, with the distant rim of sea an ever-present horizon, all belie the fact that the elements of this now remote, quiet landscape were in every way contested, and are still the locus of layers of conflict.

The place-names, as so often, betray the long pattern of land use here: many a 'lluest' and 'hafod' clearly indicating the conversion of older, summer dwellings in the last few centuries into permanent holdings.

This is the poorest of poor land: exposed, thin, stony and extremely acid soils with high rainfall levels, seen as fit for nothing but extensive summer grazing for millennia. But as the population grew in the early modern period, these became permanent dwellings, albeit surrounded still by a sea of open *rhos*.[258] The vast majority of this was Crown land, used as common land since time immemorial. But now, the cottagers of eighteenth-century Wales increasingly tried to make some of it their own; simultaneous to this, Parliament in London had accelerated a series of Acts encouraging landowners to buy common land from the Crown and make it more productive.

Technically, both the landowners and the squatting cottagers were engaged in what is called enclosure. But here – in the hills of mid Wales – it was the little people that won out. While the land magnates were clearing the Scottish Highlands of people, cattle and hearths to make way for sheep, huge swathes of open upland pasture in Wales were being squatted to make holdings for local people. This was, they could maintain, nothing new: the custom of younger offspring or other lesser folk carving out a holding from the mountain went back centuries.[259] And so what had been shared grazing, turbary, candle-rush patch and summer milking-and-churning ground became the small, hedged fields providing one small family with sustenance and a home.

It was, nevertheless, illegal by the letter of the law – if not by local perception of what the law ought to say. When the Crown appointed agents to make the very same sorts of square fields and low hedgebanks on these moors that locals were creating, but on behalf of landowners who had parted with thousands of pounds to legally buy the land, the locals' vehemence was squarely based on this customary understanding of the law. And so in 1820 on Mynydd Bach, representatives of a violent local mob testified to the court that 'there shall not be any farms or houses built on Mynydd Bach but what ... shall be pulled down; [if] any poor man shall come then he shall build a house and make a field and we will help him'. The pattern was a common one, repeated across Wales: in 1858 on Mynydd Llanfair, the Crown valuer was forced to state that he 'had the greatest difficulty in carrying out this inclosure in consequence of the encroachers ... stoutly holding out ... It would have required a military force to aid the civil power to turn out 48 families.'

Similarly on rocky, thin Mynydd Cilgwyn, home in the 1820s to 700 people living in 141 houses. There, the threatened cottagers pleaded, they wanted nothing but to de-stone the land and work it; to grow some corn and potatoes and keep a cow or two. And when the local lord attempting to enclose the land and evict them relented, these chapel-going smallholders poured a cask of home-brew to celebrate and sent another to his London dwelling. To the warblers' background song, in innumerable petty skirmishes across Wales, the cottagers overcame and remained – even though some were convicted for their crime and ended up in Australia.

Not that the outcome was in any case predetermined, and the extent of the battle to be fought was perhaps nowhere greater than on Mynydd Bach, where the saga of which the 1820 skirmish is an episode still remembered and celebrated as 'Rhyfel y Sais Bach' – the war of the little Englishman. The Englishman in question was a Lincolnshire nobleman, Augustus Brackenbury, who made the seemingly shrewd investment of £1,750 for almost 1,000 acres of Cardiganshire Crown land. He visited the area, beholding himself well and employing local workers both for land improvement work and to start construction on what would become his pleasant, new manorial pile, 'Green Meadow'.

Unfortunately for him, no sooner had construction started than it was in May 1820 knocked down at night by unknown locals. The case went to court, with witnesses going on oath to explain that the only people they would tolerate building a house on Mynydd Bach would be local cottagers. In a display of strength, that summer hundreds of cottagers from the area descended on Brackenbury's land to cut their harvest of peat without paying the 1s. fee that Brackenbury had in his opinion quite reasonably asked them to pay for what was legally his.

Dismayed but not defeated, Brackenbury started work soon afterward on a new dwelling to replace the fated Green Meadow higher up the hill and on land purchased in a different settlement. The site, Castell Talwrn, can still be seen today from the roadside as a set of ditches and dykes in a field and bears the physical imprint of Brackenbury's new wariness in the fact that the ditches are the remnants of a defensive – rather than ornamental – moat. The house was built, but in May 1826, local boy Siaci Ifan y Gof climbed to the rocky knoll of Hebrysg Fawr half a mile away and blew his horn. According to local myth, over 1,000 men gathered in response within less than half an hour.[260] Together, they stormed Castell Talwrn, threatening to burn the inhabitants alive unless they gave up its defence. All inside fled; and the building was razed to the ground. Realising his Welsh venture was lost, Brackenbury started selling off his land soon after, and departed.

Mari's cottage and acre of land high up on Mynydd Bach date from precisely this period and help ground this complex tale. As Meic tells me, this is far more than a tale of ethnic tension manifesting itself in a confrontation between the moneyed, hapless Englishman trying to carve up the *rhos* and the poor but valiant local Welsh cottagers rallying to save it. For one thing, the first significant confrontation on Mynydd Bach was in May 1815, five years before the Green Meadow fiasco, between local surveyor John Hughes and a mob of over 100 angry squatters, who threatened to murder him if he ever returned to measure their local commons.[261] When it came to Brackenbury – and despite the deliberate framing of him as the 'Sais Bach' (or little Englishman) – the cottagers' objection was much more to do with his purchase of common land than it was his Englishness or his wealth. And their objection to his purchase of common land was only partially entangled in a desire to defend their ancient *rhos* with its valuable peat, grazing, rabbits and berries. It was by their own admission just as much to do with the fact that they wanted the right to enclose it, as they had already started doing.

'The irony about *rhyfel y Sais bach* is that in the long run, the fact that they had had a long and hard-won fight to keep the *rhos* open is probably what led to so much of it surviving in this area,' Meic explains to me as we trudge up to the monument to local poets that stands on one of the highest outcrops in the area. 'They had fought so hard to keep it as it was, they couldn't very well lose it now – even to each other.' And on top of this, the war, such as it was, only ever involved local cottagers, *tyddynwyr* smallholders; established farmers and others in the area were never directly involved but bought into the myth afterwards.

We reach a high point where miles of brown lands stretch out before us, most of it arranged in the tell-tale squares of nineteenth-century enclosure. 'Most of these square fields are from Brackenbury's era', Meic explains, 'and most of these holdings are ultimately descended from that period of squatting and fighting.' It was legal mechanisms – partly brought about by locals' intransigence – that enabled this. In 1897, the Welsh Land Commission in London reported their findings: that the land was the home of the people, who thereby had 'a kind of moral right to have a means of obtaining thereon their livelihood through life'. In post-war Ceredigion, the arduous victory of the cottagers was almost total: 70 per cent of its land by then was owner-occupied, the highest percentage anywhere in Britain (followed closely by other Welsh counties) and significantly up from 19 per cent in 1887.[262]

These holdings spread out below us are by modern standards vanishingly small farms and in almost no cases are they productive enough to support an individual, let alone a family. 'If I think about my neighbours – almost all small farmers – they are also an electrician, carpet-layer, garage owner, groundsman and so on. Their identity, though, is absolutely as a farmer. That's what they want to do in life. And that's why they work so hard to improve the land.' But even to the untrained eye, it is clearer here than almost anywhere in Wales how much the land resists improvement. A minority of these small, chequered fields are green with sheep, kept by these local small-scale farmers, but the majority of the fields remain stubbornly brown, with thickets of willow dotted about the place. It turns out that horses are what keep these failed, unimproved fields open, in an approximation of the mixed grazing from centuries gone by; except that these are lifestyle horses, brought here by rural incomers who have mostly come in from England to return 'back to the land'.

A perusal of the latest census data upon returning home confirms what I had suspected: in this wild-feeling area, within sight of the sea with plenty of detached cottages attached to their own plot of land, the percentage of Welsh speakers has declined in recent decades more precipitously than in almost any other part of Ceredigion. 'They are almost all lovely people,' Meic tells me when I ask later, 'but they're largely clueless about the culture we have here. They want an area like this to be a kind of blank slate, so that's how they behave.' Communities like these have been completely hollowed out over the last few decades; school, shops, pub, chapels – everything has closed, and now people can move here, work from home and get their food delivered from a distant supermarket. That is of course a lot easier than learning a new language, sympathetically learning about a place and its story, and contributing to it. Ironically though, Meic observes that many of them are much less interested in improving the land, so their management may well be better for biodiversity. And the deeper irony is that is to a great extent because they are so much less invested in it as a massive part of identity.

I ask Meic about the role that the 'war' plays in the area now. 'People who are from here, who grew up here, absolutely they know the story – or rather the myth – about it.' He feels it still shapes the sense of identity locally in quite a major way and that this can be displayed in obvious ways: only a year or two previously there had been an anonymous plaque put up protesting against incomers and calling for a kind of new 'war of the little Englanders'. He explains that progressive groups like Cymdeithas yr Iaith know full well that the dynamic playing out here of rural depopulation and community death is also playing out on a pan-Europe level, but the myth is powerful and it can channel people's understanding of these things in a particular direction.

We wander on into the heart of the surviving open *rhos* and come across Jeff, a neighbouring farmer, on a quad bike. Meic explains that he's taking me to see Cors Pwll-yr-ych, a wetter part of the *rhos* where his late wife used to cut peat and some of her relatives still do.[263] Jeff smiles knowingly when Meic explains that I am learning about the history of Mynydd Bach, and then tells us that the sheep are too fond of Cors Pwll-yr-ych. 'It's because of that white flower that grows there in summer, the bog cotton, you know the one? They're drawn to it and they keep ending up stuck in the bog there.'

This explains to a great extent why the loss of *rhos* has continued apace. Detailed figures for the Llŷn Peninsula show just how much has been lost even in the past century, well after the end of the period for which historians generally use the term enclosure. Compared to 1922 figures, the habitat cover of dense scrub, wet heathland or dry heathland (all of which would be *rhos* or *gwaun* areas) on the peninsula has decreased by an astonishing 70 per cent.[264] And what is true of the Llŷn is also true of Wales as a whole, to only a slightly lesser extent. Few people today would believe how much the landscape has changed in its elements within the course of one long human lifetime, perhaps particularly since all its components remain present today. It's just that their composition has changed out of all recognition.

Back on Mynydd Bach, what is left of the great *rhosydd* that once covered this area is now split up into small patches, mostly isolated from one another apart from the thin threads of interlocking hedgerows. One of these, Rhos Glandenys, is now managed by the local wildlife trust with grazing horses and shows the abundance of life that a small 5-acre plot of *rhos* can sustain. Not only are Southern Marsh orchids and

Heath Spotted orchids both common enough for their grey skeletons to entrance me even on a bleak January afternoon, but the varying wetness of the land with shrubs and small trees interspersed across it support a profusion of insects and birds. Dunnock, blackbird, wren and grasshopper warblers flit among willow warblers and chiffchaff and are joined in winter by snipe and woodcock. All this in an area that is no larger than a medium-sized field and takes no more than 3 or 4 minutes to cross. So, what could *rhos* areas sustain if they were larger and joined-up, as they once were?

A great expanse of scrub

I have, to my great luck, an eyewitness to these changes in my family. A couple of fields away from Tyddyn y Rhos lies the heathery common of Crugelwin, rising to almost 250m above sea level. Both it and adjacent fields that were once *rhos* contain sheep enclosures dating back to the Cistercian sheep enterprises of Whitland abbey, 800 years ago. All my life, Crugelwin had always been there, the brown heathery expanse on the skyline that stood as a silent reminder of the former life of these hills. And then, one summer in the late 2010s, it was gone. Ploughed up, the gorse and heather burnt, and then reseeded with a productive, non-native grass. Suddenly, there was one more green hill – almost certainly illegally enclosed and all within the last few years.[265]

I ring up my Wncwl Martin, now in his ninety-sixth year, to ask about his memories of the *rhos* when growing up there with my grandfather and his other siblings. They had never been on to Crugelwin itself, though it had always been there, the brown backbone on the other side of the valley. But then on the *rhos* around the cottage 'there'd always been *ehedydd* [skylarks]. Are they still there?'

'No, though I hear them on the Frenni Fawr when we go for a walk there.'

'Oh. And what about the *chwibanwr?* There had always been plenty of curlews – do you hear them?'

'No, they're gone too since the *rhos* has gone.'

'Pity. There had been a lot of *rhosydd*, and a lot of birds, back in my day,' he says wistfully. Then a change of tone, exactly like his brother used to, 'Ah! So they've gone and filled in the other *rhos* then? There we are! It happens!' And a wry chuckle, before we change topics.

His childhood memories of another world confirm the basic observation that these spaces came with their own forms of now-vanished wildlife, that had, in all likelihood, inhabited them for countless long years. Taking just the curlew of Martin's memory, numbers of this iconic bird with its long, curved beak and haunting song have declined by 80 per cent since only 1993, and it has recently been added to the UK's red list of species at risk of extinction. The nearest breeding pair to our now-vanished *rhos* is likely over 50 miles away. That's just one species of bird; reconstructing a broader picture of the ecology of *rhos* areas historically is a painstaking task that can only be based on remarks by people whose attention was almost always elsewhere and deserves much more systematic searching than I have been able to give it. But even my broad and winding forays through the historical record, in throwaway remark here and proverb from country lore there, allow us to get a broadbrush sense of what many of these areas would have been like in the round.[266] And they were, in short, wonderful.

It's clear that a large range of plant species were found on the *rhos*. This includes raspberries, so abundant on these areas around Cardigan in the seventeenth century that visiting travellers remarked on the locals' practice of using them to make country wines.[267] Gorse was clearly widespread and appears in the very earliest reference to *rhos* in the twelfth-century Book of Llandaff – 'ros ireithin' – *eithin* being the Welsh for furze, with regulations about its use also appearing in Welsh law. Heather also features strongly in the record, as in an 1800 reference to heathery *rhos* losing its heather if allowed over time to become too wet. Rushes often appear in poetry alongside *rhos* and *gwaun,* as in fifteenth-century Glyn Cothi's 'brwyn gweunydd'. But also more uncommon plants like woad, of vital importance as a dye and clearly known in Wales above all from *rhos* and *gwaun* areas as indicated by its name 'balog y waun'. Beyond these, certain other plants seem to have been locally viewed as emblematic of *rhos* areas, including meadowsweet (*brenhines y waun* or 'queen of the *gwaun*'), cranberry (*ceirios y waun* or *gwaun* cherry) and the keen white flowers of greater stitchwort (*egran y waun*). To this we can add the wild chamomile, which thrives in its most northerly populations of all on *rhos* areas in Anglesey and Llŷn and which we know was historically much more widespread.[268]

But it's in the birds that these associations and names become most revealing. To my uncle's skylark and curlew, we can add 'cornicyll y waun', the plover, a bird known as a summer visitor that nests on heather and grass in moorland. Similarly, 'ehedydd y waun' is the titlark, known primarily as a species of open habitats, controlled by light-touch grazing and agricultural harvesting; exactly the sort of ecospace that a *rhos* is. And perhaps most poignantly, place-names open a window onto past ecological realities: just a few miles from Mari's house on Mynydd Bach lies a still-existent area of *rhos* known as 'gors caranod' – the crane bog. Cranes are generally held to have gone extinct in Wales over 400 years ago and even if by some chance they survived on this particular patch for longer, there is now no trace of them other than this name. It is however one of fifteen places in southern Wales named after cranes, almost all of which reflect wetter patches of land. Once again, we find the language encoding a knowledge of native wildlife and their habits.

These *rhos* areas were thus clearly associated in language and the popular imagination with a great range of species historically, showing us with twenty-first-century ecological lenses their value for nature. But the list also allows us to get under the skin of how these areas were used, as so many of the plant and bird species there are known as lovers of light and open areas; with some tree and shrub cover, but certainly not dense woodland. And as we have seen before, this type of scrubby habitat can only ultimately be kept in that kind of state by grazing – which is what a close look at the evidence confirms has been present on *rhos*, for millennia. Much of this grazing, for the past 1,000 years and quite possibly long before, was done by cattle (accompanied by horses), with herds providing by far the most important stock of wealth in society. Mari's sole cow surviving off the grazing on Mynydd Bach in the 1950s is one late relict of this pattern. These were later joined by sheep, with the right of common attached to different holdings providing an essential economic basis to many upland holdings.[269]

Again, words give us clues to this now-gone picture. Harebells, still common in the Welsh uplands and known to need grassy or heathery areas with generally acidic soils, are called in Welsh *clychau'r bugail* or shepherds' bells. Shepherds were known both under traditional law and in customs that still held sway in some areas into the eighteenth century, as boys and young men who spent the summer out on the *rhos* or the mountains with the cattle, tending them. And the role these plants play as evidence of continuous grazing in these heathery *rhos* areas is strong as a Swedish study of their incidence of a fifty-year period showed. Where grasslands had been abandoned, they found no incidence at all of harebells; it was only in continuously grazed sites that harebells' incidence remained high.[270] Here, as the language implies, the shepherd's shadow is directly related to the presence of these plants.

But hints as to the diversity of these *rhos* areas from a wildlife point of view emerge even more strongly when we look at the range of animals that were grazed there, beyond sheep and cattle. In many periods they were clearly important for grazing horses, with echoes of the association of horses with the *rhos* coming down to us in all sorts of ways. In eighteenth-century Meirionydd and Montgomeryshire, the grazing capabilities of these areas as pasture allowed sufficient numbers of ponies to be kept on the hills until they were three years old to form a valuable source of income when they were sold at fairs.[271] Folk songs also reflect the idea that horses were often found 'out' on the *rhos*, as in this Glamorganshire folk song which was sung while driving cows to milking:

'prw me, pre me /	'proo meh, proo meh /
prw ngwartheg i dre ... tair caseg	proo my cows in ... three black
ddu draw yn yr eithin'	stallions out in the gorse'[272]

One of the reasons for this on the wetter *rhos* areas is that on this sort of terrain, sheep are prone to developing liver disease, whereas the right sort of small mountain pony – like hardy cattle – can do well, even if they don't put on copious weight. Modern ecological science has shown time and again the extent to which mixed grazing – particularly with horses and cattle prominent in the mix – create a rich and complex habitat for insects and birds with patches of denser thorns, willows and other trees amongst an array of grassland types.[273]

Geese were a further member of the grazing mix, with the Brecon Buff goose (one of only four surviving native to the British Isles) still known for its hardiness and good grazing abilities. Although many of those in possession of such rights are now often ignorant of them, commoners across Wales continue to hold rights to graze geese on surviving commons, such as the 2,000-hectare large Blorenge common outside Blaenavon.[274] And, unsurprisingly, the way in which geese graze differs from four-legged grazers such as cattle and sheep, leading to a yet more complex vegetational mosaic.[275]

It is precisely because of this shifting combination of grazing species, wood and bracken-cutting, coupled with occasional arable cultivation and periods of lower pressure from humans and their animals, that these *rhos* areas supported such a diverse mix of wild species, shifting in exact composition over time and place. When and where grazing pressure was high, these areas would have been more open, with fewer trees and bushes. But at the many times and places where grazing pressure was lower, many *rhos* areas would have been very scrubby, with gorse and thorn thickets creating space for other tree species to move in as well. The great English landscape historian, Oliver Rackham, caught on to exactly this tendency – the normalisation of a constant flux between woodland, scrub and open pasture – in the Welsh cultural record. As a result, it struck him that 'the Welsh attitude to woods seems to be different to other nations ... [there is a] curious patchwork of fields and woods, without any sharp division between them'.[276]

The point here is that these scrubby, woody areas are not woodland proper, nor are they open pasture; they have been caught pendulating back and forth between those two extremes by the grazing and browsing of this range of domesticated animals (that were, however, by modern standards, all hardy breeds more similar to their wild relatives than their current descendants). Without that constant and varied grazing pressure, the scrub would have developed into closed-canopy woodland. Those woodland areas would undoubtedly have supported high levels of biodiversity, but the range of species – from flowers to insects and birds – would have been different. It may well have been less, as the charity Rewilding Britain states on their website: 'Many ecological surveys find higher biodiversity in the different habitats of scrub than in adjacent closed-canopy woodland.'[277] The reason for this is simple: grazed scrub can contain trees, bushes, rank grasses, close-cropped sward, exposed soil and standing water. In the same area you have both dense shade, bright light and nutrient-rich dung – the best of all worlds.

With this being so, the losses for biodiversity as the remaining *rhos* land up and down the country was transformed over recent decades into improved, permanent grassland are incalculable. Where once a great expanse of this scrub – formed by farming – covered swathes of the land, supporting many of the millions of birds and insects that we have lost even since the end of the Second World War, we now have nitrogen-rich, monocultures of reseeded grass, bereft of shrubs, flowers, insects, birds and everything that depends on them.

Restoring areas of *rhos* with free-ranging native breeds of herbivores ought to be a priority for any sensible land-use policy for the future, as a part of the farmed landscape providing useful grazing particularly for cattle but most importantly providing a semi-natural refuge for wild species across the country. Instead of dead conifer plantations, areas like Mynydd Bach could benefit enormously by much of the land returning to what it visibly wants to revert to, which is the rich, brown expanse of scrubby, wet *rhos*. Using, for instance, the 1888 OS maps as a baseline, existing farms could become a large archipelago of improved land surrounded by open and interlinked *rhos* common land, stretching in this one part of Ceredigion from the sea at Aberarth to Llangeitho inland, and from Trefilan in the south to Llangwyryfon in the north; an area of 50 square miles or around 13,000 hectares.

Crucially, this would not be rewilding – though it would be re-insecting, re-birding and nature recovery broadly defined. What it would be is ecological restoration at a medium-sized scale that was entirely in line not just with the cultural history of the area and its biodiversity potential, but also with the strong and ancient desire here as in all parts of Wales that the land be farmed.[278] Of course, for such a restoration to happen, the livestock mix would have to move towards cattle, with a mix of other species (perhaps Tamworth pigs, ponies and sheep) playing a supporting role. We have hard data from history that suggest in areas like the Llŷn Peninsula this would only represent re-establishment of a long-standing historic norm where cattle and oxen outnumber sheep;[279] and despite necessary protestation against the greenhouse gas emissions cattle can produce, much of this is based on current ways of producing beef in the Americas – a world away from grazing native Welsh Blacks on Ceredigion *rhos*.

This is where the question of how many livestock – and of what sort – becomes of singular importance, and why the seemingly technical agricultural term 'stocking rate' ought to be part of the public's general knowledge. As we saw earlier, a given area of land can only produce enough feed (in the form of grazing and hay/silage for winter) for a certain number of animals. Much of the farmer's knowledge and skill comes in at this point: how much each field will produce, what of and for how long. How will it do in a wetter or colder season than usual? How will the animals do on that land – and how long for? The stocking rate comes closest in a single number to capturing this: the number of animals on a given area of land for a specified period of time. Unsurprisingly, the stocking rate on well-drained grassland in a mild area can be kept notably higher than on an exposed, wet area of *rhos*.

Using the standard measurement in livestock units (LUs), where 1 LU corresponds to one mature cow, the stocking rate per hectare for a dairy cow on improved lowland grassland in Wales comes out at 1.0, while on unimproved wet grassland this could be as low as 0.3. What this means in practice is that on good pasture one hectare would support one dairy cow year-round, while on *rhos* land you would need an area of just over three hectares to support that one dairy cow. This is on first glance a less efficient use of land; but the figure might reduce with the right breed of cattle raised for the right purpose (e.g. the native Welsh Black is a hardy forager, which although now known as a beef breed is also perfectly capable of producing high quality milk).[280] And since, as we have seen, different animals graze differently, a given area of mixed vegetation can also support a greater number of livestock units if those units represent different species.

In practice, this might allow a grazing population of 1 cow, 1 pony and 10 ewes over a 10-hectare area of *rhos*. If the entire Mynydd Bach were returned to *rhos* with a stocking rate around this level, the area would support 1,300 cows, 1,300 horses and 13,000 sheep. That number is directly comparable to stocking levels known from Cistercian holdings in north Wales that stretched from the mountains down to the lowlands around Aberconwy, which from surviving figures seem to have varied between 0.05 and 0.25 LU/ha, in line with current recommendations for conservation grazing.[281]

Those figures come out at around a quarter of what the current stocking rate might currently be in the area, based on 2017 figures for Ceredigion as a whole and extrapolated downwards.[282] But, in practice, since the same farmholdings as now would continue to dot the landscape and continue to have their own more productive hedged infields, hay meadows and perhaps small-scale orchards, agroforestry or vegetable/forage production, the overall area might conservatively be able to support up to double that (or half current stocking levels). And this same area would also be home to unimaginably greater levels of wildlife than currently, with farmers producing these livestock – and the associated meat, milk and wool – with almost no inputs other than what the land provides, driving down their costs. Could this support the current number of farmers? Yes. Under the principle of public money for public goods, farmers could be compensated for lower stocking levels than currently by virtue of the public service they provide in CO_2 sequestration, wildlife recovery and landscape recovery.

With *rhos* returning – which it would within a matter of years were stocking and grazing regimes at the right levels – the stage would be set for the arrival and spread of many iconic species, from the lost crane to, magically, the nightingale.[283] But that would only happen because so many other, lesser-known and celebrated species would also make their homes in these now hospitable extents of scrub and heath: A. fimerarius and E. pusillus dung beetles for instance, larvae of wood-boring insects and currently rare caterpillars.[284] And as *rhos* areas expanded across the different soils and microclimates of Wales once more, the stage would be set for the return of the outfield; filled with wildly different wildlife from one region to another. Brown lands, stretching across the landscape, cattle bellowing, dragonflies buzzing, deliberately unenclosed in a recalibration of what represents real value in this world.

8
Perllan

A planted fruit-bearing woodland/ fruit, grazing

It is a balmy September day down on these coastlands, and the living world has thrown itself full-throttle into one final explosion of vitality before autumn proper sets in. The air is humming with flies and bees, a marsh harrier swoops dramatically from a perch ahead while all around are the gorgeous bright gold and red baubles that form this orchard's ultimate *raison d'être*: pears, apples, damsons and plums. We are in a different world here, a patch of creation that is simply alive in uncountable ways, hidden away in a remarkable landscape only 3 miles in each direction from the bustle of Wales's two largest cities.

'I think the oldest of 'em must be 400 years' old,' says Linda, the farmer and owner of this place, in her urbane Cardiff drawl. She's talking of the perry pear trees, five magnificent specimens that dominate her farmhouse orchard. It's impossible to know for sure, but what is certain is that these survivors are rare perry pear varieties, representatives of an entirely forgotten Welsh perry tradition that formed an essential part of the living landscape in eastern counties of the country for centuries. In no other part of the British Isles do you find traditional orchards in the middle of mountain country as you do here in south-east Wales, and nowhere else does the orcharding heritage run from trees grown in the shadow of 800m peaks right down to places like this, where the trees' roots lie almost beneath sea level. But more than this, these maligned and overlooked orchards running from summit to shore – human creations through and through – harbour an as yet unknown quantity of unique biodiversity.

I am here at Cherry Orchard farm with Beccy, a friend and field officer with the Gwent Wildlife Trust, which over the last decade has championed the importance for biodiversity of the orchards on the Gwent Levels. She first met Linda in her early days working on the Trust's levels project, as she drove around this Dutch-like landscape on the hunt for old orchards. 'You'd been selling eggs on the road,' she remembers with a laugh as we have tea with Linda, 'and when I stopped to buy some I just couldn't get away for chatting. And then you invited me in to see the orchard.' Invisible from the road, the 1.1-acre orchard here lies directly behind the farm buildings, only a few hundred metres inland from the sea wall and the waves of the Severn Estuary beyond.

Linda, born in 1934, had married the farmer here, Gordon, and through the oral memories of their parents' generation, can recount events in the area spanning back to the days when Lord Tredegar from the nearby manor house would travel around to visit his tenants on horseback. They had farmed cattle on 30 acres or so, a small-scale way increasingly unviable as the twentieth century rolled on; but had been happy. Linda had bred ducks, and even now with Gordon gone and approaching ninety, she takes great pride in her little flock of chickens. When we arrive, she hurries us into the kitchen, pressing on us tea, coffee, biscuits, cake – and a sharp, warm desire to find out all the news. There are tubs of apples and pears in the back utility room as we make our way back out to the farmyard, and I spot among the concrete cracks a now-uncommon herb peeping through. I exclaim in surprise, 'Feverfew!' stopping Linda mid-flow. She glances over, 'Yes dearie. It's good for headaches you know,' before pointing out the swans in the *reen* (the local name for a type of water channel) and continuing her story.

'It was terrible though, Beccy, back in the summer. They've come shooting again, down near the sea wall and it's wrong. They know it's wrong! I think they've come out from the city to get the birds, but I wasn't 'aving it. So I goes out down near the big hedge when they were last shooting – a few weeks ago this was – and I shouts at 'em, 'shame on you! You're not allowed to shoot here!' And they went quiet. They knew it was wrong!'

Nothing escapes Linda, and it becomes increasingly clear as we talk that the trees' survival on the watch of this nature-loving farmer is no accident, bound contentedly as she is to the tradition of her place.

That place – the Wentlooge Level (the name deriving from the ancient kingdom of Gwynllwg, which fell out of existence by 1100 AD) and by extension the related Gwent Level on the east bank of the Usk – has been created and maintained by human tradition as tangibly as anywhere in Wales. It is arguably the most thoroughly human of all Wales's landscapes, the roads, reens, fields, orchards and stone buildings extending for miles, all bearing hardly any resemblance as habitat to the tidal salt-marshes that preceded them. Now an area of fertile agricultural land some 4 miles wide and 10 miles long, it was reclaimed from the sea in a manner comparable to the Dutch polders or East Anglian Fens. Roman engineers started the process, building an embankment on the outer edges of the marshes and digging ditches to drain the newly created farmland. Some of this is likely to have reverted to fenland during the following centuries of skirmish between the British (Welsh) here and the West Saxons on the other side of the estuary, but the foundation of the Norman Goldcliff Priory on the shore in 1113 right next to where a Roman marker-stone was discovered also suggests a degree of continuity within the landscape.[285]

By the thirteenth century, an increasing number of the villages on the levels emerge into recorded history as a productive, agricultural landscape created by the imposition of a drainage system, now extending in total to over 1,000 miles. It starts in the fields with a web of shallow surface ditches called grips, which to the casual visitor look like nothing more than light furrows across the land. But water from here then flows into proper field ditches and then out into larger channels or reens, which often line the roads or separate blocks of fields from each other. These flow into 'main reens', which take the water to the sea wall where it can pass through tidal gates called gouts into the estuary itself. The terms themselves – grips, gouts and reens – sit alongside others such as 'brinker' (a person who owns land alongside a reen and is responsible for maintaining it), all within a native form of English that has developed within this Welsh landscape for over 800 years; there is no historic Welsh name for the levels villages of Goldcliff or Redwick, in sharp contrast to Llanwern or Magor (Magwyr) just inland. And this ancient, gravity-driven drainage system (as opposed to one dependent on the operation of pumps) spans the entire levels landscape, almost all of which lies under the spring high-tide mark.

The communities, both human and non-human, that have inhabited these levels for the past 800 years or more have lived off a landscape maintained above all through continuous human labour.[286] Dredging the drains of silt, scouring them clear of vegetation by hand ('drashing') using long-handled hooks, controlling water levels in the reens by means of 'stanks' – holding ponds used to drain reens in winter and refill them in summer; all this requires countless man-hours each year. This work is needed in all sorts of ways for livestock, hay production and human comfort. But for some species of aquatic insects and wetland birds, the enormous length of stable watercourses created by it is of incomparable value: the assemblage of water beetles found in this area is unique to Wales, the now rare shrill carder bee manages to hold on well here, while lapwings and shelduck and many other waterbirds feed off the rich invertebrate life.

I grew up in Cardiff, in a family enmeshed with the city for five generations and both interested and invested in its heritage and future. But even as the city threw up high-rises and re-landscaped factories into business parks, unsung and unnoticed, this overlooked area on its periphery conserved something of inestimably greater value: knowledge of the land and its inhabitants. For Linda, this is the world that has marked her life, punctuated not only by the antics of swans and cygnets, calving and feeding the horses but also by neighbours' accidents and church fêtes. She remembers the cider-making that marked late autumn around here until the 1960s, and that played a huge part in the seasonal calendar as neighbours gathered and the year's vintage ranked with others. And despite government grants to grub up orchard trees and the decline of the cider-making tradition across the region, the memories embodied in the orchard itself mattered to Linda and Gordon.

Because this overlooked estuarine landscape also contains some of the richest remnants of Wales's lost orchard landscapes, that previously covered swathes of both the country's lowlands and uplands. 'We 'ave tried to keep the trees, see, but there did used to be a lot more,' she explains slightly apologetically. That much is clear from the beautiful veteran trees that remain in the orchard field, and the types of apple and pear varieties represented here – all pre-twentieth century, and most pre-1800 in origin, and clearly chosen by someone who knew their top fruit.

I ask her what she remembers in the orchard that is now gone. 'Oh, there was a lot! One of them was called 'Sheep's Nose' I think – is that right?' It is, of course – and though she can't have known it, proof of the living tradition she represents, as the modern 'Sheep's Nose' apple was only introduced in 1951, but this was in fact a supplanting of a pre-existing older variety by the same name, now presumed lost.

We leave Linda behind at the garden gate and make our way round a shed to the orchard itself, the sun beating down on us. I hear myself taking a quick intake of breath and Beccy looks over and smiles. 'I said you'd want to see this!' The place is resplendent: ivy hanging from trees, passerines twittering from the hedgerows, tall grasses singing with grasshoppers and all dotted with yellow, bronze and red-skinned fruit. We wander on between the trees, tasting a sun-warmed plum and one of the finest pears Beccy has ever bitten into. There is dead wood all over the ground; several of the trees have fallen over and are regenerating into new uprights. The place, to the untrained eye, is a riotous mess. But once you know what you are seeing, the natural riches start multiplying.

A recently commissioned invertebrate survey by Gwent Wildlife Trust, which looked at twenty surviving orchards on the levels, found that six of the species of insect identified there had never before been recorded in Wales.[287] This included the burgundy-coloured beetle *Gastrallus Immarginutus*, whose habitat niche lies in pear trees (13 specimens found at 3 different orchard sites during the survey), and *Cleonymus laticornis Walker*, a tiny parasitoid wasp associated with common ivy. That, in itself, is evidence enough for the role of these sites as wildlife reserves, but an even more noteworthy observation from the data collected is that 76 per cent of the invertebrate 'species of interest' found at these sites were identified in a single orchard only.[288] In other words, not only are the orchards as a whole home to species found rarely if at all elsewhere in Wales, but the same conclusion can be drawn for almost any one of these orchards individually. Each individual orchard acts as a wildlife reserve in its own right, with its own range of species – different even to its neighbours.

Why is this? Here we see once again the unintended fruitfulness of judicious human stewardship on the natural world. According to the ecological survey, in an orchard like Porton Cottage, a couple of miles away: 'senile fruit trees with glade-like clearings, veteran ivy shrouding marginal crack willows, a standard oak tree and a fine Black Poplar [form] a combination with no exact regional parallels'. The site becomes a distinct island of habitat, as species are thrown together by human intervention in ways that would never have 'naturally' occurred down here, creating a true 'biological hotspot', in which the fruit trees play an important role.[289] And all this in a place far from propitious for fruit-tree cultivation: as a rule, fruit trees hate having wet feet. If that makes most of Wales marginal for top-fruit cultivation given the high annual average rainfall, then that is even more true of the levels with its high water table and ever-present risk of flooding. Even on this warm early September day after one of the hottest, driest summers in decades, the water in the reens here is only metres away from the fruit trees.

'Oh yes,' Beccy chuckles, 'these trees often get wet feet.' But despite this, and despite (or is that because of?) years of hands-off management with no fungicides or pesticides, the trees are producing vast quantities of fruit while harbouring more wildlife than almost any dryland site for miles around. Partly, the unexpectedness of this productivity is because there is so much we simply don't understand yet about traditionally cultivated fruit trees, despite the millennia of practice we have now collectively had. We don't really know how long they can live for; standard modern reference works will tell you that an apple tree lives to about 100 years, and a pear tree perhaps 150. But countless documented examples of individual trees – including the original Bramley's Seedling in Nottingham and a specimen from the Gwent Levels[290] – attest that apple trees commonly reach 200 years of age, while pears may well commonly live to 300 or 400 years of age, as traditional lore asserts.[291] The same variety will demonstrably produce different-tasting fruit when grown on different soils, even only a few miles apart. Some varieties defy standard practice by not responding well to being grafted onto ubiquitous modern rootstocks; while others resolutely propagate themselves by suckering.[292]

But partly, the traditional practice of orcharding on the levels will have contributed to fruiting by mitigating some of the danger from wet feet, as Beccy shows me at another orchard, The Willows, over in the village of Whitson. In this larger orchard (extending to 2.4 acres), the pattern of planting the fruit trees on the tumps remains visible to the naked eye, as the whole field is scoured by the ribcage effect created by the grips. Here also, the fauna of the site is markedly different to Cherry Orchard in no small part due to the flock of sheep that has grazed it for decades. Stumps of old trees abound, with their specialised insect communities slowly eating away at them,[293] while massive hawker dragonflies cross our path in the late afternoon breeze. The Willows's orchard is also remarkable for hosting one of the few lost Welsh varieties of apple to have been rediscovered in recent years, the lovely 'Brith Mawr' ('large and speckled'). This tree had been popularised in the 1930s by a local nurseryman, John Basham, but it fell out of favour with the decline in orcharding in the 1950s. Serendipitously, one of the last people alive to remember the variety confirmed its identity when a tree was rediscovered here a decade ago – and died only two months later.

In all this, ownership matters – as the underlying impetus and the decisive factor for the survival of orchards like these, and the cultural and living heritage they contain. Without Linda and Gordon's affection for the orchard, it could have become just one more acre of improved grassland among hundreds of others around their farm. In recent years, Cherry Orchard has had some of the undergrowth cleared by volunteer teams working with the Wildlife Trust, which has enabled light penetration and maintained the mostly herbaceous character of the site as an orchard; an act of local ownership expressed in charitable activity. And at the Willows, the consistent grazing regime continues the pre-1950s' norm for orchard management almost everywhere in Wales – essential for the wildlife that had adapted itself to precisely those kinds of conditions but reflecting farming practice in the teeth of faceless 'expert' advice.[294]

This continuity in management matters enormously for biodiversity; not only because of the adaptation of different species to the orchard's conditions (fruit, muck, ivy, flies), but also because of the cycle created by the trees as they age, with dead wood slowly accumulating and decomposing. The more of this there is at different stages, the better for the many and varied species of beetles and flies that depend entirely on this habitat for their life-cycles; and in turn for the birds that feed on them. As a rule of thumb, the greater the age of the orchard and the trees within it, the more potential life it can harbour. It is therefore entirely plausible that very old orchards may represent living links for some species with early Welsh post-medieval deer parks, or other now vanished habitats.[295]

So how old are these levels orchards? In the case of Cherry Orchard farm, the first mention by name is found in a local newspaper in 1869, though the 1842 tithe map depicts a house and garden on the site.[296] Significantly, however, it also depicts an extensive orchard, now grubbed up, just over the road. For so many species, that neighbouring orchard would have been an extension of this one. Two of the entirely new beetles to Wales found at Cherry Orchard in the recent survey – *Gastrallus immarginatus* and *Vanonus brevicornis* – are listed as highly sensitive grade 1 indicator species for ancient woodland. On this coastal plain there is only one woodland within a mile and a half of the site; these rare beetles are almost certainly only present in this landscape thanks to the orchards.[297] Although we can't be certain, the existence of extensive orchards by the early 1840s, combined with archaeological evidence from the sites and the varieties present suggest they were gradually established over the period between the late seventeenth century and then.

These rich levels orchards and their living communities are all, however, notable exceptions. Although the proportion of surviving orchards here is probably higher than almost any other part of Wales, nevertheless only 12 per cent of orchards present on the levels in the early twentieth century remain today. And of those survivals, all too many have now declined to only one or two decayed trees.[298] Some villages – notably Goldcliff and Redwick – may feel a little like one large orchard when you pass through with an attentive eye during blossom season or late summer; but a quick glance at an OS map from 100 years previous shows that even this is only a fraction of what had been. Indeed, until the mid-twentieth century it would have been easy to chart a journey starting from the coastlands here tracking north along the eastern marches of Wales for three days' walk without leaving orchard country.

Orchard country

On a warm July evening in 1869, Miss Johanna Thomas, maidservant, was going about her business on the farm when she spied an unfamiliar man in the orchard. She beckoned another maid, Margaret Williams, and together they approached the man, who was making his way away from a clothes line fastened to some fruit trees. 'We went up to him and asked him what he wanted there. He said, "it is hard that a person cannot lie down", and he was on his knees; he told us to search him, as he had not got anything; he then went towards the gate which leads towards the road,' she recounted later in court. But upon returning to the orchard the maids noticed that one of the night shirts drying there was gone. They rushed to tell the master, John Jones, and he rushed after the intruder, the maids in tow. The confrontation was dramatic, as Miss Thomas explained to the court: 'he swore at me and threatened to strike me and Mr Jones. I saw a knife in his hand.'[299]

The intruder ended up serving two months in Brecon gaol for this misdemeanour, but its significance for us lies in the orchard setting for the crime, which is far from atypical. A search in Welsh newspaper articles from 1806 to 1919 for entries including both 'Talgarth', where this incident happened, and 'orchards', comes up with over 3,300 hits. Orchards were an integral part not just of the wider rural landscape, but the urban townscape too. A century ago this whole town, like so many, was one veritable fruit-scape; an entire orchard spanning the gardens and stone cottages, extending out into the hedged landscape beyond. There is little now in this sleepy place of 1,700 souls, nestled in the shadow of Mynydd Troed (609m) and Pen Rhos Dirion (713m) to suggest this past glory, beyond the occasional apple tree rearing its head above back-garden walls.

Orchards have in fact been a major presence in the Welsh landscape for at least 1,000 years, though that may surprise anyone familiar with the shape and feel of the country by the early 2000s, by which point well over 95 per cent of orchard land had been lost.[300] The land-use survey of the *Journal of the Royal Agricultural Society* notes over 6,000 acres of orchard in the country in 1899, with Anglesey the only county singled out for having no orchards to speak of.[301] Even here, however, caution is needed: there is abundant documentary evidence of orchards in walled gardens and great houses on the island, as well as first-hand recollections of peasant gardens containing half a dozen apple trees as early as the late eighteenth century.[302] All this suggests that when virtual orchards spanning farm or cottage gardens and townscapes, such as Talgarth [see map in plate section], are included, the total acreage of orchard land at the time is likely to have been higher still – and the concomitant destruction over recent decades even greater.

Significantly, this fruitscape formed a part of cultural conceptions of the Welsh landscape from at least 1,000 years ago. The very first eyewitness account of a Welsh orchard comes in the poetry of the twelfth-century

Gwalchmai ap Meilyr, who sings of apple-blossom filling the Severn valley near Welshpool.[303] But the depth to which orchards had already penetrated cultural conceptions as places of bounty and fruitfulness can be seen most clearly in a couplet by Dafydd ap Gwilym, not to a rural setting but a townscape, that of fourteenth-century Newborough in Anglesey. He describes the town as: '*Perllan* clod y gwirodydd, / Pair Dadeni pob rhi rhydd' ('The praiseworthy *orchard* [i.e. vessel] of drink / Cauldron of rebirth for every free sovereign'). Orchards were known landscape features, evocative enough to serve as metaphors for urban areas' buzz and hubbub.

This interweaving of orchards and their produce in culture continued into early modern folk culture, with orchards featuring in place-names,[304] folk songs, bird names (a bullfinch in Welsh is 'coch y berllan', 'the orchard red', reflecting the birds' love of fruit) and other traditions – like that of carving applewood lovespoons in the Talgarth area. All this came to an end not primarily because of farmers and landowners turning away from fruit production, or even because of the changes in the rural economy that made conventions like paying labourers' wages partly in cider a thing of the past. The primary reason for orchard destruction in Wales, through the middle and latter decades of the twentieth century, was government policy.

Farmers were paid to grub up orchard trees, and because a greater proportion of Welsh land is marginal for production, and more of Wales's orchards produced fruit for local rather than market consumption, a perfect storm of conditions was created that led to the rates of orchard loss here far outstripping that of England. And with the twentieth century's state-sponsored destruction and the disappearance of orchards and cider from both landscape and culture, the cultural awareness of the fruit heritage also disappeared – leading to a widespread but misplaced impression that 'Wales has never produced much fruit, as the soil and climate are not suitable'.[305] This has been slowly rectified in recent years as the traditional varieties have been rescued and reintroduced, and the place of apples and cider have received some cultural recognition.[306] But there is another, still entirely neglected facet to the place of orchards in the historic cultural landscape of Wales.

I come across this forgotten story first when standing in a field with a retired journalist-turned-cider-maker a few miles outside Talgarth one fresh autumn morning. Andrew Jenkins is a native of this area, and well-remembers cider being served on the farms as part of the hay harvest. 'That was the first experience a lot of us kids had of alcohol, helping out with the hay. They'd get them tipsy at 13.' He is now trying to put the orchard heritage of the area back in the spotlight – and is doing so to no small extent by means not of cider but of perry. And that is why he has suggested we meet today in this particular field, on this particular farm.

To get here we left our vehicles on a quiet country lane a stone's throw from Middle House farm, on whose gable end stands inscribed the date 1620. We follow a slightly overgrown green lane, jump across a little brook and swing over the fence into a field. We're out of sight of the road now, over the brow of the hill and in a large field with a notable ridge running down its middle. Only a few short miles to the south the backs of the Black Mountains stand sentinel. I look around for an orchard, and Andrew points towards the hedge to our left. 'I told you there wasn't much left! But there they are.' Hugging the line of the hedge, on a steep slope at the field's edge, stand five mature pear trees, laden with golden fruit.

'We had these DNA tested,' Andrew explains, 'and four of them are unique varieties.' The one 'known' variety, Oldfield, is a classic English variety, several centuries old and so highly regarded for perry-making that it was known as the queen of the perry pears. Whoever planted this tree knew what they were doing, and made a very deliberate choice of the other four too, which as well as being genetically unique are all different to each other. Now named by Andrew and the farmer here, Phil Price, who died in 2019, they are all productive trees that make delicious perry.[307]

I tasted the year's vintage six months later, from a perry Andrew made out of the haul from these trees. This, it's worth saying, is *fine* perry, made in the traditional way; nothing put in other than pears and their naturally occurring yeasts, and nothing taken out.[308] The golden, warming wine that fills my mouth with bouquet on a warm morning in Andrew's garden all those months later is a revelation. At around 6.5 per cent volume, this is like a lighter version of a natural rosé wine, but wider in flavour somehow than most I have tried. I gave some to friends: the immediate reaction from one who'd grown up on a very traditional small farm was 'summer hay!' while another went for pear drops. My mother, poetically, called it 'the flavour of summer, sweet as honey, smooth as mead, aromatic like apples in a crumble'. For my part, it's easily one of the best tipples I have tried, with a balanced but deep flavour similar to an Ashmead's Kernel.[309] I am gratified that these trees have made such a fantastic perry; but I'm not surprised.

Andrew is self-effacing, but also very clear about how the magic comes about. 'Nature makes cider', he repeats at more than one juncture, 'it may just need a nudge'. The apples and pears are hand-picked from unsprayed orchards and then slowly fermented without filtration. The proof of any method is always in the pudding, and for him, having received numerous awards, the greatest accolade was serving cider a decade or so ago to an old lady at the farmers' market in Brecon. She had commented that you didn't see much around anymore. But on tasting some of Andrew's vintage cider she beamed with joy: it was just like what they used to make on the farm.

But these four trees, now hidden away at the edge of a field, are all that remains of what had previously been acres of orchard. Phil remembered the orchard as was, and the cider-making season when the travelling cider maker visited the farm each autumn. It was his grandfather who grubbed it up after the Second World War, at the behest of a central government initiative; but he also knew the special value of the perry pear trees, and left them, along with the old cider press that still lies dormant on the farm.[310] How old are these trees? The entire field (along with several others on the farm) was already established as orchard by the 1847 tithe map, while the farmhouse itself dates from 1620. We know that there was a great wave of orchard-planting after the civil war from the 1660s onwards, and that perry pears can live for centuries.[311] It is far from implausible to suggest that some of these pear trees may date from between these two dates.

As I talk to Andrew it becomes clear that there are several relict sites like this, dotted around the Black Mountains. 'Yes, there are six perry trees like this in Scethrog – unique varieties – and one on a farm down in Crickhowell, and another nearby.' All are at risk of passing out of memory as the last generation who were involved in farmhouse perry- and cider-making in this area pass away. But the clear, balanced flavours of Andrew's perry, and the sheer number of unique varieties among the surviving trees, reflect something of the pervasiveness of perry culture in this area at one time.

And the place of pears – and perhaps perry pears above all – turns out to be deeply embedded within Welsh-language culture, despite the way this has in recent decades fallen into complete oblivion.[312] The very word *perllan*, the title of this chapter and the Welsh word for orchard, occurs in writing for the first time in a thirteenth-century redaction of Welsh law, which may itself originate several centuries earlier. A compound noun, it combines the common element 'llan', originally meaning enclosure and appearing in places across Wales from Llandudno to Llandrindod, with 'pêr', one of three Welsh words for 'pear'. Despite its similarity to the English, this is no recent anglicism but rather a borrowing from the Latin 'pira', whose appearance in Cornish and Breton suggests an origin stretching back at least to the fifth century AD if not before. Both this term and the two others for pear – *gellyg* and *rhwning* – are widely used in Welsh literature over the last millennium, and all three terms survive into modern Welsh. A basic principle of lexical semantics is that multiple words for the same phenomenon are unlikely to survive in the vernacular if that phenomenon doesn't form a part of speakers' lived experience. *Gellyg*, *rhwning* and *peren* together hint that Welsh speakers, or in other words most inhabitants of the country, for the past 1,000 years, have needed words for pears.[313]

We can make sense of this by reference to more copious records from late medieval and Tudor England, where both 'wardens' (a type of culinary pear) and 'pears' proper are often listed separately as though they were different types of fruit. The great value of both pears and apples during these periods was in cooking and as a safe, fermented drink – in comparison to water, with its attendant perils. When the first pomonas and fruit lists appear in the early seventeenth century, they tend to feature as many if not more pear varieties as apple varieties – including ones that have survived to the present as perry pears.[314] Welsh documentary evidence, always slightly sparser, nevertheless corroborates this pattern for perry and cider – 'perai' and 'seidyr'. There are numerous references to both drinks in late medieval documents, with a 1545 Welsh definition of perry given as 'drink of green fruit viz perry wine cider'.[315] Tellingly, one fifteenth-century Welsh poet from north Wales relates how he was served wine and beer in Rome – and notes that 'it was no perry', suggesting either that he missed the familiar perry of home, or that he much favoured Rome's offering to the perry he was used to at home. Either way, the contrast between Wales and Italy is clear in the context and is interestingly refracted through the prism of perry as in some way representing Wales.

So, despite almost complete contemporary neglect, the Welsh perry tradition has deep roots – and is arguably one of the country's unique contributions to the world's food and drink heritage. In the British perry world, the only area regarded as having a tradition worthy of interest is that part of the English three counties (Herefordshire, Gloucestershire and Worcestershire) that lies within sight of May Hill. But the Welsh perry country, stretching down from the northern slopes of the Black Mountains through hilly Monmouthshire to the levels, has its own tradition and varieties, all lying a full 50 miles away from May Hill in very different landscapes and climates. Annual rainfall in Talgarth is around 1,200mm; around May Hill, nearer 700mm. In the sheltered English three counties, trees can root in well-drained, deep and fertile red soils; on the levels, they sit on alluvium, at or under sea level and face coastal gales and sometimes salt spray. There is something worth paying attention to here.

The secret lies of course in the varieties. Quite apart from Andrew and Phil's rediscoveries at Middle House farm, the list of Welsh perry pears now extends to a dozen or so cultivars: Llanarth Green, Berllanderi Green, Gwehelog Red, Berllanderi Red, Littlecross Huffcap, Chapman's Orange, Monmouthshire Burgundy, Early St Brides, Potato Pear, Gwehelog, Welsh Gin. Unsurprisingly, it was the Early St Brides that was identified as growing so majestically at Cherry Orchard; a variety generally unknown in England but known on the Continent. The relevance of this to the Welsh landscape is simple: without good, suitable fruit varieties and their produce, there would have been no orchards in the landscape in the first place.

I visit one other Black Mountains orchard before I leave the area, to try and get a better handle on why some orchards have survived. This one, at Maesydderwen farm, is a beauty. Extending to well over an acre of mature apple, pear and walnut trees a stone's throw from the farmhouse, and also lying just a mile or two from the high mountain peaks, its autumnal beauty is a heart-wrenching evocation of what this land has lost. In a corner of the orchard a bull is tethered; there are owls here, and bats; dead wood aplenty filled with crevices and cracks. In autumn, the orchard field is full of mushrooms. 'We have loads of mushrooms!' Tom exclaims when I ask him. 'Dad will pick and fry up so many that Mum gets annoyed.'

Dad is the farmer here, in his seventies and the proud owner of a beef herd of 70 cows that range these 270 acres. And the mushrooms, and the mistletoe, go a long way to explaining why the orchard is still here. 'Yeah, he picks the mistletoe to bring in at Christmas – that's a family tradition.' I ask about the fruit, and the story is similar. 'There are just so many. We always pick crates full in October, and we're still eating some of them next Easter. There's more here than we need, but obviously Mum makes pies and things. It's just part of the farm really.' They don't know what the varieties are, so I take several specimens home to ID. They turn out to be a connoisseur's mix – Lord Lambourne, Ribston Pippin, King of the Pippins, Yorkshire Greening. Good apples, clearly selected by the previous owners of the farm, the nearby estate.[316] Now part of a small family farm, practising a slightly old-fashioned form of mixed farming with low inputs, the reason for the orchards' survival lies ultimately in its owners – and the traditionalism that shapes their farming and view of the land.

It is a delightful setting, and the family are pleased to find out a little about some of the varieties they have. I promise, of course, not to disclose where the site is – they don't want troublemakers or meddlesome authorities to come and interfere. And Tom is clear he wants the orchard to remain into the future – along with its owls and bats. On a gentle September day it is one of the most delightful of all settings; and within this Welsh context it is a survivor of a type of place long celebrated in poetry and song, that has produced tipples comparable with the finest wines and graced these landscapes for many hundreds of years. They did so in a productive marriage of human taste and labour with trees' fecundity, providing by default a home to innumerable other denizens of the landscape, from owls to lichens. The cultural knowledge that lies behind tasty cider and cultivar development is also what led to the only area in the British Isles where large and productive orchards were (and still are) juxtaposed with high mountain peaks – and that alone is worth celebrating, though sadly entirely absent from any guidebooks or other accounts of the Black Mountains' cultural heritage.

It may, however, have more of a role to play in our future.

Welsh agroforestry

Driving through the tranche of countryside between Cardiff and Newport today, with its identikit houses, business parks and monocultures of grass or corn, and overlaying that with the knowledge of what had been and now survives only in corners, is like seeing a tree suddenly shorn in summer of all its leaves. A landscape that had been pulsatingly alive reduced to a shadow of what it had been. But much of the structure itself in the form of varied fields, miles of hedges and bands of woodland is still there; merely dormant. And that very structure could provide the outline for the most rapid drawdown of carbon dioxide from the atmosphere, while also integrating neatly into an improved version of the current agricultural economy. This potential lies in a massive expansion of the orchard principle, under the guise of agroforestry.

To get my head around this, I go to the verdant Tywi valley on a gusty early spring day to meet Richard Edwards, forester and one of the directors of Clo Carbon Cymru. Over tea, he explains to me pithily the concept his company has been working on: 'When you have interlinked global crises, the most effective solutions are those working at the nexus of them all.' Originally from Neath and with a background in forestry both in Sri Lanka and working at DEFRA in Westminster before moving on to the UN, as well as a stint supplying Raymond Blanc's restaurant with pork and mushrooms from his own land, Richard has a wide-angle approach to land use, climate change and farming.

'I'd been on the verge of retiring to be honest,' he explains, 'but we're so completely f**ed at the moment with catastrophic climate change heading our way, and there seemed to be some scope to do things in Wales with the Future Generations Act and the flurry of intent to get to net zero, I decided to roll my sleeves up further.' The community-interest company's self-designated remit is to develop strategies for farmers in Wales to reduce emissions drastically, capture carbon and transition away from conventional agriculture to systems that produce more food, more employment and are better for biodiversity.

I am curious as to why they have chosen to focus on agriculture and land use, given their primary focus clearly lies in reducing CO_2 emissions. He refers me to a report in the *Nature* journal, published that month, that highlights the figures involved in all other methods of carbon drawdown: at the cutting edge of technological means of doing so, $3.5 billion spent equates to 1 million tonnes of CO_2 extracted from the air; a drop in the ocean compared to the 41 billion tonnes currently emitted annually, compounded by the fact that this is highly experimental technology.[317] This is why the primary focus from government and environmental organisations more widely lies in tree-planting potential; a low-cost, more-than-proven method that can also produce many other benefits. The problem Richard has with this is twofold: a lack of joined-up thinking added to a poor understanding of forestry that means time-costly mistakes are made continually.

On the forestry and carbon accounting front, Richard is acerbic. 'Government calculations, right up to IPCC [Intergovernmental Panel on Climate Change] level, take the 'global warming potential' of a generic, planted tree over a hundred-year time period.[318] If you stop to think about it, it's nuts when at the same time the UN tells us we only have until 2030 to avert complete climate catastrophe. On top of that, the amount of carbon different tree species sequester differs massively – by more than an order of magnitude – and it also changes over the tree's life-cycle. Then the other big blind-spot is the fact that many of those trees planted are also intended to be felled – and may then be used in a way that releases that carbon right back into the atmosphere. Of course, there is a need to plant more trees, but that need must benefit the farmers today – not in 100 years' time when the planet may be uninhabitable.'

He explains that they are working with Coed Cadw – the Woodland Trust in Wales – to develop a model for quick-growing broadleaf trees that can be coppiced in a very quick rotation by cutting for a crop every other year. These include willow, grey alder, poplar and small-leaved lime trees. This gives the farmer a crop and a product immediately, but it also means that the tree and its root system stay in the ground – which is better for soil health, for biodiversity and for CO_2 drawdown. Every year those trees stay in the ground – and you could reasonably expect a lifecycle of around thirty years with the trees intensively cropped like this – they sequester more and more CO_2 into the soil. That woody biomass can then be converted on-site into biochar, which is one of the most exciting products currently being investigated for combating climate change.

'Biochar' is a generic term describing organic material that has been burnt at high temperatures (up to 1,000°C), in the presence of little or no oxygen. This process produces oils and gases and leaves a solid residue of at least 80 per cent carbon which is termed biochar: similar in principle and appearance to charcoal. Biochar takes a long time to decompose (centuries or even millennia) and as a result has real potential to store significant amounts of carbon in the soil. The excitement around it, as Richard explains, arises from the fact that biochar is known to increase the energy-density (calorific value or CV) of slurry. Increasing the CV of slurry would, among other things, aid with retention of beneficial soil minerals (phosphorous, potassium, etc.) in the digestate, creating a fertiliser product with less run-off risk and more benefit to soils and CO_2 emissions. The product helps farmers deal with a current costly waste product, and simultaneously fertilises their soils using on-farm materials.

All this is done within an existing Welsh farm layout, with the trees densely planted in rows on a few fields and animals allowed to graze in between. But there is a second, parallel component to this plan, in the form of a species of mallow native to North America. *Sida hermaphrodita* is a long-lived perennial plant that seems to have the potential to contribute significantly to both decarbonisation and farming viability in places like Wales.[319] Cropped, it can yield around 30 per cent protein; only a few percentage points lower than soybeans. And being a perennial, it will regrow from a June harvest year-on-year, again stabilising soil and reducing tillage.

Richard shows me a tray of young *Sida* seedlings he has been cultivating at home. 'This has taken three years of trial and a lot of error to get to this point. I reckon we started by sowing around 100,000 seeds to get our first 25 plants! But by this year we'd increased our success rate to near 80 per cent, so a massive but successful learning curve.'

He also brings out a stack of dried *Sida* stems, which have hardened to form poles similar in feel and appearance to bamboo. I am impressed, given how soft and fleshy the plants look when growing.

At the time of writing, the crop is being trialled at the farm of NFU Cymru president, Abi Reader, alongside strips of 3,500 trees per 0.5 hectare, 'which is significantly more than the planting regimes funded by Welsh Govt that stand anywhere between 1,110–2,500 trees per hectare,' Richard explains. 'What you end up with from the farmer's point of view is another low-input crop produced on-farm that gives a significant amount of high-protein feed every year – replacing bought-in feedstock, which is a major outlay on a dairy farm like this one.' But on top of this, you're producing biogas from an anaerobic digester that can be used to heat polytunnels (for fruit or veg production) or buildings, and the biochar combines with the slurry to provide a very efficient carbon storage solution on-farm that also improves soil structure.

Although the combination of these varied elements to create a unified whole is new and needs prototyping, the various elements are already tried and tested. There are, for instance, already around 6,000 hectares of *Sida* grown annually in Europe, primarily in Ukraine and bordering countries. Then the trees: the CO_2 sequestered annually from fast-growing hybrid poplars in Richard's garden, for instance, comes to 20.4 tonnes in comparison to only 330kg from a wild cherry tree nearby. The potential of applying biochar to slurry to create an on-farm fertiliser for soil use is far from experimental, with the dairy conglomerate Arla presenting reports on its development to UK Government. In their own words, 'manure management systems, including farmyard manure (FYM) and slurry present the ideal conduit for applying biochar to soil'.[320] One of the differences between the corporation's model and Richard's community-interest company's concept is the way Arla's plans depend on (conifer-plantation sourced) softwood rather than fast-growing broadleaf trees, including from hedgerows.

I ask about biodiversity: are they talking about a complete redesign of the landscape to achieve this rapid carbon drawdown on farms? Richard is adamant that one of the advantages of this approach is that it works within the current landscape. Wood from the hedgerows could be integrated into the biomass production and the system could also benefit wildlife massively by letting the hedgerows grow to twice or three times their current volume, then cutting them on a longer 7–12-year rotation. Only somewhere in the region of 20 per cent, as a very ballpark figure, of a 150-head dairy farm would be used for agroforestry. 'This is about working with the farming system and thinking holistically: sequester carbon, improve soil life, reduce run-off, increase on-farm jobs, reduce costs for farmers, produce more and extra food. Socially beneficial carbon dioxide removal!'

In general, agroforestry systems imitate structural patterns that have been lost in many of our ancient woodlands, from the presence of coppices at different stages in their cycle to coppice-with-standards, rides and mini clearfell areas. As in the trials at Abi Reader's farm, they can include grazing livestock or indeed ground-level crops in between the rows of productive trees. With sensitive design, they can significantly benefit the farm's system and economic autonomy while also benefitting biodiversity, water retention and carbon drawdown.

Traditional orchards are just one of the major forms that agroforestry has long taken in this landscape. As is still the case at Maesydderwen in the Black Mountains and the Willows near Newport, orchards have always been grazed in Wales both by sheep and cattle. The 1840s tithe map series demonstrates this beautifully: time and again at sites displayed on the maps as orchards and listed on the apportionments as 'perllan', the land use is noted as 'pasture'. With a modern ecological lens, grazing is viewed as one of the essential components in maintaining the rich orchard habitat, contributing through dung among other things to the incredible wealth of species that can inhabit these spaces. A notable study of a traditional orchard site in Worcestershire in 2006 found a total of 1,868 individual species encompassing vascular plants, bryophytes, fungi, lichens, vertebrates and invertebrates, many of which were known to be nationally rare.[321]

Many of Wales's old orchards do indeed lie in that long-favoured arc for fruit production extending from the Gwent Levels near Newport up to the Wye valley between Brecon and Hay, but traditional orchard distribution covers the whole of lowland Wales, including all the counties to the damper west of our central mountain backbone even more suited than Worcestershire to moisture-loving bryophytes.[322] In these areas, old orchards take on many of the same characteristics as the native woodlands here, sometimes called Atlantic rainforests, draped in stunningly rich communities of mosses, lichens, ferns and liverworts sustained by the mild temperatures and year-round moisture. In the surviving acre or so of orchard at Abergwili Palace just outside Carmarthen, this creates an utterly otherworldly sense of the fruit trees' bountiful fecundity married with the green-grey beards and cushions of the bryophytes. If the woodlands deserve the moniker of 'lost rainforests of Britain' and long overdue attention, then the lost rainforest orchards of Wales have a prized place within that, as entirely human creations graphically taken up into the biophysical community of these moist western lands. Western or eastern, the age of the habitat is an essential part of its wealth with old, gnarled trees creating niches for everything from beetles to owls, and processes ranging from the hanging lichen to microbial industry in the unploughed soil all contributing to a whole that is significantly greater than the sum of its parts. Unsurprisingly, the majority of the traditional orchard sites in Wales I investigated in researching this chapter had never had an ecological survey carried out, but they, along with our other remaining 650 hectares of orchard, form one of the biodiversity jewels of the nation.[323]

Just as agroforestry lies at the nexus of food production, carbon drawdown and whole-farm systems thinking, so orchards lie at the nexus of biodiversity, cultural heritage and high-value food production. If we wanted to design land-use systems that brought the maximum possible benefit for food production, human community and wild species while also conserving the soil microbiome and drawing down carbon, then in areas across the Welsh lowlands we would almost certainly land with something very close to agroforestry and traditional orchard systems. This would be a way of working with the grain of current land use and its history while maximising the potential for all the other things that matter, whether human employment, food production, biodiversity or carbon sequestration. The obstacles, other than a failure of imagination, lie primarily in the domain of knowledge and skills: the skills to plant and run agroforestry or orchard systems and to create the infrastructure for processing the produce – whether getting fruit to local shops or turning coppiced rods into biochar. The alternative to such a landscape of orchards may well be more conifers.

9
Epilogue

adnewyddu/renewal

It's a brilliant summer's day in a field in west Wales, and this particular farmer hands me a brilliant yellow tomato, and its warm, sweet, summer juices really do explode in my mouth. He laughs, 'Our Ceredigion tomatoes are pretty good, aren't they? To be honest, these cherry tomatoes would have done better grown outdoors than in the polytunnel this year – that's probably the future.' We walk through the late summer glow along the tousled field edge on to the next poly, where quite a sight awaits me: a whole row of healthy, vigorous Mediterranean stone fruit trees. Peaches, apricots, cherries, etc. 'People have been delighted with these! When we planted them it was quite experimental, but they're now starting to make a real difference to the veg boxes in season.'

Not that there is a season, per se, at Troedyrhiw, this organic vegetable farm on the Ceredigion coast that for me has come to represent much of what the future Welsh landscape should hold. It is a place in profound alignment with the landscape's past, but oriented firmly to providing for current and future human food needs. And it does this while sharing the land with a veritable panoply of wild denizens. 'We're now in a place where we send out our boxes 52 weeks a year and sell to regulars at the local farmers' market 51 weeks,' explains Alicia, co-farmer here with Nathan. 'And that is exactly what we want to do.' Nathan jumps in and repeats to me one of the most profoundly humane lines I think it is possible to utter: 'what we really want to do here is to feed our local community'.

That is exactly what this place is doing on less than 40 acres of terrible, thin, shaley soils. 'I mean, let me be clear here', Nathan chuckles, 'this soil is just boot-strippingly sour.[324] I mean, to the point where in the early days you'd walk around on it and I'd wonder how the leather on your shoes wasn't being corroded by it.' There are stones of every size in the yellow-ish beds that are a far cry from the deep browns or blacks that convey fertility; it brings to mind the proverbial tight-fistedness of the *Cardi*, the Cardiganshire farmer of this region, a cultural product of being wed to land of this sort.

'You really have to treat the soil here carefully,' Nathan explains. 'It's also quite clayey, so it will compress quickly and obviously we have copious levels of autumn and winter rainfall here, but we're still cropping throughout that and we do use a fair bit of machinery on our operation – which can compress the ground. But I *know* this land. We've been farming like this here for fifteen years now and with every passing year I feel that more and more deeply – and I feel the importance of that knowing more acutely too.'

That intimate, farming knowledge is a key part of what allows him, Alicia and three other farm workers (one full-time, two part-time) to produce 200 boxes of fruit and veg each week for households across an area within a roughly 10-mile radius off soils of this sort. Pumpkins, potatoes, broccoli, rocket, aubergine, onions, beans, five sorts of tomato, raspberries, apples, plums and much more go out week by week from these five fields and the cluster of unheated greenhouses. There is no magic here; nothing that couldn't be replicated on land in any part of Wales to feed people in their area with the very best organic produce at the same price as the major supermarkets. And it is all happening within a mixed farming system that goes completely with the grain of how the Welsh cultural landscape has evolved over the last few millennia.

And that is why I have come here. Because although the farm's output is entirely and deliberately fruit and vegetables, this is a mixed farm with pigs and cattle both integral parts of its system. And once again, to understand how this place works and why it can both produce copious amounts of food on terrible land and be many times more biodiverse than any of the surrounding land, we need to talk about fertility.

'We produce between 60 and 80 tonnes of compost here a year to spread on the beds', Nathan explains, 'and that compost has two main components – farm waste, and animal manure.' The farm waste includes all sorts of vegetable matter – weeds, stalks, grade-out produce, grass clippings – that is turned onto the heap. This is essential: every bit of plant matter that leaves the farm includes trace phosphorus, potassium or other elements that over time would draw the fields' fertility down even lower.[325] Woodchip is also created and added in, using in recent years ash from the hedgerows that has needed thinning because of ash dieback. And then the animal manure.

'Our pigs are a really key part of our farm economy … we are virtually zero-waste here and the pigs are a major part of that, as well as one of the main reasons why we both gave up veganism after many years of eating that way.' In a process replicating countless ancestral cycles, the pigs here are fed grade-out potatoes and other kitchen waste. They defecate – conveniently, pigs are very tidy in their habits – and that muck is also added to the compost. 'We are also very fortunate to still have a very small-scale local abattoir near us in Tregaron, so I also take a pig there every now and then to butcher, which I do myself. None of it is wasted.'

On top of the pigs' manure, Nathan also shovels out two neighbouring horse places where the horses have a diet compatible with Troedyrhiw's organic licence conditions. That has been an established practice with them for a number of years, but over the past couple of years, Alicia and Nathan have deliberately brought back cattle to the farm, which are now a key part of the farm's ecosystem. 'I mean, we are talking about very low stocking rates here – no more than four or five cows at any one time and often as few as two.' They purposefully chose to go with an old-fashioned breed, that is small and hardy and can winter outdoors.[326] The cows are taken off to be slaughtered at 4.5 years, rather than 18 months, and are naturally weaned.

This is not in any sense an outfit designed around maximising beef production, though they do provide 'the best-tasting beef I have ever had the pleasure of tasting', as Nathan adds laconically. It is, rather, a horticultural operation where meat is an incidental by-product of vegetable production – much as it was an incidental product of dairy and corn production in much of Welsh agriculture historically.

'These cows graze our land and eat the hay we produce off the meadows here – which have increased in diversity and in production since we added lime. And yes, the manure could go into the compost or onto the veg beds in some way if we wanted to do that, but we are happy with our set-up with the stables. That isn't actually the main role the cows play in our system.' Their main economic contribution to the farm is in fact on the biodiversity front.

I know from trying to grow as much veg as possible wherever I've lived since being a teenager in the early 2000s that growing good quality Mediterranean veg in a northern, oceanic climate is challenging. But one of the most notable things about walking around Troedyrhiw (as is true of all organic veg farms I have visited in Wales) is the minimal pest damage, even compared to my own small garden. And this is of course in a system where pesticides are expressly forbidden, and as Nathan tells me, a lot of the biological control mechanisms simply cost too much for a small-scale enterprise like theirs to invest in.

'So we're dependent on a healthy ecosystem to do it for us. Yes, ok, I'm a messy farmer!' he says emphatically, gesturing around him to borders that are a riot of weeds, creepers, flowers and grasses. 'And the docks I've inherited on this land are still going to be here for my grandkids to deal with.' But it's precisely all that wildlife, prime among it the hedgerows and corridors they naturally form between the different areas of the farm, that keeps his crops healthy. 'We really need the hedgerow trees we've inherited here – ash, oak, sycamore, hazel. Not only do they make a massive difference (along with the hedgerows themselves) as a wind break, which is all important for many veg and fruit, but they also give our cattle shelter and many other types of birds and beetles which we depend on to control pest levels.'

It's the ecological interactions that happen here on every scale, from the bacterial level up to predators like owls. They have had ecologists visit their site several times, looking at what they have, and they have identified mosses that they are convinced are only here because of how the land is managed. And as Nathan tells me, if he comes out of an evening to where we're sitting, he can just stand and enjoy the nightly chorus from the owl in the oak above us. That delights him – quite beyond the beautiful cries – because they keep the vole population down, which is directly beneficial to their crops. And that is why they brought in the cattle.

At this low stocking rate, the cows poach up the land lightly by their trampling, but without causing damage or compaction. That poaching in a climate like this creates slightly less well-draining areas where puddles form. Multiply that across a certain acreage and you have plentiful habitat for fleas, beetles and other insect predators that keep down things like aphids. You also have a growing and more diverse insect population, as the wider range of habitats (as compared to trampled, grazed land with no hedgerows or meadows, or all meadows and hedgerows with no trampled, grazed land) allows a wider range of insects at the bottom of the food chain to inhabit this same small area of 8 or so hectares. In other words, were these 8 hectares all 'hedgerow habitat' or 'woodland habitat', or pastureland or meadowland or arable land, it would provide one type of habitat only. As it is, for reasons entirely aligned with producing healthy and plentiful food from the land, the small Troedyrhiw parcel contains all the above.[327]

The presence of the cows has widened the range of habitats – a key reason of course why rewilding advocates are so keen to see large animals reintroduced to areas – and hence the range of insects.

'When we brought the cows in,' Nathan tells me, 'we saw the number of birds and bats on the farm increase. And that in turn is great in terms of keeping pest levels down. It really is everything for us – I like to tell people that come here to visit and learn that even the hedgerow blackberries are essential for us. Of course we enjoy them in season, but they and the bullaces and the sheer amount of them we encourage by keeping our hedgerows thick all also play a real role in feeding the insects and birds we want here.'

The whole point of this kind of farming is that pests are not eradicated – it is called land sharing for a reason – but that levels are kept down, and manageable.

As a result, both the outside inputs onto this farm and the waste output are negligible. The real output of this small farm is food: good food, plant food, and a *lot* of it that really does go a significant way towards Alicia and Nathan's dream of feeding their local community. But in order to do this – and particularly to do this with the basic soil conditions here – the farm depends on two key landscape-scale features that stand in profound alignment with how the Welsh agricultural landscape has developed: the hedgerows and the presence of livestock.

The challenges that face our society – prime among them the challenge of feeding everyone in a growing population a decent, healthy diet that doesn't destroy the living earth as it's produced – are too urgent for us to engage in large-scale landscape re-engineering. But the reality is, for once, profoundly good news: we don't need to. Since the key components of the landscape, and even their precise locations, have evolved over millennia alongside traditional, mixed farming that didn't use fossil fuels, it is unsurprising that the key building blocks *as they lie now*, in a Welsh context at least, are eminently suitable for both producing food and protecting biodiversity. And as Troedyrhiw eloquently demonstrates in everything from leeks to tomatoes, the landscape as it is structured provides the backdrop for producing significantly more good food per unit of land than late twentieth-century agriculture ever managed.

Over lunch – gnocchi with tomato and onion salad, all grown in the next field from where we sit in the shade – I want to hear more about Alicia and Nathan's relationship with this land, and in particular with its cultural heritage. 'I'm not religious', says Nathan, 'but I love going down to the old medieval church a mile down the lane. Every time I have a chance to go past I go and find Morgan Davies's grave: Here lies Morgan Davies of Troedyrhiw – *hunodd Rhagfyr 19eg 1782, aged 60 years*. I like to reflect on him and his family – Catherine, John, Griffith, whoever they were – and how they lived here and depended on this land. And one thing I know, is that he knew this land. He *knew* this land.'

Ownership

Knowing the land, in the broadest sense of that phrase, will matter for any liveable future for humans on this planet. And, whatever its blind spots and failings, it has been one of the central contentions of Welsh culture since its first appearance in the written record that it does indeed both know and belong to this particular area of land: the claim of being *brodorol*.[328] But readers coming to this book perhaps hoping for indigenous wisdom on living within the natural world by, say, a European version of Native American land-management practices, embodied within an ancient Celtic language, have doubtless been disappointed. I am sure such a book could be written, but it would concentrate only on peripheral aspects of people's interactions with the land and would be at risk of drifting into spuriousness. No; the tale of Welsh culture's relationship with the land, for much longer than it has in any sense other than geographical been 'Welsh', is the tale of an agricultural worldview.

I have not argued in these pages that Welsh ecosystems or traditional farming are either unique or uniquely biodiverse. Both the ecospaces of this small country and its traditional farming methods contain many similarities with neighbouring parts of north-western Europe, albeit with salient and interesting local adaptations. But I have made what I hope is a nuanced and often implicit argument about ownership, and given examples across all the landforms that make up Wales about the happy outcomes that can come about when felt local ownership has a practical relationship with the land.

Often, over the past seventy years or so, that has meant asserting something against the teeth of official advice, government policy and economic pressure. It is a stunning indictment of arrogant and short-sighted government policy under the leadership of every mainstream party that there has often been an almost perfect inverse correlation between the degree to which landowners and farmers in Wales have followed official directions and the degree to which nature has flourished on their land. To put it another way: it took a combination of a particular sort of rural traditionalism alongside independent-mindedness and marginality within the economy for almost all the survivals we have seen in this book to make it to the 2020s. I am talking about Erwyd and Linda, Maesydderwen and Cwm-yr-Alaw, the *ffridd* and the *corlannau* and the not unremarkable fact of their existence today.

I have also suggested that this sort of attitude is fostered and supported by strong, underlying and longstanding currents within Welsh-language culture in particular.[329] We could trivialise this by relating the example of the high-profile country poet and farmer Dic Jones, asked by a prominent Radio 4 presenter how it felt to live in his area of Ceredigion so far away from civilisation. What did she mean by that, Dic was curious to know? 'Well, how many miles is it to the nearest Marks and Spencer?' Dic's answer, after a short pause, 'So, that's what you mean by *civilisation*.' The point, however, is a serious one. The Welsh language has long sustained a discourse about a relationship with this land that has highlighted two important things: first, a defiant claim to spiritual ownership both of and by the land and, secondly, an insistence along the lines that a practical working knowledge of the land is not parochialism, but the very essence of patriotism.[330]

The lineage of the first claim, that of a spiritual (for want of a better word) tie to the place of Wales is masterfully dissected by Dorian Llywelyn in his volume *Sacred Place, Chosen People,* 'in the Welsh mind ... one's place and one's society play a significant part in who one is as an individual. Place – understood as a social and geographic reality – defines, shapes and guides each human being.'[331] It is precisely this basic double-sidedness to place, both social and geographical, that stands in such sharp contrast to the attitudes towards place and indeed nation (in Wales for many centuries now a nation but without a nation-state) generally prevalent across the Western world. As Llywelyn notes, 'my Welsh approach to landscape was notably very different from that of my American classmates ... none of whom had the experience of awareness of ancestral belonging to place which so typifies Welsh consciousness.'[332] Had he, however, shared a class with American friends of First Nations background, he would have found many commonalities in exactly that space where among European Americans he found incomprehension.

This is intensely relevant to the key question that forms the context within which and for which this book is written: the question of appropriate responses to the ecological catastrophes of our time. Those responses are ultimately decided by people, and people's decision-making apparatus is formed by their accumulated and shared cultural knowledge. Within the Anglosphere, the leading edge of the debate around what true sustainability looks like has finally realised the importance of listening to indigenous voices. As Lucy Jones, the London-based author of *Losing Eden: Why Our Minds Need the Wild*, put it, 'How do we put things right?' To answer this she quotes the Native American writer and ecologist Robin Wall Kimmerer to the effect that we need to 'become indigenous to place'.[333]

Applying this valuable insight becomes in Wales – for all the reasons implied above – highly problematic. There is an existing cultural and linguistic community here that, for nearly a millennium and a half, has and continues to claim precisely that mantle of indigeneity to place.[334] We have a culture that is as close as you can come to being indigenous to place in Western Europe, and asserts precisely that in everything from the national anthem to recent football chants.[335] That is a highly inconvenient fact to others, who, motivated by different considerations, come and act on what they perceive as the relatively empty canvas of Welsh landscapes. Among those groups are some who move to Wales and try to act to create ways of being 'indigenous to place' driven by exactly the kinds of realisation of ecological alienation underlying Jones's prescient question. They, repeatedly, have ended up in confrontation with the surrounding Welsh culture, both groups perceiving the other to be in the position of power and bafflingly unable to see what they are trying to do, which is build a long-term and healthy relationship with the 'Welsh place' in question.

All of this happens – and arguably has happened in different ways for centuries, as the Brackenbury episode demonstrates – in a political context where the government apparatus that frames all high-level decision-making remains unmoored to place. I am talking in the first instance about centuries of distant Westminster rule that pursued policies with nary a regard for the question of what good land governance in Wales might look like.[336] That of course is what led both to the well-known hot disputes about reservoir creation in inhabited Welsh valleys to water English cities but can equally be demonstrated by eighteenth-century agricultural policy or the twentieth-century conifer blight.

These plantations, purely ecological considerations aside (which tended in any case to come later), were despised from the off by rural Welsh culture as alien impositions. This is not because the culture has inherently been against innovation or adopting alien practices, as the wholesale adoption of tea-drinking in the early modern period or the integration of the domestic apple tree into the landscape in an earlier period demonstrate. It is because of a locally grounded perception that these particular innovations – mass conifers plantations – could not well integrate into the fabric of the existing landscape. That this still continues for different reasons and in different ways is also amply shown by the new conifer wave, facilitated among other things by Welsh Government policies that want measurable tree-planting results and laudable CO_2 reductions, but prefer to borrow from global discourse rather than sensitively understand place and its dynamics. Governance in Wales remains, from a biophysical point of view, insufficiently Welsh.

In this context, it is interesting to consider whether an argument could be made for a more indigenous-style relationship with the land before the 1282 Conquest of Wales by the English Crown. Certainly, at this time, the extractive industries underpinned by imperialism did not exist; indeed, almost all the large megafauna supported in Wales since the last Ice Age still shared the land with human culture. Wolves, beavers, deer and wild boar were not only present in the landscape but featured strongly alongside domesticated animals and plants in native mythology, replete as it is with tales of shapeshifting and talking creatures.[337] In this sense, some of the hallmarks of true indigeneity seem to come to the fore in the Welsh cultural record as it exists pre-1282,[338] including also laws that, as we have seen, strictly limit land use to its carrying capacity.

It is the strong memory of this state of affairs (albeit with a focus on the political rather than the ecological) that animated much of Welsh politics over subsequent centuries; and if a strong form of dispossession is a key element of indigenous encounter with imperial power, then the land struggles in Wales that lasted into the late nineteenth century show an element of dispossession from the land even within what was a core 'home territory' of the British Empire. This, to use the jargon, is about a marginalised discourse, and it is one that applies differently to Welsh-language culture than to Wales as a whole (not that there is any sort of clear disjuncture between those two phenomena, as noted previously). But with all those caveats in place, some of the contours of this semi-spiritual sense of inherited cultural ownership of the land may be starting to shine through.

The other aspect to this claimed ownership of and belonging to the land is an intensely local one, valorised within Welsh culture as being therefore of universal rather than parochial value. This is the strand of that culture that has long insisted that a practical working knowledge of the land is not to be seen as folksy but as one of the cornerstones of a healthy human society. As Margaret Jenkins put it (in Welsh), 'when the folk poet has disappeared from Wales we might as well turn out the lights, because it will be proof that there is no longer life or force enough here to take inspiration from the soil, scatter a handful of seeds and see it blossom on hill and hedgerow'.[339] This is not a yearning for old country bygones, but something much more insistent: an assertion that human 'life or force' becomes null and void if people lose a meaningful connection to the assembled life-forms of their place. Reading her words today ought to give us pause for thought.

Within her context, Jenkins's point is an uncontroversial one, and relates to the widespread appreciation within Welsh-speaking Wales that the language is rooted in this place. It contains encoded within it (particularly in the demotic literary tradition) the memory of the sum total of human interactions with this land, from the stories behind places and their names down to the names of plant communities, birds and proverbs.[340] This is often intensely local in its manifestation, as of course it should be. The poetry of Snowdonia muses on the *ffridd* and shepherding traditions, absent from the sea-facing culture reflected in the produce of Cardigan Bay. I encountered this time and time again as I talked to people across the country for this book – and strikingly, among people of all generations. Dion, on our walk up to Waun Lydan, exemplified this in his first reaction to my explanation of this book. 'O, dach chi'n mynd i son am betha fel Cae 'Sbyty felly?' – 'Oh, so you'll be writing about things like the "Cae 'Sbyty" then?' These are 'hospital fields' near the homestead on farms and smallholdings where a rich mix of flowering meadow species were traditionally kept in order to nourish sick animals to feed and recover. The fact that I haven't had the space to do so implies something about the extent to which so many of these land-related traditions remain alive.

That all this often manifests in the form of a poetic idealisation of the place of the farmer is often remarked upon in studies of the phenomenon; it is equally true that images of the forager, craftsman or hunter are prized, from the era of the eighth-century 'Pais Dinogad' to Isfoel's own mid-twentieth-century 'Cywydd Diolch am Eog' ('Cywydd Poem to thank for a salmon'), caught by a friend of his with an old-fashioned trident in the river Teifi.[341] Today, that same poetic tradition lacerates our Western consumerism as being a mindless rape of the earth's life, as another old farmer-poet put it in a recently published volume:

Am a ddaw, oes maddeuant
I ni a lygrodd y nant
A gwagio'r môr? Am greu
    maeth
O wenwyn, a'i droi'n lluniaeth,

[For what comes, can there be
forgiveness
For us who polluted the stream
And emptied out the sea? For
creating nutrients
Out of poison and turning it to
sustenance
And raising you with chemicals?][342]

Throughout, a close relationship with the land and all its inhabitants is assumed, discussed, bemoaned when lost, celebrated when expressed in anything from a caught salmon to ploughed field or a swallow's nest built in the eaves. This culture also, by virtue of a noted tendency to look to the past, tends to foreground a vocabulary and framework for land management as practised universally until the advent of mechanised agriculture in the mid-twentieth century: a form of agriculture that allowed now-fantastic levels of biodiversity to flourish within a mostly renewable, non-fossil-fuelled farming system. It is precisely this kind of low-input mixed farming system that could lead again to higher levels of sustainability, farm profitability, rural employment, healthier diets and greater biodiversity. The cultural framework for any such transition in this land lies latent within the Welsh language.

Flux

That is one vantage point from which to view some of the arguments I have been advancing in this book, and to the extent that human beings make decisions with reference to inherited and shared cultural frameworks, it is an important one. But this book is intended more as a work of historical enquiry, drawing on principles from experimental archaeology, than it is as polemic. To that end, an entirely different set of implications needs to be drawn out here about this story of the Welsh landscape, and that is this central idea of flux; the ebb and flow of tendencies within the landscape's tale.

There is no one period within Welsh landscape history which represents an equilibrium to which we should or even could return. Wales is now home to more people than ever before, growing from 500,000 to over 3 million over the course of the last 250 years. As we have seen, every element of the landscape had seen considerable flux even before then with periods of growth, decline and stasis. There have been elements of continuity, and it may well be that certain small parts of the country would still be recognisable to a visitor from the late Iron Age; but that continuity is dwarfed in many details by stupendous change, with the extent of that change sometimes obscured rather than clarified by language. Rhiannon Comeau's point that the relevant part of a *clawdd* before *c.*1500 was a ditch rather than a dyke stands alongside the fact that peat bogs have co-evolved with us over the last several millennia. It's a reminder that in both the purportedly 'human' and 'natural' parts of the landscape, change is constant and boundaries are blurred.

But none of this means that this history is of no more than academic interest: a nuanced understanding of landscape history that gets under the skin of the drivers of change, the whys and wherefores, might be able to give us key reference points for existentially crucial questions about the future of life in this corner of the Earth. We stand here at the intersection of (primarily human) history and science; humility in interpretation is called for. Nevertheless, some important conclusions about the nature of this ebb and flow in the landscape present themselves.

The first of these is that over the last several thousand years until the mid-twentieth century, many of the main characters in this long landscape drama – plants, insects, animals and humans that have been the actors in this flux – have remained much the same. Sphagnum and heather on the uplands; rapidly colonising 'native' tree species such as birch or willow; honeybees; humans and our ungulate livestock; golden eagles and wolves. Modern ecological science gives us the beginnings of confidence in the types of interactions we would expect to play out on a landscape scale between those elements; principles rather than laws. For example, that grazing inhibits tree domination, that predation moves livestock and thus nutrients around the landscape, and that humans and our domesticates can occupy a similar ecological niche to otherwise absent species.

The second is that, almost by definition, the most biodiverse sites in Wales both today and historically are part of this *human* landscape and would not exist without human influence. This is not just true in a negative sense (i.e. that semi-natural ancient broadleaf woodlands have been conserved in their surviving locations because of human decisions) but also in a positive sense: no ecospace resembling hay meadows nor orchards would exist without strong human intervention,[343] and neither would ecologically important spaces like *ffridd*, *cloddiau* or, possibly, peat bogs. This is even more true at a meta-level. Closed-canopy woodlands abutting a patchwork of meadows, arable fields, permanent pasture with farm orchards in the valley bottom and heather moorland on the open mountain that could be found in many parts of Wales a century ago represents a dense patchwork of quite distinct ecospaces that, in sum, may potentially support a greater overall number and range of species than that same valley completely rewilded.[344]

Thirdly, and leading on from this, it is indisputably the case that even if the potential for rich biodiversity exists within the landscape's basic structures, almost all of these landscapes in Wales today are degraded. And the single-biggest cause of this has been the fossil-fuel driven intensification and simplification of agriculture. This was of course a global phenomenon and viewed on a global scale with the narrow metrics of feeding more mouths, more cheaply, and as quickly as possible, and was an enormous success. But those narrow metrics are now coming back to haunt us: the cheapness of this food came at the cost of almost unlimited trashing of the oceans, the air and the soil as well as the continuing human cost of exploited labourers and genetically damaged animals.[345] In Wales, we have lost many of our most biodiverse spaces – orchards, peat bogs, hay meadows, *ffridd* and *rhos* – and drastically impoverished those remaining. Ancient woodlands no longer coppiced, mountains grazed only by sheep, hedgerows flailed to within a metre of their lives and rivers poisoned by chicken manure. Almost all of this has happened within the last seventy years, and its consequences are severe: never mind wild boar or wolves, we are now at a stage where we are losing flies and swallows from our skies en masse.

Based on our understanding of ecological systems and of the history of this landscape, this is clearly aberrant; it goes well beyond the bounds of what we might call 'flux' and into a completely different space. Change may be constant, but viewed on the grand canvas of archaeological time, the last seventy years or so do not fit into that pattern: it's that hockey stick graph again, so devastatingly familiar from representations of CO_2 in the atmosphere. This is not because humans have been uniquely rapacious over the last seventy years, just that we have had a qualitatively different type of power and potentiality than ever before and knew not what we were doing.[346] We can pinpoint one of the central underlying drivers of this by looking at fossil fuels and how they have fundamentally altered the dynamics that, until the 1950s, had always dominated our landscape use. We are back at nutrients again.

As well as mechanising agriculture and pushing both horses and people from the land (not an insignificant change in itself), fossil fuels also allowed the development of long-supply chains and artificial fertilisers, pesticides and herbicides. Fossil-fuel subsidised global supply chains made it more economical to produce fruit, vegetables and grains halfway across the world and ship them to Western countries like Wales,[347] meaning the only niche left for local food producers was high-end produce or government subsidy farming. The latter, in most of Wales, pushed for production of the goods perceived to be most economical and suited to the landforms, namely livestock (dairy and meat).

On top of this, the chemical suite of fertilisers and biocides (fungicides, pesticides and herbicides), all created from fossil-fuel hydrocarbons, completely disrupted for the first time in human history the more-or-less closed nutrient loops that had previously dictated the upper bounds of land use. It was now economical on fragile upland soils or poor *rhos* heath to use heavy machinery to drain the moorland; economical to apply nitrogen fertiliser to pasture; economical to keep more stock and more demanding stock than the land could support if the market signals were there (not least because of cheap supplementary feed); economical to push the land to produce more and larger animals. It became uneconomical or, at best decidedly old-fashioned, not to get into these self-reinforcing cycles, supported of all things by debt.

In stark contrast to this, in any renewable, solar-powered economy we need to skim the flows of the land's carrying capacity, rather than mine our planet's stocks.[348] The energetic basis for past agricultural economies was the renewable energy derived ultimately from the sun (with the water cycle and wind both ultimately products of solar inputs to the earth system), and that was the underpinning of the agricultural land-use patterns that had shaped the Welsh landscape until the twentieth century.[349] It is not, though, the basis for the agricultural economy of the past several decades, the structures and dynamics of which have been reshaped around fossil-fuel derived inputs. Take those out, as we know we must, and the basic shape of agriculture in any number of important ways reverts naturally to something more akin to a traditional mixed-farming model.[350] In no way does this imply a simplistic return to the past, as though that were desirable. Rather, with the enormously greater levels of knowledge we now have about everything from soil health to animal genetics and ecosystem function, it represents a synthesis of real scientific progress with the basic nutrient-cycling, renewable principles that always underpinned good husbandry.

Encouragingly, the UK's Food, Farming and Countryside Commission found in 2021 that such a transition back towards mixed farming 'in UK countries would allow us to grow enough healthy food for a growing population, entirely remove pesticides and synthetic fertilisers, free-up agricultural land for nature and other uses and reduce net greenhouse gas emissions by 80%'.[351] In Wales, this would lead to more land use for fruit and vegetable production, land returned to arable cultivation for pulses and grains for human consumption, more trees in the landscape and generally lower stocking rates in the uplands, all within a more mixed, rotational model. It would represent a return to the old ebb and flow of human pressure on the land; restoring the dial on the flux back to something closer to what we had in the past.[352]

Crucially, any transition of this sort is more a question of *how* we use the current landscape structure we inherited than it is a question of *what* that landscape structure is. We already have a landscape evolved for mixed use, with nutrient cycling, extensive grazing of the uplands and sensitive, lower-fertility areas like *rhosydd*, stock control to conserve woodlands and more intensive arable or horticultural production on the best land. Working with the grain of this is the route forward for us towards true sustainability that has both the lowest entry barrier, and the highest return on investment across society.

It is also the only way of working that respects the current mixed and distributed land ownership we enjoy in Wales and that satisfies broadly defined outcomes that encompass all that is desirable in this debate: food production, sovereignty, better human health, maximum biodiversity, rapid carbon drawdown and cultural flourishing. Reformulating the landscape in order to rewild as much of it as possible in the purest possible way, or to generate as many carbon credits as possible for maximum shareholder returns, or to allow it to continue being hollowed out of people and wildlife as at present; all these other routes focus on narrowly defined goals and would lead, ultimately, to a landscape changed out of all recognition from the thousands of years of co-evolution has lent us.

What, though, of more moderate proposals for rewilding – which we have circled several times in the book, without yet landing?

Grazing and wild

We could simplify much of what has been described in this book as the interplay of place with three main factors: grazing livestock, trees and human choices. That explains some of the polarisation currently characterising debates around land use, with trees (and rewilding, veganism and environmental activism) at one end of the spectrum and livestock (and farmers, meat-eating and a more traditional rural politics) occupying the other. This seems to me a peculiarly late modern way of understanding our relationship both to land and to animals that does no justice to a nuanced understanding of how our landscape evolved in the first place, nor how it subsequently spiralled into its current crisis.

In other words, I believe there is a fertile middle ground in this debate. It starts from the recognition that any landscape-scale rewilding project is utterly dependent on the presence of both large, grazing herbivores *and* the significant presence of self-seeding trees. Rewilding, as an umbrella term, has three main meanings. First, allowing a patch of land as small as a backyard square metre and up to grow as it will. Eventually, in almost all parts of Wales and indeed the temperate world, that results in domination by trees. Secondly, that process can be moved into a more complex dynamic by introducing untended grazing animals, that browse the trees and create space for a wider range of species (flowers, grasses, etc.) to inhabit the landscape too.[353] The other way of doing that though – thirdly – is by introducing large predators such as wolves, bears and golden eagles, that will keep the grazing animals' populations in check by their predation, thereby allowing trees and their dependent species to persist in the landscape.

That third, full-bodied manifestation of rewilding is practically impossible and politically undesirable in Wales; above all because there is no qualifying area of land large enough to sustain the necessary numbers of predators for a genetically viable population.[354] Politically, it would only be possible by government-led compulsory acquisition of land and the forced cessation of all cultivation in an area the size of the whole of Carmarthenshire, surrounded doubtlessly by an enormous perimeter fence to keep in the wolves. Much of the history of popular protest in Wales, as touched on above, concerns land use and the perceived robbing of agency from local actors and stakeholders. To imagine that such a proposal could happen without enormous violation of democratic norms would represent a level of political and cultural naivety on a par with the suggestion that the Western aversion to eating insects could be overcome on any timescale relevant to responding to our current crises. It is why there is currently no serious organisation planning such a project in Wales.

That leaves both the first and, most pertinently, the second form of rewilding for consideration. Since, in this model, human intervention is needed to keep herbivore populations in check in the service of maximum biodiversity, we end up with something closely related both to conservation grazing and to significant elements of traditional pastoralism as practised in Wales. In conservation grazing, native breeds of grazing animals (primarily horses and cattle) are used to maintain an inherited habitat – such as heathland – with its vegetation cover that of the mid-twentieth century. It mimics elements of the agricultural practices that had created that habitat but is in the service now of conserving particular species rather than food production within a mixed farming economy. In rewilding, similar numbers and breeds of grazing animals are used to imitate the action of their wild relatives on the landscape and, theoretically, without a particular end in mind. The intended outcomes may differ, but the methods used are in important respects similar.

I saw a candidate site for this sort of rewilding – albeit not called that – on the northern slopes of Carn Ingli in northern Pembrokeshire. Stephen Jenkins is a local lad who grew up here and has made it his mission to see as much wildlife return to this area as political structures and local opinion will allow. To that end he has co-set up a charity, Tir Natur, that advocates for models of agricultural rewilding suited to the Welsh context. In the patch of beautiful, mixed countryside Stephen shows me, the abandonment of fields over the last few decades has led to a compact but significant area of perhaps 300 acres to rewild in the first sense of the word above; with no or minimal grazing, trees and shrubs have sprouted up and created a beautiful, dappled area of wood pasture that echoed to a cuckoo's song on the misty morning I visited. Immediately adjoining this land lies the lower boundary of Carn Ingli common, extending to hundreds of acres of grazing land, large swathes of which are now being overrun by invasive bracken.

'It's got a lot worse over the last two decades or so,' he tells me. 'Twenty years ago I remember a couple of dozen graziers who'd put animals out on the common, and you had a lot more cattle than now, and fewer sheep. We're now down to just three remaining graziers and there's over 800 sheep and hardly any cattle. That's why the bracken has gone rampant.'[355]

Stephen's plan was to demonstrate the effect that reintroducing native breeds of pig – to mimic the action of now-absent wild boar – could have on the landscape by rootling the land and disturbing the bracken.

'It's all tried-and-tested science. The pigs disturb the bracken and push it back, and that perturbs areas of soil that releases the seedbank of wildflowers and so on lying in that soil. Bring them back, and you'd have a profusion of butterflies and insects such as hasn't been seen here for decades.'

It's an ostensibly uncontroversial plan, but one that nevertheless would need thousands of pounds worth of forms to develop, not to mention significant liaison with bodies like the National Park, the Welsh Government, the local Graziers' Association and Natural Resources Wales to implement. 'The benefits would have been significant: as well as biodiversity, by lessening bracken cover you de-acidify the soil, reduce the need for costly mechanical or destructive chemical interventions to control bracken and create a blueprint for extensive pig-keeping that could have been integrated into the sustainable farming scheme.' Unfortunately, a combination of Covid-19, the pig business collapsing and the loss of support from one of the aforementioned public bodies put paid to this trial run of a very restrained form of agricultural rewilding.

I asked Stephen what his charity would advocate for as an ideal, biodiversity-maximising, strategy for managing this land in the long term. His answer was a grazing regime that centred on a low-stocking rate of cattle, with free-ranging ponies and pigs also a part of the mix. Could he see a place for sheep, I wondered? Once the heather had recovered, and at low stocking rates, he could also see a place for sheep without significant negative impacts to the restored biodiversity. Stephen is keen to impress upon me that his charity is not advocating a one-size fits all approach to the Welsh landscape. What they would like to see is some areas – farms, nature reserves – dotted across the landscape and managed in this sort of way for biodiversity but with high-quality and high-welfare meat being one of the outcomes. That is a far cry from the blanket, carnivore-centred rewilding advocated by some, and to my mind is more a form of low-input agriculture than anything else.

That assertion is borne out above all by two main considerations, the necessity of culling aside. First, the fact that the stocking rates Stephen's charity has in mind for a project like this would be in the region of 0.3 LU per hectare; if anything, slightly higher than historic stocking rates practised for centuries in Wales on *tir mynydd* by people for whom biodiversity outcomes was not a factor in stocking level decisions at all. Adopted in areas with historic *rhos* or *mawnog* cover, Tir Natur's aspirations would only represent a return to the past. The second consideration here is the key place of free-ranging native breeds in this. Whether cattle – such as the Welsh Black or Highland – pigs or ponies, the main contenders for use in projects of this nature in Wales as in Europe generally are hardy, native, domestic breeds. Though they retain more of the characteristics of their wild relatives than their high-performing domesticated relatives, they are nevertheless domesticated animals, developed by people whose main consideration was agricultural output suited to the confines of their context.

It is highly instructive to consider what farming might have looked like over the last sixty years if we had never had fossil-fuel inputs in agriculture, or only minimal application thereof. Imagine all the insights of modern plant and ecological science, as well as those of nutrition and health, applied to early twentieth-century farming. Significant development and change would undoubtedly have happened in that fantasy scenario; but rather than try to indiscriminately push the land, or decouple livestock from arable, we would have worked with closed loop systems, and continued to develop the right breeds of animal for the right locations– nowhere more so than in upland contexts. Get the variety right, and you can grow pears or apples in surprising locations; get the breed right, and you can create food from a semi-natural landscape with minimal inputs.

Importantly for Wales, this is also true of sheep. Cultural icon embedded in our traditions they may be, but sheep are at best a threat from a biodiversity point of view. That doesn't that mean they have no place or only a marginal one in any low-carbon future where nature thrives once more alongside us. But only if we choose to farm the right sheep in the right places.

Future

As Debby Mercer – wool-expert extraordinaire – explains to me on her Ceredigion smallholding, the potential uses of wool in a renewable, circular economy are immense, and with judicious use of the right sheep breeds, could be coupled with all-round benefits for farmers and nature. Currently, wool is a near worthless by-product of rearing sheep for meat, and so, as a result of that current structure of the agricultural economy, the larger your sheep the more meat – and thus profit – you will accrue. The problem with this in a context like Wales is that the larger breeds of sheep are by nature unsuited to wet, upland environments and succumb to diseases like footrot or strawberry foot, while also requiring supplementary inputs of feed. In other words, the current agricultural economy is unsustainable at every level, not rewarding farmers, trashing biodiversity and encouraging the wrong sheep to be raised in the wrong places.

But most native breeds of sheep – of which Wales has many – were bred for their fleeces and to cope year-round with the prevailing conditions in the Welsh uplands. 'You see it in lambing,' Debby says with a laugh. 'I talk to friends in England with lowland breeds who talk about having however many hours once the lamb is born to check it over before it can run off. Ha! For me with this Welsh hill breeds it's literally a couple of minutes!' Breeds like the Torddu or Welsh Mountain can cope year-round with tough outdoor conditions, without feet diseases and even without trimming. But currently, for purely cultural reasons, the potential of their wool is ignored, depriving farmers of an income source that could make their businesses viable.

It is, once more, cheap fossil fuels that have pushed wool to obscurity. Plastic-derived textiles clothe us, and the wiles of fashion have dictated in the UK that wool (other than merino) has no place to play in that. That this is a cultural misstep can be seen in comparison with Iceland, where a national culture of slow fashion makes knitted woollen jumpers a treasured item to be handed down the generations, and where such a garment is expected to be worn for many decades once it has been made. All wool, not just merino, naturally has antibacterial properties and, as such, doesn't need washing.[356] The idea is not, of course, to wear a woollen jumper next to the skin, but above a base-layer.

Beyond this, wool has an enormous number of uses that would immediately come into their own in a non-fossil-fuel driven economy. These include as insulation (with a long-life span, naturally fire-retardant, hypoallergenic, non-irritant and a decent U-value for insulation of 0.16); in compost and mulch (as part of a suite of abundant resources to replace peat) and as a hard plastic replacement in the form of bio-composites. Being 50 per cent carbon, all these uses of wool also represent a carbon sink, the production of which, using the right breeds, requires nothing more than low-input grazing sheep. As Debby hands me a beautiful purple scarf made out of 100 per cent Beulah sheep's wool, it strikes me that, if only people were aware of the extent to which we could fashion a sustainable, circular economy using the familiar resources of sheep, cows, crops and trees as opposed to untested, experimental technologies, demand for policy-makers to sculpt systems that allowed this would be loud indeed. This purple scarf, without an ounce of merino in its fabric, is light and soft to the skin. In truth, I would to my shame have mistaken it for a soft synthetic fibre rather than the product of a hardy, native Welsh breed.

The unrealised potential of wool shows how there is a clear pathway that involves replacing fossil-fuel products from plastics and fibres to construction materials and above all food, and which includes a key place for native, grazing livestock within a restored, biodiverse landscape. Whether your interests lie in minimising CO_2 output as quickly as possible, maximising the potential for nature recovery, food security and health, or indeed an informed cultural conservatism, the overlap in terms of potential routes forward and what that would mean for the Welsh landscape is substantial.

To take just one strand of this – the idea of the land producing the maximum amount of healthy, nutritious food as possible, with people equitably recompensed for their labour in its production – we end up with a proposition that could bring significant employment back to the countryside while also benefitting biodiversity. That the land should produce food is both the most radical and conservative of starting points, uniting the broadest possible swathe of voices across the range of human experiences and perspectives.

That this seems both from left and right to be overlooked or dismissed is one of the symptoms of the naive myopia that has increasingly gripped Western civilisation over the last few centuries and allowed us to drag the rest of the world into the confounding crises which we all now face. That this production of food should happen in a way that works with the grain of the naturally occurring vegetation and climatic conditions was for all human history until our recent fossil-fuel powered rush both a given and a constraint. Now, it becomes an imperative that we choose to prioritise the integrity of the ecosystems and living species we live alongside: the alternative, quite simply, is a world where not only spring but all our seasons do indeed fall silent. It is the prospect, now rendered imaginable, of a semi-sterile world of which the dead rivers Wye in Wales or Po in Italy are already the unwelcome portents.

Given the scale of the threats facing us, and the urgency of the need to act, here are ten concrete actions that could be taken at a landscape scale in Wales, at low cost and with very quick benefits to biodiversity, human health and food security:

1. Continue public investment in farming post-Brexit as the only equitable, socially just and culturally rooted means of managing the vast majority of the Welsh landscape; but do so in a way that clearly rewards protection of the living world with public money.

2. Encourage farmers and landowners to allow existing woodlands to expand in size across the country by natural regeneration, so that *overall* total woodland tree cover in Wales doubles from the present and wood pasture/scrub cover expands to 20 per cent of overall land use by 2040. This could be done in practice in our fecund and hilly land almost entirely by identifying appropriate (sloped) areas and excluding stock from those areas rather than adopt a one-size-fits-all model. Those farmers for whom this might work with their system and farm can opt-in to this natural afforestation and be rewarded for doing so.

3. Invest significantly in farmer education and peer-to-peer mentoring so that ideas and technical expertise can be shared; one of the outcomes of this should be that more financially profitable low-input, nature-friendly models of farming become normalised.[357]

4. Rewet all peatland areas as rapidly as possible.

5. Encourage landholders to identify hedgerows that can be left to double in thickness, with disincentives for flailing.
6. Encourage the creation of a new, scalable infrastructure to process wool into marketable products, from textiles to insulation to plastic replacements.

7. Learn from ventures like Troedyrhiw and pioneering work in the Brecon Beacons to devote 12,000 hectares of good quality land to vegetable production, making us as a country self-sufficient in local vegetables and creating thousands of jobs in rural areas into the bargain.

8. Invest in pilot projects to find routes to market for fresh produce grown in Wales (such as top fruit) for local consumption, enabling the creation of traditional orchards with standard trees under which stock can be grazed all across the country.

9. Invest in financial incentives that allow farmers to keep native, hardy breeds of cattle specifically in the uplands, as well as some to allow suitable areas of land to be developed as semi-rewilded reservoirs of nature.

10. Facilitate training in skills for the development of agroforestry for whole-farm systems, timber, fruit/nuts, coppiced wood and biochar.

These measures, or anything like them, have the potential together to revivify our landscape, making it more productive on every measure – not just financial.[358] Our current crisis – to which Wales with its heavy industry and massive coal extraction has contributed an outsized part – is both ecological and cultural in nature. That's why it is crucial that we understand one of the core insights of modern ecology: that people form an essential, shaping part of the living world. We are the apex predator, the keystone species above all others; to quote the writer of Genesis, we are the species that 'rules over the fish in the sea and the birds in the sky, over the livestock and all the wild animals, and over all the creatures that move along the ground'. We depend, as we always have done and always will, on the bountiful resources of our living planet for all our needs: food, clothing, clean air, shelter, energy.

This crisis which forms the backdrop now to all our lives stems from our *abuse* of nature – not our use of it in the first place. It also stems from the outsized negative contribution the Western world has made to pulling humans deeply out of kilter with the rhythms of life on this planet. Wales is part of that, and despite its smallness, must bear its moral responsibility to act rapidly towards the solution. This does not call for self-negation (as some on the activist end of the environmental spectrum tend to do), nor does it call for a greater dose of precisely the sort of pursuit of high-technological and utopian interventionism that landed us in this mess in the first place.[359] When it comes to the landscape, which is one of any country's first-order assets, ecological history suggests that most of the benefits of 'wilderness' can in fact be gained alongside a human presence shaping the environment. In Wales, that presence has to look more like the human presence of 1900 than of 1990. That's why this understanding of Welsh ecological and cultural history, though not a panacea, presents us with a hopeful way forward.

To close, then, let's imagine this way forward after it has had time to grow and develop into maturity, and visit a future Wales several decades from now where this radical, ambitious but also deeply conservative potential for the land's future has been realised. How does the country look, feel and sound?

On this summer's day in the Wales of the early 2080s, the sun is of course hot, and no rain has been seen for many weeks, as now happens every year. Average temperatures year-round are 4°C warmer, because although ambitious and drastic political measures were taken, built-in warming ended up towards the mid-to-upper end of scientific estimates in the 2010s. So it's warmer here; a fair bit wetter in winter and dry and hot in summer. That gives Carmarthen a climate very similar to that of Bilbao in the 2010s: good country for growing chillies, yes, but a temperate climate still. There are enormous changes from an ecological point of view, but the country is still recognisably itself.

I'm sat on the slopes of Bryn Amlwg overlooking the Tywi valley not far from Cwmyrarian and am musing on the structure of the rural landscape below me. It's still a patchwork, hedged landscape and the villages, roads, woods and rivers are on the whole all where they used to be. It's mid-July and the land is starting to look pretty parched, and that is one of the most significant changes from how things had been: fewer shades of green and more yellows and browns at this time of year. More of the green that there is comes now from tall rows of hedgerow trees swaying in the breeze, among which there are now many more poplars, and just generally more trees, in the now usually quite thick hedges. But all the ancient oak woodlands are still here, and pleasingly they still have some ash trees on north-facing slopes, though these are now stressed and at the very southern limit of their range.

Alongside more trees, another of the major changes is that there are more people in this landscape. I can see a great many small landholdings clustered around the villages, with intensive, organic horticulture taking up a significant part – almost half perhaps – of the valley bottom land that isn't floodplain.[360] They produce a lot of food from a comparatively small amount of land, and coupled with the need for people in the country to do everything from grow and process food to working with wool, energy generation and timber produce of all sorts (this is now for the most part a renewable, circular economy), the villages have also grown significantly. It's true to say that there has been an urban exodus of sorts over recent decades; and places like Cwmyrarian that were derelict sixty years ago now support a dozen people once again. There are now electric minibuses running through rural villages like Nantgaredig, Pont-ar-gothi and Llanegwad every ten minutes from 6 a.m. until 10 p.m. These kinds of mass transit systems criss-cross the country and their quality and affordability have also significantly reduced personal long-range vehicle use and ownership, primarily as an economic calculation made over decades by many millions of households.

Immediately below me lies a vineyard, one of the better ones for natural red wine production given the steep south-facing gradient and free-draining soil on this hill. But nearby I can see a more representative field of *joualle*-type cultivation, an ancient method of agroforestry from southern France, where vines are cultivated up to 15m above ground level along elms, and field crops (beans, potatoes) are cultivated in summer in the shade underneath.[361] Many of these fields contain a tree crop alongside sheep or cattle, and as I scan the hillsides I can count two dozen herds, even through all the trees, and see many cattle lolling in the shade.[362]

These trees are a godsend given the relentless summer heat, but I shouldn't give the wrong impression. Comparing this view with a photo taken in the then hot summer of 2018, I'd say somewhere around half the fields remain just as open now as they were then, and most of those are pasture or meadow. Those meadows are a joy, particularly in mid-spring, abuzz with the first flush of heat that comes in March and are still a pleasure now as in centuries past after the dark, wet days of winter. There are more trees on the mountain too – the still-brooding Mynydd Du a few miles way to the east. This now has a clear area of *ffridd* extending up to 600m or so above sea level, giving it a more similar feel to how mountain areas in parts of southern Snowdonia used to feel. It's grazed by mixed herds of cattle, sheep, ponies and pigs, and though I don't eat meat often, mutton in winter and rose veal in spring are both delectable treats from that land.

Much has changed by the 2080s, and the landscape has shifted in a number of important ways. But does it still feel like Wales?

I fish my copy of *Gwaith Dafydd ap Gwilym* out of my rucksack. The best part of another century now divides me from Dafydd, and Wales has changed further from when he was writing. I skim through the pages, listing some of the titles that resonate still with this living landscape – 'Y Pwll Mawn', 'Yr Ehedydd', 'Y Mwdwl Gwair', 'Serch fel Ysgyfarnog' ('The peat-pit', 'The skylark', 'The haystack', 'Lust like a hare'). Then a sheet of paper with a handwritten copy of 'Gorhoffedd Hywel', 'Hywel's boast', falls out in the breeze. This is a poem from almost two centuries before Dafydd's time, in which the court-poet conjures all the reasons he can boast of his homeland in north-west Wales:

> Caraf ei morfa a'i mynyddoedd
> A'i chaer ger ei choed a'i chain
> diroedd
> A dolydd ei dwfwr a'i
> dyffrynnoedd
> A'i gwylanod gwynion a'i gwymp
> wragedd.
> Caraf ei milwyr a'i meirch hywedd
> A'i choed a'i chedyrn a'i
> chyfannedd.
> Caraf ei meysydd a'i mân
> feillion arno,
> Myn yd gafas ffaw ffyrf orfoledd.
> Caraf ei broydd, braint hywerth
> A'i diffaith mawrfaith a'i
> marannedd.
> Wy a un mab Duw, mawr a
> ryfedd!

> [I love its saltmarsh and
> mountains
> Its castle by the trees and
> its fair lands
> Its watermeadows and valleys,
> And its white gulls and lovely
> women.
> I love its soldiers and proud
> stallions
> Woods, strong men and
> homesteads.
> I love its fields covered in clover,
> Where honour could take pride.
> I love its vales, privileged in
> valour
> Both its great wilderness
> and its plains.
> By God's only son, what
> a wonder!]

Much has changed, but is this land I am surveying on this hot 2080s evening still recognisably that Wales?

I think it is.

Notes

Introduction

1. See *https://www.wwf.org.uk/future-of-uk-nature* (accessed 27 May 2023). The 'corporate power' here refers not just to recent examples but also to early precursors of the modern corporation, that mined and poisoned the vale of Rheidol and Ystwyth, left gaping pits where previously had been mountains on Anglesey, and raped much of the lower Swansea valley, to give just a few early examples.

2. The only notable exception to this are chalk downs, with their wonderful flora and threatened chalk streams – all entirely absent from Wales.

3. And is a great deal higher than that of nearby Ireland at 1,211 species; a country almost four times as large as Wales.

4. See *https://herbaria.plants.ox.ac.uk/bol/ancientoaksofengland/Numbers* for comparative figures for England and the rest of Europe; note the westerly distribution of such oaks in England and compare with the ancient oak map produced by the Woodland Trust in 2013, showing comparable densities of such oaks on the Welsh side of the border in Monmouthshire, Breconshire and Montgomeryshire; *http://www. landscapearchitecture.org.uk/ancient-and-veteran-oaks-and-natural-capital/* (accessed January 2022).

5. It is hard to know for sure, as hard data are scarce and assessments of this necessarily rely on proxies. But reports like this from a team at the Natural History Museum – *https://www.nhm.ac.uk/discover/news/2020/ september/uk-has-led-the-world-in-destroying-the-natural-environment. html* (accessed 9 November 2023) – estimate that half of biodiversity has been lost since the Industrial Revolution.

6. See *https://community.rspb.org.uk/getinvolved/wales/b/wales-blog/posts/how-*

much-of-wales-is-really-protected-for-nature (accessed 9 November 2023).

7. See, for instance, discussion of the traditions around the idea that 'it is not too much to say that classical civilisation [and its later instantiations in European culture] has always defined itself against the primeval woods'. This and many other well-commented aspects of the set of attitudes towards the land inherited from Greek and Roman civilisation – the Arcadian idyll, the rural retreat from urbanity, etc. – although also influencing educated opinion in Welsh, nevertheless shape the overall discourse to a strikingly small degree. Much the same could be said of Irish. See discussion in S. Schama, *Landscape and Memory* (London: HarperCollins, 1995).

8. Or, at a minimum, for the future of this particular landscape both insofar as it remains a home for people and as the ways they use it has rebound effects on other people's ability to provide for themselves.

9. I am indebted to Seimon Brooks for his heuristic term, 'yr archif Gymreig', that has done so much to enlighten my work, both here and in my previous *Welsh Food Stories* (Cardiff: Calon, 2022).

10. From 'Gwahodd Dyddgu', by Dafydd ap Gwilym. Translation by the author.

11. Dylan Foster Evans and Sara Elin Roberts, 'Y Bardd', *dafyddapgwilym. net* (accessed 12 January 2022). That they are reflections doesn't negate the likelihood that they are stylised, as any fictional depiction of, say, central London in film amounts to a stylised-yet-realistic reflection that an audience can recognise.

12. A further 600 miles south, in Florence, the poet Petrarch was composing his sonnets and writing within the same broad tradition of love poetry. Petrarch's sonnets are written to Laura, who was very much a real woman who had refused his amorous advances. But his birds, his trees and even his stream are all nameless – present in the poem in order to create an atmosphere and conform to poetic norms and no more:

> Se lamentar augelli, o verdi fronde
> mover soavemente a l'aura estiva,
> o roco mormorar di lucide onde
> s'ode d'una fiorita et fresca riva,
> là 'v'io seggia d'amor pensoso et scriva,

[The birds' sad song, the young leaves' rustling play,
In the soft summer air, the hoarser sounds
Of lucid waters as they rush away
Between their verdant flower-enamelled bounds,
Where, lost in Love's sweet fantasies, I lie]

13. See, for instance, extensive discussion of this in H. Fulton, *Dafydd ap Gwilym and the European Context* (Cardiff: University of Wales Press, 1989).

14. See comparison e.g. of ap Gwilym's use of concrete agricultural terminology with that of the *Roman de la Rose* in D. Johnston, *Iaith Oleulawn* (Cardiff: University of Wales Press, 2020), p. 196 or the contrast between ap Gwilym's 'sheaf of dry stubble' and the trouvérian's bland 'fencing' in poems using the same core imagery as discussed in H. M. Edwards, *Dafydd ap Gwilym: Influences and Analogues* (Oxford: Clarendon, 1996), p. 210.

15. T. Jardine, 'Indigenous knowledge as a remedy for shifting baseline syndrome', *Frontiers in Ecology and the Environment*, 17/1 (February 2019), *https://esajournals.onlinelibrary.wiley.com/doi/full/10.1002/fee.1991* (accessed 9 November 2023).

16. G. Monbiot, *Feral* (London: Penguin, 2014), p. 198.

17. P. Tinsley-Marshall, A. Skilbeck and A. Riggs, 'Monitoring of ecosystem function at landscape-scale demonstrates temporal difference in invertebrate abundance in Kent and South-East England', *www.kentwildlifetrust.org.uk/sites/default/files/2020-02/Bugs Matter report website version_0.pdf* (accessed 9 November 2023); D. Goulson, *Silent Earth: Averting the Insect Apocalypse* (London: Penguin, 2021), p. 53.

18. M. Benbough-Jackson, *Cardiganshire: The Concise History* (Cardiff: University of Wales Press, 2007), p. 100.

19. D. Owen, *A Wilder Wales* (Cardigan: Parthian, 2017), p. 89.

20. Paul Jepson and Cain Blythe, *Rewilding: The Radical New Science of Ecological Recovery* (London: Icon, 2020), p. 91.

21. See, for instance, the survey of Welsh historiography in H. Pryce, *Writing Welsh History: From the Early Middle Ages to the Twenty-First Century* (Oxford: Oxford University Press, 2022).

22. Cf. S. Brooks, *Hanes Cymry* (Cardiff: University of Wales Press, 2021) or N. Thomas, *The Welsh Extremist* (Talybont: Y Lolfa, 1971). It is commonly accepted within the field of psycho-linguistics that the

average human brain has the capacity to learn between three and seven languages to functional fluency. Some readers may raise eyebrows, but school French lessons are a poor approximation of the type of context that gives humans a real incentive to learn a foreign tongue.

23. Quoted in Diarmuid Johnson, *Pen and Plough: 20th Century Poets and Bards of Ceredigion* (Llanrwst: Carreg Gwalch, 2016), p. 13.

24. S. Wynne-Jones, G. Strouts and G. Holmes, 'Abandoning or Reimagining a Cultural Heartland? Understanding and Responding to Rewilding Conflicts in Wales – the Case of the Cambrian Wildwood', *Environmental Values*, 27/4 (2018).

25. Technical definitions exist that are centred on 'restoring trophic complexity, dispersal, and stochastic disturbances'.

26. It has been demonstrated, for instance, that impala, deer, European badgers and mountain lions fear hearing playbacks of humans (simply conversing calmly) far more than hearing the vocalisations of their non-human predators; and even elephants flee at hearing people speak. See Liana Y. Zanette and Michael Clinchy, 'Ecology of fear', *Current Biology*, 29/9 (2019), pp. R309–R313.

27. F. Pearce, *A Trillion Trees: How We Can Reforest Our World* (London: Granta, 2021), p. 86.

28. Pearce, *A Trillion Trees*, p. 7.

29. Not that 'science' is a good translation of the German *Wissenschaft*, which effectively conveys the sense of 'branch of knowledge'. The technical definition of what constitutes a 'science' in German differs materially from the definition of *Wissenschaft* in German. A perhaps relevant example of the sort of cultural relativism and caution I am propounding in these pages.

30. K. Bharatdwaj, *Physical Geography: Landscape Appreciations* (New Delhi: Discovery Publishing House, 2009), p. 6.

31. Whereas the incentive for government officials to prevent logging or poaching in national parks in Congo or Brazil may be very little compared to the lure of a significant bribe, for native and indigenous people who depend on intact forests, coastal waters or other 'natural' landscapes for their livelihoods and ways of life, the incentive could hardly be greater.

32. Other needs and desires have of course played a significant part, not least for fibre and shelter, and these have been alluded to at various points in passing. Beyond this, industry, and in particular the mining industry, has been an important presence in Wales for millennia. My

major reasons for neglecting this here are to do both with the fact that these industries' presence in the Welsh landscape has been well covered and the dynamics driving their development and shaping of land have, on the whole, been different in nature to food production; and generally more localised in impact.

33. It has recently been acknowledged, for instance, that there are Australian 'Aboriginal stories about the time, perhaps 10 millennia ago, when the Great Barrier Reef was the coastline … recent research has demonstrated the plausibility that humans can pass on memories for several thousand years without the assistance of literacy'. P. Nunn, *The Edge of Memory: Ancient Stories, Oral Tradition and the Post-Glacial World* (London: Bloomsbury, 2018), p. 205.

34. Jardine, 'Indigenous knowledge as a remedy for shifting baseline syndrome'.

35. Myth is powerful, and I have no interest here in contributing to the creation of a new myth. But as Schama notes, if these powerful subconscious forces are not discussed, we 'concede the subject by default to those who have no critical distance from it at all, who apprehend myth not as a historical phenomenon but as an unchallengeable perennial mystery'. *Landscape and Memory*, p. 134.

36. As Schama, again, puts it: 'Not all cultures embrace nature and landscape myths with equal ardour, and those that do, go through periods of greater or lesser enthusiasm. What the myths of ancient forest mean for one European national tradition may translate into something entirely different in another. In Germany, for example, the forest primeval was the site of tribal self-assertion against the Roman Empire of stone and law. In England the greenwood was the place where the king disported his power in the royal hunt yet redressed the injustices of his officers.' *Landscape and Memory*, p. 15. Neither of these, incidentally, maps well onto the Welsh cultural conception of old woodlands – as we shall see.

Coed

37. O. Rackham, *Ancient Woodlands of South-east Wales* (Dorset: Little Toller, 2022), p. 210.

38. Coed Cefn-y-crug is by a fair distance the highest naturally occurring ancient woodland in the British Isles, topping out at 517m above sea level; almost 100m higher than the highly celebrated Wistman's Wood in Devon.

39. *Provisional Woodland Statistics: 2021 Edition, www.forestresearch. gov.uk* (accessed 1 February 2022).

40. For an exploration of these and their importance, see G. Shrubsole, *The Lost Rainforests of Britain* (London: William Collins, 2022).

41. Wales has, for its size, the highest diversity of lichen species in the world. See this website by an alliance of conservation organisations: *https://wales-lichens.org.uk/*.

42. W. Condry, *Woodlands* (London: Collins, 1974).

43. See for instance the values for ecological continuity for ancient woodland sites in Wales – joint highest with the New Forest and those in Cornwall: Francis Rose, 'Ancient British woodlands and their epiphytes', *British Wildlife*, 5 (1993), 83–93 (92).

44. Tamás Rédei et al., 'Plantation forests cannot support the richness of forest specialist plants in the forest-steppe zone', *Forest Ecology and Management,* 461 (2020), 117964, *https://doi.org/10.1016/j. foreco.2020.117964* (accessed 9 November 2023).

45. W. Condry, *Natural History of Wales* (London: Collins, 1981), p. 69.

46. Condry, *Woodlands*, p. 14.

47. Malcolm Lillie, *Hunters, Fishers and Foragers in Wales* (Oxford: Oxbow Books, 2015), p. 31.

48. A time characterised by wild swings in climate, with a roughly 1,500-year period before the start of what is known as the 'Holocene' period marked by shorter phases lasting between a few decades and a couple of hundred years of either a return to extreme cold or milder climates.

49. Lillie, *Hunters, Fishers and Foragers in Wales*, p. 37.

50. Mesolithic finds at the former site include a flint blade; cf. C. R. Musson, with W. J. Britnell and A. G. Smith, *The Breiddin Hillfort: A Later Prehistoric Settlement in the Welsh Marches*, CBA Research Report 76 (1991), 19.

51. Peter Rhind and Barbara Jones, 'The Vegetation History of Snowdonia since the Late Glacial Period', Field Studies, 10 (2003), 539–52.

52. This site is important as we have cores allowing for pollen analysis extending back to this period; there are very few others in Wales meaning that we have to extrapolate for the landscape as a whole. But the chances of this one site being the only one controlled in this way in Wales during this period are of course vanishingly slim.

There would have been many, many others; *https://coflein.gov.uk/en/site/401580/* (accessed 9 November 2023).

53. Lillie, *Hunters, Fishers and Foragers in Wales*, p. 91.

54. Quoted in I. Tree, *Wilding* (London: Picador, 2018), p. 81.

55. Tree, *Wilding*, p. 83.

56. Nicola Strange, 'Holocene to Bronze Age Woodland in the British Isles' (conference paper 2018).

57. Lillie, *Hunters, Fishers and Foragers in Wales*, pp. 192, 181.

58. Lillie, *Hunters, Fishers and Foragers in Wales*, p. 47.

59. Lillie, *Hunters, Fishers and Foragers in Wales*, p. 47.

60. L. K. Petersson et al., 'Influence of canopy openness, ungulate exclosure, and low-intensity fire for improved oak regeneration in temperate Europe', *Ecology and Evolution*, 10/5, 2626–37, *https://doi.org/10.1002/ece3.6092* (accessed 9 November 2023).

61. Rhind and Jones, 'The Vegetation History of Snowdonia since the Late Glacial Period'; Lillie, *Hunters, Fishers and Foragers in Wales*, p. 84.

62. Lillie, *Hunters, Fishers and Foragers in Wales*, p. 46.

63. The climatic fluctuations that were still happening through this Mesolithic period (up to around 4,000 BC) had significant effects on different plant, insect and animal species' ability to survive and reproduce, and so shape what is present in the landscape. And alongside herbivores, coastal sites include evidence of aurochs, red deer, pig, roe deer and brown bear, while cave sites also show evidence of foxes, wolves and hares. Cf. Lillie, *Hunters, Fishers and Foragers in Wales*, p. 93.

64. C. Fychan, *Galwad y Blaidd* (Talybont: Y Lolfa, 2006), p. 22.

65. H. J. Birks, 'Mind the gap: how open were European primeval forests?', *Trends in Ecology & Evolution*, 20/4 (2005), 154–6, *doi: 10.1016/j.tree.2005.02.001*.

66. F. Pearce, *A Trillion Trees: How We Can Reforest Our World* (London: Granta, 2021), p. 164.

67. Lillie, *Hunters, Fishers and Foragers in Wales*, p. 91.

68. D. Austin, 'Reconstructing the upland landscapes of medieval Wales', *Archaeologia Cambrensis*, 7/165 (2016), 1–19.

69. F. Pryor, *Making of the British Landscape* (London: Penguin, 2011), p. 67.

70. Miles Russell and Stuart Laycock, *UnRoman Britain: Exposing the Great Myth of Britannia* (Cheltenham: The History Press, 2019), p. 163.

71. T. Driver, *Hillforts of Cardigan Bay* (Hereford: Logaston Press, 2016), p. 52.

72. Driver, *Hillforts of Cardigan Bay*, p. 52.

73. See *https://archaeology.co.uk/articles/features/roundhouses.htm* (accessed 9 November 2023).

74. Pryor, *Scenes from Prehistoric Life* (Apollo, London, 2021), p. 254.

75. V. Smil, *How the World Really Works* (London: Viking, 2022), p. 99.

76. It is worth taking a little foray into the highly sensitive territory of ancient DNA analysis to understand this. Recent work has demonstrated the extent to which tides of incoming farming migrants from further south and east in Europe replaced the existing local populations during this period. In the case of the British Isles this seems to have happened thrice over, once at the onset of the Neolithic period and again during both the early and later Bronze Age – it was the last of these waves of migration around 1,000 BC that seems to have been responsible for bringing the Celtic languages to the British Isles, including older forms of both Irish and Welsh. However, peoples' ancestries do not map neatly or simply onto their culture. Even where the DNA record seems to suggest that the local population is wiped out and replaced by incoming migrants, deeper analysis reminds us that a variety of factors lead to us having that data in the first place, such as the funerary practice of burial, which may have been accorded to higher status individuals and not others, meaning the very samples we have to work with are biased. This means we need to try and form a view of the past based on the widest possible range of sources, and to return to prehistoric Wales as there is important archaeological 'evidence for significant cultural continuity across the Late Neolithic–Chalcolithic transition' in question ranging from ceramic styles through to use of the landscape, despite the genetic shift. See for instance Selina Brace et al., 'Ancient genomes indicate population replacement in Early Neolithic Britain', *Nature Ecology and Evolution,* 3/5 (15 April 2019), 765–71; T. Booth et al., 'Tales from the Supplementary Information: Ancestry Change in Chalcolithic–Early Bronze Age Britain Was Gradual with Varied Kinship Organization', *Cambridge Archaeological Journal,* 31/3 (2021), 379–400, *doi: 10.1017/S0959774321000019.*

77. Ludovic Orlando, 'The first aurochs genome reveals the breeding history of British and European cattle', *Genome Biology,* 16/225 (26 October 2015), *doi: 10.1186/s13059-015-0793-z.*

78. Driver, *Hillforts of Cardigan Bay*, p. 41.

79. W. Linnard, *Welsh Woods and Forests* (Llandysul: Gomer, 2000), p. 18.

80. D. and Rh. Ifans, *Y Mabinogion* (Llandysul: Gomer, 2007), p. 115.

81. From Lady Charlotte Guest's translation.

82. Llanmelin hillfort.

83. The hills to the north of Cardiff include the prominent 'Wenallt' or white-'allt'; Breconshire has the parish of Allt-mawr or Great 'Allt' and in Ceredigion we find the village of Alltyblaca or the muddy 'allt'. Beyond these there are countless other *elltydd* dotted around the landscape to be found on any OS map of Wales.

84. *Geiriadur Prifysgol Cymru.*

85. *Geiriadur Prifysgol Cymru.*

86. In the Welsh of south-west Wales *allt* only means wooded slope down to the present day. The pattern of words expanding their meaning in some dialects but not others is common in the world's languages. Cf. also Fenton's comments in 1696, as quoted in *Geiriadur Prifysgol Cymru:* 'They call here hills glennydd ... and *gallt* a wood.'

87. The only notable exception to this being the *gwernydd* or alder carr in wet valley bottoms.

88. P. M. Perrin and O. H. Daly, 'A provisional inventory of ancient and long-established woodland in Ireland', *Irish Wildlife Manuals,* 46 (2010). National Parks and Wildlife Service, Department of the Environment, Heritage and Local Government, Dublin, Ireland.

89. Linnard, *Welsh Woods and Forests*, p. 21.

90. See Gerald of Wales's *Journey Through Wales,* including for instance the description of Carmarthen as 'surrounded by woods and meadowlands' and nearby Cantref Mawr containing 'impenetrable forests' and 'lush woodlands'.

91. From which root we have the Welsh *derwydd* and English 'druid'.

92. G. Graves, *Welsh Food Stories* (Cardiff: Calon, 2022), p. 123.

93. G. Jenkins, *Crefftwyr Gwlad* (Llandysul: Gomer, 1971), p. 39.

94. From 'Marwnad Gruffudd Llwyd' by Rhys Goch Eryri, translation by the author.

95. By Robin Clidro, *Welsh Poems: Sixth Century to 1600*, trans. Gwyn Williams (Berkeley: University of California Press, 1974), pp. 87–8.

96. Cf. Glanffrwd, *Llanwynno* (Caerdydd: University of Wales Press, 1949), pp. 58–67.

97. Christine James, 'Coed Glyn Cynon', in Hywel Teifi Edwards (ed.), *Cwm Cynon* (Llandysul: Gomer, 1997), p. 47.

98. Verses 1–7; the full 13 verses can be found in James, 'Coed Glyn Cynon', pp. 53. Translation my own.

99. See James, 'Coed Glyn Cynon', p. 59.

100. Rackham, *Ancient Woodlands of South-east Wales* (Dorset: Little Toller, 2022), pp. 200 and 204.

101. Rackham, *Ancient Woodlands of South-east Wales*, p. 196.

102. Rackham, *Ancient Woodlands of South-east Wales*, pp. 214, 208.

103. See also nearby Coed Cefn-fforest and Cefn Fforest farm above Treharris; Coed Ty Dan Darn and Ty Dan Daren above Ynysboeth, and Coed Fforest Isaf and Fforest Isaf Farm also above Mountain Ash.

Cloddiau

104. For a full discussion of the landscape of Dinas and its antiquity, see Rh. Comeau, 'Cytir and Crosses: the archaeological landscape of the parish of Dinas', *Archaeologia Cambrensis*, 158 (2009), 225–53.

105. Comeau, 'Cytir and Crosses', 234.

106. This is in contrast to known sites in Cornwall and Ireland where there is discontinuity of settlement in the early medieval landscape but parallel other known sites in north Pembrokeshire. All such conclusions are necessarily of a preliminary nature given the lack of excavated evidence and radiocarbon dates for local sites. See Comeau, 'Cytir and Crosses', 234.

107. Rh. Parry, *Cerdded y Caeau* (Talybont: Y Lolfa, 2022).

108. Fishing and seafaring have also been important at different points in the parish's history; though as far as we know over the course of recent millennia, always combined with farming.

109. Taller and thicker within limits; see J. Wright, *A Natural History of the Hedgerow* (London: Profile, 2016), p. 271.

110. Wright, *A Natural History of the Hedgerow*, p. 134.

111. This is known to have been the case in lowland Ireland, most of central England and large swathes of France.

112. There is a slightly different dynamic at play in lowland Glamorgan, where the landscape was reorganised to a great extent by the Normans.

113. This is also true, though the detail of the history is different, in parts of the west of England (Cornwall, Devon, the Marches and Cumbria) and patches in the south-east in Sussex, Kent and Essex.

114. There is, for instance, no Welsh 'Domesday book' describing the entire country at one point in time; fewer charters have survived, and more needs to be read into law texts and throwaway references in other documents, such as literature or trials.

115. See D. Austin, *Ystrad Fflur: Hanes a Thirwedd Mynachlog Gymreig* (Strata Florida: Ymddiriedolaeth Ystrad Fflur, 2022); also the following: 'This is suggested by comparing the distribution of archaeological records for deserted settlements with pre-1500 place names, the latter – given the restrictions of historical and archaeological records – providing useful proxies for medieval settlement (Fig. 5). Almost all the place names are located on soils of greater fertility and are frequently close to boundaries with less fertile soils that are often, in modern times, liable to seasonal waterlogging. These variations in fertility and drainage determine whether areas are better suited for arable or for seasonal pasture, with the siting of settlements at soil-zone interfaces providing optimal access.' Rh. Comeau and B. Silvester, 'Transhumant settlement in medieval Wales: the *hafod*', in Piers Dixon and Claudia Theune (eds), *Seasonal Settlement in the Medieval and Early Modern Countryside* (Leiden: Sidestone Press, 2021), p. 120.

116. Heather James and David Thorne, 'Toldar: a place-name in Meddyfnych, a ninth-century estate in Carmarthenshire', in Gareth A. Bevan et al. (eds), *Ar Drywydd Enwau Lleoedd* (Talybont: Y Lolfa, 2021), p. 69.

117. Eight became demesne farms and were renamed in the process. The other twelve became part of the new abbey's wider charter within the 1184 grant from Rhys ap Gruffudd. See Austin, *Ystrad Fflur*.

118. E. La Trobe-Bateman, 'Snowdonia's early fieldscapes' (PhD thesis, University of Sheffield, 2020).

119. OSL (optically stimulated luminescence) date rather than radiocarbon. From Mike Alexander, *Skomer Island* (Talybont: Y Lolfa, 2021), p. 46.

120. See discussion by Andrew Fleming, 'Welsh landscape history: notes from the edge', in Rhiannon Comeau and Andy Seaman (eds), *Living off the Land* (Oxford: Oxbow Books, 2019), pp. 202–4.

121. There is, of course, debate about the detail. For a different emphasis, see the three-field system as outlined by M. Stevens, *Economy of Medieval Wales* (Cardiff: University of Wales Press, 2019), p. 36.

122. Welsh *cytir*, though also occasionally *rhos*.

123. P. Davies, *Yr Efrydd o Lyn Cynon a Cherddi Eraill* (Llandybïe: Llyfrau'r Dryw, 1978), p. 35.

124. As always, a blanket statement like this obscures plenty of important nuance across time and space; not least the fact that in some areas a four-fold division seems closer to the mark (with outfield, *rhos* and *mynydd* distinct), while in others the outfield and *rhos/mynydd* may be entirely synonymous, creating a basic two-fold division.

125. From the archaeological evidence at Bayvil, see: Rh. Comeau, 'Crop processing and early medieval settlement: the evidence for Bayvil, Pembrokeshire', *Medieval Settlement Research*, 36 (2021), 61–7.

126. S. Vervust et al., 'Optically stimulated luminescence profiling and dating of earthworks: The creation and development of prehistoric field boundaries at Bosigran, Cornwall', *Antiquity*, 94/374 (2020), 420–36, *doi: 10.15184/aqy.2019.138.*

127. La Trobe-Bateman, 'Snowdonia's early fieldscapes', 3.

128. The extent to which landscape division reflects intimate knowledge of the land right down to its underlying geology and minute differences in soil quality can be seen in the chapter on Dinas and Bayvil (Comeau, 'The practice of *in rodwallis:* medieval Welsh agriculture in north Pembrokeshire') in Comeau and Seaman (eds), *Living off the Land.*

129. Shepherding was an important part of this, and there is linguistic and historic evidence for cattle-herds keeping livestock off crops in what we take were outfield or *mynydd* locations both in Wales and nearby. But then there are the night-times, indicated by fields near the home called *cae nos* or 'night-time field'. See D. Jenkins, *Ar Lafar, Ar Goedd* (Aberystwyth: Cymdeithas Lyfrau Ceredigion, 2007), pp. 148–9, for discussion.

130. See extensive discussion in Jenkins, *Ar Lafar, Ar Goedd.*

131. T. Driver, *Hillforts of Cardigan Bay* (Hereford: Logaston Press, 2016), p. 45.

132. See image at *https://rcahmw.gov.uk/castell-nadolig-a-christmas-hillfort-with-hidden-secrets/* (accessed 9 November 2023).

133. Irish/Welsh parallels are fraught with difficulty, but it is nevertheless illuminating that at a time of significant cross-channel contact towards the end of the first millennium AD, the main Irish law text on farming, the *Bretha Comaithchesa*, contains specific descriptions of what constitutes a proper field-boundary, including a type called *clas* defined as a trench and earthen bank.

134. Driver, *Hillforts of Cardigan Bay*, p. 41. At the very latest, by the time the poet Guto'r Glyn is writing in the mid-fifteenth century, *cloddiau* were common enough in north-east Wales and clearly included hedges in their meaning frequently for him to complain about lambs getting entangled in them in his poem 'Euthum innau i borthmona' (with the line 'Pob clawdd y glynawdd eu gwlân' ('To every hedge their wool stuck')). See discussion in E. A. Rees, *A Life of Guto'r Glyn* (Talybont: Y Lolfa, 2008), p. 104.

135. Parry, *Cerdded y Caeau*, pp. 62–72.

136. This is part of a wider context of change in agriculture as there is a move away from lots of young men herding cattle to the need for hedges to do so instead as traditional *bugeilio* declines.

137. Jenkins, *Ar Lafar, Ar Goedd*, pp. 145–69 and Parry, *Cerdded y Caeau*, pp. 31–41.

138. La Trobe-Bateman, 'Snowdonia's early fieldscapes', 201.

139. Parry, *Cerdded y Caeau*, p. 52.

140. See paintings by Richard Wilson and Moses Griffith, both active in the 1760s and 1770s and drawing locations across north Wales. Their rural paintings clearly show an enclosed landscape with hedges and plentiful hedgerow trees.

141. H. Warwick, *Linescapes* (London: Vintage, 2018), p. 38.

142. Warwick, *Linescapes,* p. 40.

Cae

143. These things are notoriously difficult to measure accurately as a margin of error is always produced by the definitions used. For one figure see 'Manifesto for the Wild Meadows of Wales', Flora locale and The Grasslands Trust, April 2008. A lower-end figure of 90 per cent lost since the 1930s is given in 'National Meadows Day Senedd Cymru Briefing', Plantlife, 2020.

144. 'Wales Farmland Report', Plantlife, 2014.

145. Edward Armstrong, 'The Farming Sector in Wales: Research Briefing for Senedd' (National Assembly for Wales, 2016).

146. In Welsh, in order: Trilliw bach, Gweirlöyn y glaw, Glesyn cyffredin, Gweirlöyn y ddôl, Gwibiwr bach, Gweirlöyn brych, Gweirlöyn y perthi, Mantell goch, Gweirlöyn bach y waun, Gwyn gwythïen werdd, Gwibiwr mawr, Mantell dramor, Mantell paun, Copor bach, Gweirlöyn y cloddiau, Britheg berlog fach.

147. A term like 'large' is necessarily relative and varies from place to place – we are talking about an area typically several acres in size, but nowhere near as large as the Midland open fields or the vast prairie fields of modern northern France or the US Midwest.

148. A partial survival, in an area dominated by Welsh law rather than Norman custom, can be seen still today on the Ceredigion coast near the village of Llannon.

149. A hay meadow would usually be a *gweirglodd*.

150. See the distribution for Atlantic wet heaths here, for instance: *https://jncc.gov.uk/jncc-assets/Art17/H4010-WA-Habitats-Directive-Art17-2019.pdf* (accessed 9 November 2023). With only localised distribution in England and Northern Ireland, it is present in almost every grid square of Wales, both lowland and upland. Not that a *gwaun* is entirely synonymous with this ecologically based, scientific jargon term in English, but it encapsulates how different ways of knowing can converge.

151. 'Gweirgloddiau, *parcau heb hyn / Ŷnt iddo, deucant tyddyn*' from the fifteenth-century *Gwaith Hywel Cilan*, cited in *Geiriadur Prifysgol Cymru*; cf. also D. Jenkins, *Ar Lafar, Ar Goedd* (Aberystwyth: Cymdeithas Lyfrau Ceredigion, 2007), p. 111.

152. In a similar development a few hundred miles north, in the Scots language the term also came to mean any enclosed field, particularly pasture.

153. Cf. Parc-y-meirch in Denbighshire, Parc in Gwynedd or Penparcau in Ceredigion.

154. Rh. Parry, *Cerdded y Caeau* (Talybont: Y Lolfa, 2022), p. 114.

155. Parry, *Cerdded y Caeau*, p. 149.

156. Parry, *Cerdded y Caeau*, p. 44.

157. Parry, *Cerdded y Caeau*, p. 172.

158. See recent discussion of the background to this poem attributed traditionally to Taliesin: 'Introduction', in Gwyneth Lewis and Rowan Williams (eds), *The Book of Taliesin* (London: Penguin, 2019); as well as excellent translations of many other poems attributed to Taliesin in the same vein.

159. Among others, Robin Wall Kimmerer has written movingly on the importance of native American indigeneity and language in understanding the ecology of that continent, and the profound alienation within modern North American culture between the colonial English

language and native ways of inhabiting the land as expressed in their languages and cultures. That historico-cultural experience is of course profoundly different to that of Welsh-language culture in Britain; the only parallel to ancient indigenous knowledge we have here is the native knowledge passed down in the oldest Welsh writings.

160. See for instance the cycles of verse called *Canu Heledd* and *Canu Llywarch Hen*, with the poignant references to cold hearths and fields of stubble.

161. Tony Conran, *Welsh Verse* (Bridgend: Seren, 2017), p. 136. This is one verse from the poem entitled 'Sadness in Springtime'.

162. Iolo Goch, 'Y Llafurwr', translated extract taken from, *Welsh Poems: Sixth Century to 1600*, trans. Gwyn Williams (Berkeley: University of California Press, 1974).

163. Ff. Payne, *Cwysau* (Gomer: Llandysul, 1980).

164. Parry, *Cerdded y Caeau*, p. 172.

165. There is a notable exception at Llannon on the Ceredigion coast, which is still subdivided into strips dating back to the Middle Ages and quite plausibly beyond.

166. See *https://www.plantlife.org.uk/uk/nature-reserves-important-plant-areas/important-plant-areas/mwnt-arable-fields* (accessed February 2022).

167. Respectively, around 900mm and 1,600 hours, compared with over 1,300mm and 1,400 hours in the hills above the Teifi a few miles away. For comparison purposes, this is almost identical to areas on the north Cornwall coast such as Bude or Newquay.

168. Quoted in Jenkins, *Ar Lafar, Ar Goedd*, p. 111. But note that there was variation of all sorts – some of the 'best errable' land is recorded as having been kept under barley 'since time immemorial', just as there is a folk tradition in west Wales that the best grazing field was never ploughed.

169. Such as at Llanbedr in Gwynedd, where an *arddlas* is noted as being 'pasture', one talar field is arable and the other pasture, while a field called wern is described as arable.

170. Hay meadows and other high-yielding permanent grasslands were a valuable part of the farming system in the Middle Ages, and some were positively revered; you get a sense from some old writers of the idea of ploughing a good meadow being to all intents and purposes taboo. But such meadows were comparatively rare, amounting in England

at the time of Domesday to only 1 per cent of land area, albeit well dispersed (O. Rackham, *History of the Countryside* (London: Weidenfeld and Nicholson, 2020), p. 334). This site doesn't seem to have any of the characteristics of such ancient, productive meadows, and if it was managed as hay land historically, the balance of evidence in this part of the Upper Teifi valley suggests it would have alternated between different land uses.

171. Anonymised and slightly simplified (in terms of detail of landholding structure) to protect the place and its inhabitants.

172. A mix of native Welsh blacks, dairy crosses and Limousins, all put to a Charolais bull.

Ffridd

173. A form of musical performance where the tune played on the harp and that sung by the soloist or choir are at counterpoint to each other. Utterly beautiful but also a slightly otherworldly, disorientating thing to listen to for those unfamiliar with it. For an initiation, see: *https://www.cerdd-dant.org/*.

174. In southern Wales, the term *ffridd* generally doesn't appear and isn't commonly known among Welsh speakers; but in hilly Breconshire and Glamorgan, the term *coedcae* seems to have denoted areas with a similar function within the landscape. This habitat does appear in places in other upland parts of the British Isles, sometimes under the name 'intake', but hasn't such a clear function or ubiquity within the upland farmed landscape. See R. Hartnup, *Gold Under Bracken* (Talybont: Y Lolfa, 2011), pp. 88–92.

175. But beware armchair travelling! 'Ffridd' place-names as implied above occur more frequently than remaining *ffridd* areas; many places called 'ffridd' are now moorland or improved pasture.

176. Rhian Parry, *Cerdded y Caeau* (Talybont: Y Lolfa, 2022), p. 13.

177. Colin Thomas, 'Place-name analysis in the geographical study of the rural landscape of Wales', *Studia Celtica*, 8/9 (1974), 308–12.

178. Thomas, 'Place-name analysis in the geographical study of the rural landscape of Wales', 314. Though it seems equally likely that many of these were areas already known as *ffridd* that were simply enclosed for the first time during this period; this pattern can be clearly seen in the word lists compiled by G. Melville Richards, where some attested medieval occurrences are accompanied by numerous additions – many bearing

names like 'ffridd newydd' in the seventeenth and eighteenth centuries: '*ffridd / ffrith* as a Welsh place-name', *Studia Celtica*, 2 (1967), 29–90.

179. *Y Bardd yn ei Henaint yn Dwyn i Gof fel y Bu Gyn*, in Blodeugerdd Barddas o Ganu Caeth y Ddeunawfed Ganrif, Ed A Cynfael Lake (1993), p.212

180. T. H. Blackstock et al., *Habitats of Wales: a Comprehensive Field Study, 1979–1997* (Cardiff: University of Wales Press, 2010).

181. R. J. Fuller et al., 'Breeding bird communities in the upland margins (ffridd) of Wales in the mid-1980s', *Bird Study*, 53 (2006), 177–86.

182. See *https://www.rspb.org.uk/our-work/conservation/projects/resilience-of-biodiversity-to-habitat-change-in-the-marginal-uplands-or-ffridd-of-Wales/* (accessed 17 December 2022).

183. G. Conway and R. Fuller, 'Multi-scale relationships between vegetation pattern and breeding birds in the upland margins (ffridd) of North Wales', *BTO Research Report No. 566* (2010).

184. 'In Wales there is special interest in the motives of operators of farms classed as economically Very Small or Small, as these account for 87 per cent of all Welsh farms and thus carry social and political weight in agricultural and rural matters; they also occupy 60 per cent of the agricultural land area. Using questions developed from a review of literature (and especially work published by Ruth Gasson), a survey in early 2021 of over 400 farm households found that respondents overwhelmingly reported intrinsic factors as very important reasons for them being in farming, a categorisation that included motives such as enjoyment of the various production activities of farming, providing a healthy outdoor life, and giving them independence and control': B. Hill and D. Bradley, 'What Motivates Households with Very Small and Small Farms in Wales?', *EuroChoices*, 21 (2022), 58–65, *https://doi.org/10.1111/1746-692X.12344* (accessed 9 November 2023).

185. See *https://businesswales.gov.wales/farmingconnect/news-and-events/technical-articles/benefits-mixed-grazing-approaches-grassland-livestock-systems* (accessed 17 December 2022).

186. RSPB Cymru and Natural Resources Wales, 'Ffridd: A Habitat on the Edge' (2014).

187. These hills had in fact long been famous for their good grazing, with medieval poet Lewys Glyn Cothi singing their praises: 'Blaen Marchdeg ei wartheg oedd / yn eu lliwiau yn lluoedd / Rhai mlaen Gwy fwyfwy a

el / Rhai ar ddaear Hirddywel.' Leland also mentions them, saying 'ther be left al maner of catail all winter, and prove welle': Ffransis Payne, *Crwydro Sir Faesyfed* (Llandybïe: Llyfrau'r Dryw, 1968), p. 109.

188. Tim Thompson, 'Agriculture and Change in a Nineteenth Century Radnorshire Valley', *Radnorshire Society Transactions*, 69 (1999).

189. David Jones, 'The Influence of Religion on the Survival of the Welsh Language 1801–2011: A Tale of Two Centuries' (MA dissertation, University of Wales Trinity Saint David, 2013), 22.

190. G. W. Griffith et al., 'The international conservation importance of Welsh "waxcap" grasslands', *Mycosphere*, 4 (2013), 969–84, *doi: 10.5943/mycosphere/4/5/10*.

191. See *https://andrewsforest.oregonstate.edu/sites/default/files/lter/pubs/pdf/pub3759.pdf* (accessed 9 November 2023).

192. See *https://www.rspb.org.uk/our-work/conservation/projects/resilience-of-biodiversity-to-habitat-change-in-the-marginal-uplands-or-ffridd-of-Wales/* (accessed 17 December 2022).

Mynydd

193. For comparison, the percentage of Gaelic speakers in the mainland Highlands ranges from 2 to 5 per cent, whereas in Snowdonia away from one or two anglicised coastal towns, the range runs from 40 to 88 per cent.

194. I am not, of course, asserting that the Welsh mountain environments are not nature-depleted; they are (just as they are linguistically threatened). What I am interested in is exploring the nuanced questions around *to what extent* and *why*. As part of that, it is almost undeniably the case that the Welsh mountain areas, had they suffered similar politico-cultural pressures as upland Scotland or Ireland (clearance and famine, respectively), would be markedly more denuded on all three fronts.

195. As Schama perceptively notes, 'The starkness of Welsh scenery had long been imagined in London as the epitome of barbaric rudeness, and the language spoken by the natives as the phonetic equivalent of the landscape.' *Landscape and Memory* (London: HarperCollins, 1995), p. 469.

196. There are numerous other terms used for mountains, including *Moel* denoting a bare summit, Pen for a particularly prominent peak, tarren signifying a rocky prominence and also carn, amongst others.

197. For the coastal Mynydd Aberporth, see discussion in Jenkins, *Ar Lafar, Ar Goedd* (Aberystwyth: Cymdeithas Lyfrau Ceredigion, 2007), pp. 104–96.

198. Wales shares these majestic, multicellular stone sheepfold structures with only three other countries: Croatia, Switzerland and Iceland. Cf. *https://www.cofnodicorlannau.org/corlannaur-carneddau-sheepfolds/english/sheepfolds-in-other-countries* (accessed 9 November 2023).

199. These ponies form a distinct breed, as recent DNA work has shown, and live as a wild flock under ideal rewilding conditions, with losses in hard winters. But they are also owned animals, and are rounded up once a year for health checks with some sold to keep numbers low enough.

200. J. Perrin, *The Hills of Wales* (Llanrwst: Carreg Gwalch, 2016), p. 31.

201. R. Elfyn Hughes et al., 'Studies in Sheep Population and Environment in the Mountains of North-West Wales I. The Status of the Sheep in the Mountains of North Wales Since Mediaeval Times', *Journal of Applied Ecology*, 10/1 (1973), 119, *https://doi.org/10.2307/2404720* (accessed 14 January 2023).

202. Glanville Jones, 'Field Systems of North Wales', republished in P. S. Barnwell and B. K. Roberts (eds), *Britons, Saxons and Scandinavians: The Historical Geography of Glanville R. J. Jones* (Turnhout: Brepols Publishers, 2011), p. 245.

203. Rh. Comeau and B. Silvester, 'Transhumant settlement in medieval Wales: the *hafod*', in Piers Dixon and Claudia Theune (eds), *Seasonal Settlement in the Medieval and Early Modern Countryside* (Leiden: Sidestone Press, 2021), p. 114.

204. This could simply be an allusion to the practice of transhumance or *hafota* in Welsh: bringing stock onto the mountains in summer to make use of grass growth then. But it could also imply a varied vegetation, with browsed shrubs and trees alongside a range of herbal growth part of the varied pasture available for the animals in a diverse, scrubby (*ffridd*-like) landscape with lower overall grazing pressure than today. Certainly, pollen records from this period imply noticeable increase in tree presence, which by no means need imply closed woodland.

205. Rh. Comeau, *Land, People and Power in Early Medieval Wales: The Cantref of Cemais in Comparative Perspective* (Oxford: BAR Publishing, 2020), p. 81.

206. See the striking image of multicellular sheepfold from this period abutting the massive Penrhyn slate quarry: *www.cofnodicorlannau.org/ corlannaur-carneddau-sheepfolds/english/history* (accessed 6 May 2023). The small cells are all of the same size, indicating roughly equal-sized flocks. Cattle are much more labour intensive to keep than sheep; sheep lend themselves well to being kept by a bi-vocational smallholder community.

207. See *https://www.cofnodicorlannau.org/corlannaur-carneddau-sheep folds/english/history.*

208. See *https://coflein.gov.uk/en/site/418821?term=llanllechid%20sheep fold&pg=4* (accessed 6 May 2023).

209. Used to capture kid goats in order to lure the mother in and milk her: *https://www.cofnodicorlannau.org/corlannaur-carneddau-sheepfolds/ english/structures* (accessed 6 May 2023).

210. Gerald of Wales famously describes flimsy temporary structures that are in all likelihood *hafod* dwellings, and a widely quoted piece of the *Breuddwyd Rhonabwy* myth set in the mid Wales mountains also depicts a peasant's summer encampment.

211. A vivid account of exactly this can be found in *Fferm a Thyddyn* (May 2022), 31, where an account of gathering the mountain from the Carneddau from the 1890s is reprinted in full (in Welsh).

212. The traditional solution to this in these mountains was a different sort of sheepfold, the *corlannau cynefino: https://www.cofnodicorlannau. org/corlannaur-carneddau-sheepfolds/english/structures.*

213. Llanllechid Community Council hold the grazing rights and jointly administer the grazing with the help of Cwmni Mynydd Llanllechid.

214. See a detailed discussion of this in a south-west Wales context in Jenkins, 'Ail-lunio Mynydd y Dyffryn', *Ar Lafar, Ar Goedd,* pp. 104–99.

215. And also until the early nineteenth century for occasional arable cropping in a process known as 'beat-burning' or, in Welsh, *betingo.*

216. See discussion in Vicki Cummings and Alasdair Whittle, *Places of Special Virtue: Megaliths in the Neolithic Landscapes of Wales* (Oxford: Oxbow Books, 2004), pp. 70–7, *https://doi.org/10.2307/j.ctvh1djh5* (accessed 8 May 2023).

217. J. Perrin, *Snowdon: Story of a Welsh Mountain* (Talybont: Y Lolfa, 2012), p. 103.

218. Llyr D. Gruffydd and Robin Gwyndaf, *Llyfr Rhedyn ei Daid*

(Caernarfon: Gwasg Dwyfor, 1987), p. 4.

219. 'codi mawn' in his dialect – 'lifting peat'.

220. See *www.climate.mit.edu/ask-mit/how-much-co2-emitted-manufacturing-batteries* (accessed 9 November 2023). Carbon emissions from burning peat to heat a small dwelling for one person over one year estimated by comparison at 2,000kg, producing around 10,000Kwh. Erwyd tells me that on a farm he knows in the 1940s, they estimated that 50 cartloads of peat would cover the households' fuel use for an entire year.

221. Not that they are the same thing; and if there has been a decline in agricultural employment in Wales and the Western world over the span of one lifetime, that has been an order of magnitude greater in the rest of rural employment that is directly tied to countryside production. Less noticed in the UK because of the early advent of industry and its precipitous decline, this has nevertheless also been a substantial change in the pattern of life that has had a measurable effect here, among other things, on biodiversity.

222. Cf. D. Elias, *Shaping the Wild* (Cardiff: Calon, 2023), p. 83, for a Snowdonia site where the remnant hand-cut peat beds have given rise since abandonment to a healthy, rewetted bog.

223. Anonymised for the family's privacy.

224. See *https://www.iucn.org/resources/issues-brief/peatlands-and-climate-change* (accessed 9 November 2023).

225. The CO_2 currently released from degraded peatlands across the UK accounts for 4 per cent of annual greenhouse gas emissions.

226. In the region of 2,300mm a year according to official Met Office data.

227. See *https://www.bbc.co.uk/news/uk-wales-58548745* (accessed 9 November 2023).

228. J. H. Tallis, 'Forest and Moorland in the South Pennine Uplands in the Mid-Flandrian Period: III. The Spread of Moorland – Local, Regional and National', *Journal of Ecology* (June 1991), 79/2, 401–15.

229. Tallis, 'Forest and Moorland in the South Pennine Uplands in the Mid-Flandrian Period', 413.

230. Comeau, *Land, People and Power in Early Medieval Wales,* p. 81.

231. F. M. Chambers et al., 'Recent vegetation history of Drygarn Fawr (Elenydd SSSI), Cambrian Mountains, Wales: implications for conservation management of degraded blanket mires', *Biodiversity and*

Conservation, 16 (2007), 2821–46, *https://doi.org/10.1007/s10531-007-9169-3* (accessed 9 November 2023).

232. As watery places commonly are in Welsh mythology and folk tale. See for instance the riparian encounter between Pwyll and Hafgan that leads to his adventures in the underworld kingdom of Annwn, or the well-known lake-maiden tales associated among others with Llyn y Fan Fach in Carmarthenshire.

233. E. Wyn James and Tecwyn Vaughan Jones (eds), *Gwerin Gwlad* (Llanrwst: Carreg Gwalch, 2008), p. 82.

234. Wyn James and Vaughan Jones (eds), *Gwerin Gwlad,* p. 55.

235. See, for instance, John Owen Huws, *Straeon Gwerin Ardal Eryri* (Llanrwst: Gwasg Carreg Gwalch, 2008), pp. 322–8.

236. Though it recognises that the age of oral storytelling in the region has now drawn to a close, and that, yet again, it will only be the oldest generation now alive that retain a memory both of the stories and of the social contexts in which they were told. See Huws, *Straeon Gwerin Ardal Eryri,* pp. 122–6.

237. Perrin, *Snowdon: Story of a Welsh Mountain,* p. 58.

238. Huws, *Straeon Gwerin Ardal Eryri,* p. 174.

239. Huws, *Straeon Gwerin Ardal Eryri,* p. 172.

240. The name Arthur being Old Welsh in origin, and first attested in writing in texts such as the *Gododdin* and the Cambro-Latin *Historia Brittonum.*

241. See discussion in C. Fychan, *Galwad y Blaidd* (Talybont: Y Lolfa, 2006), pp. 63–87. Some English-language sources place the date of the wolf's extinction in Wales centuries before this, but these discussions seem unaware of the substantial Welsh-language material relating to wolves, including place-name, proverbial and documentary evidence for wolves' presence across the country throughout the Middle Ages. As Camden notes when describing Meirionydd in the late sixteenth century, the county's flocks were now able to graze in peace as there were no longer wolves to prey on them – strongly implying that wolves' banishment remained a fresh memory. George Owen paints a similar picture of Pembrokeshire in the same period, noting that 'the wolves are banished from the land'; a strange comment to make if such had taken place centuries previously.

242. The existence of the poem and the reply to it by Guto'r Glyn do not prove the existence of wolves in the mountains around the Berwyn

in the mid-fifteenth century. But in a medieval poetic tradition known for its exaggeration rather than its propensity for fiction, the encounter has a ring of truth.

243. It is also worth mentioning here the topographical tradition of *Englynion y Beddau* extending back into the ninth century, which contain a lore of place and persons similar in nature to the Irish *Dinnseanchas. Here too mountains are clearly linked to persons and events as known parts of the human landscape rather than belonging in some sense to a 'wild' other.*

244. Jenkins, *Ar Lafar Ar Goedd,* p. 141.

Rhos

245. High moor, *ffridd* and coastal zones account between them for 27 per cent of Welsh land use currently. Cf. T. H. Blackstock et al., *Habitats of Wales: a Comprehensive Field Study, 1979–1997* (Cardiff: University of Wales Press, 2010), p. 193. None of these has changed much in the past five centuries. Arable land and native woodland account for 20 per cent of current land use; although we can't be certain, both these figures would likely have been a little higher in the early sixteenth century. Meadowland, permanent pasture, settlements, rivers and lakes would around 1500 have accounted for a few per cent together giving a total of around 55 per cent and leaving almost half the land unaccounted for in this period; 'waste'. This is in line with the figure of 40 per cent of all land in Wales being open moor at the end of the eighteenth century, given by T. Jones Pierce in Joan Thirsk (ed.), *The Agrarian History of England and Wales: Vol. 4* (Cambridge: Cambridge University Press, 1967), p. 379.

246. Gwynedd County Council, 'Habitat Action Plan: Rhos' (2004).

247. In some areas of Wales the word *gwaun* is also used; for historical purposes as well as in this chapter this is to all intents and purposes entirely interchangeable in meaning with *rhos*.

248. The nearest neighbours, my grandfather recalled, were monolingual Welsh speakers who would have died in the 1960s. Many others, including elderly folk I recall, would at best have been uncomfortable speaking English.

249. The name of the cottage has been lightly modified for familial privacy.

250. Though with a tendency to being slightly drier heathland or moorland, as opposed to *gwaun/gweunydd* which often denotes wetter,

boggy moorland or indeed fens. Some of the areas I am including in this chapter will be locally known as 'gwaun'. Most points apply, mutatis mutandis.

251. T. Driver, *Hillforts of Cardigan Bay* (Hereford: Logaston Press, 2016), p. 45.

252. With temporary outfield cultivation of small strips of arable – stipulated in medieval Welsh law and still practised in the nineteenth century in parts of north Wales as evidenced by Hugh Evans's recollections in *Cwm Eithin* – also contributing significantly to the agrarian economy. See Joan Thirsk and Stuart Piggott (eds), *The Agrarian History of England and Wales: Vol. 1* (Cambridge: Cambridge University Press, 2011), pp. 351–9.

253. Rh. Comeau, *Land, People and Power in Early Medieval Wales: The Cantref of Cemais in Comparative Perspective* (Oxford: BAR Publishing, 2020), p. 76; see also Rh. Parry, *Cerdded y Caeau* (Talybont: Y Lolfa, 2022), p. 171.

254. D. Thomas, *Cau'r Tiroedd Comin* (Lerpwl: Gwasg y Brython, 1952), p. 10.

255. Sixteenth- and seventeenth-century accounts suggest that at this period large numbers of deer roamed freely in Snowdonia; *Agrarian History of England and Wales: Vol. 4*, p. 139.

256. *Geiriadur Prifysgol Cymru.*

257. Gwynn ap Gwilym and Alan Llwyd (eds), *Blodeugerdd Barddas o Farddoniaeth Gymraeg yr Ugeinfed Ganrif* (Abertawe: Barddas, 1987), p. 268. This celebrated and long *awdl* (similar to an ode but in strict metre) won the National Eisteddfod chair in 1946. This poem, so normal from within the Welsh tradition, is remarkable when seen from the perspective that it not only in the 1940s gives the earth a voice, but in lyrical language celebrates her (deliberately feminine) invitation to humanity to dwell within her alongside the bullrushes, birds, trees and heather of the *ffridd*.

258. D. W. Howell, *The Rural Poor in Eighteenth-century Wales* (Cardiff: University of Wales Press, 2000), p. 8.

259. Arising, ultimately, in inherited understandings of Welsh law which in practice continued to be the customary method by which patterns of land use were governed in many rural communities until the late eighteenth and early nineteenth century. As T. Jones Pierce notes, until the mid-seventeenth century, 'it was insistently asserted in

the face of repeated threats from manorial lords that the wastes were not "commons" but *cyd-tir* (joint land), the ownership of which was vested in *cyd-tirogion* who ... were entitled to enclose and improve them without licence and at their will and pleasure': *The Agrarian History of England and Wales: Vol. 4*, p. 380.

260. Immortalised of course in verse:

'Fe chwythwyd yr utgorn / ar ben yr Hebrysg fawr
Daeth mwy na mil o ddynion / ynghyd mewn hanner awr'

261. E. Jones, *The War of the Little Englishman* (Talybont: Y Lolfa, 2007), p. 39.

262. There is of course nuance here: though freehold was always an aspiration, the cottagers were trying to defend on Mynydd Bach the right to enclose common land (with community approval) to create officially *tenanted* smallholdings. There was of course a separate but related set of battles known during the nineteenth century as the 'Welsh land question', which related to a greater extent to the relations between tenant farmers and (mostly) absentee landlords. This was exacerbated – and given a strongly different twist to land battles in England – by the longstanding cultural assumption in Wales that much of what authorities called 'common land' was *cytir* and available for community use by rights established in Welsh law. Cf. P. S. Barnwell and B. K. Roberts (eds), *Britons, Saxons and Scandinavians: The Historical Geography of Glanville R. J. Jones* (Turnhout: Brepols Publishers, 2011), p. 260.

263. On a very small scale, on private land where peat is already exposed.

264. From 5,795 hectares to 1,734 hectares, out of a total surveyed area of 8,196 hectares. These figures demonstrate eloquently the key place *rhos* areas had almost within living memory within the farmed landscape; in 1922, the vast majority of the land in Llŷn was *rhos* of one form or another.

Figures from Blackstock et al., *Habitats of Wales*, p. 14.

265. The OS map still shows the moorland expanse of Crugelwin as common land, in a shallow reflection of the past.

266. Notwithstanding, of course, the fact that every single *rhos* will have been different with underlying geology, aspect, rainfall, annual temperature, wetness and land use over time all playing a part. But

just as it can be meaningful to talk of pubs in the round, even though each has its own character and history, so *rhos* areas have important characteristics in common across the written record. I am not saying that everything on the below list would have been true of every *rhos* at all times, or even of every *rhos* at some time; but together they form a kaleidoscopic image of things that the record suggests were true of a broad swathe of *rhos* areas when viewed across time.

267. Thomas Dineley (1684), quoted in D. Owen, *A Wilder Wales* (Cardigan: Parthian, 2017), p. 60.

268. Lauren Marrinan and Tim Rich, *101 Rare Plants of Wales* (Llanelli: Graffeg, 2019), p. 25.

269. Howell, *The Rural Poor in Eighteenth-century Wales*, p. 35.

270. See *https://botanykaren.net/2020/08/10/enchanting-harebells-at-risk/* (accessed 9 November 2023). Restored grazing gave rise to a reduced incidence of harebells, meaning the results of this are indicative rather than conclusive; but when combined with the historical record we hold for Welsh agriculture, we can confidently surmise that very few *rhos* areas would have had even a year without some sort of grazing up to the twentieth century.

271. Sir Leonard Twiston Davies and Averyl Edwards, *Welsh Life in the Eighteenth Century* (London: Empire Press, 1939), p. 17.

272. Glanffrwd, *Llanwynno* (Caerdydd: University of Wales Press, 1949), p. 156.

273. B. Macdonald, *Cornerstones* (London: Bloomsbury, 2002), p. 133.

274. See *www.gov.wales/sites/default/files/publications/2018-01/common-land-blorenge-common-report.pdf* (accessed 9 November 2023).

275. See *https://cdnsciencepub.com/doi/abs/10.1139/b95-010* (accessed 9 November 2023).

276. O. Rackham, *Ancient Woodlands of South-east Wales* (Dorset: Little Toller, 2022), p. 32.

277. See *https://www.rewildingbritain.org.uk/blog/natural-regeneration-its-key-role-in-reviving-britains-woodlands* (accessed 21 April 2023).

278. For some, this could be termed a form of 'agricultural rewilding'. The key point is that most people in these areas are much more sympathetic to the fact that it does represent cultural landscape recovery that goes *with* the grain of how the land has been used and viewed in this part of the world, and that is built not on the human

introduction of large predators but rather on the ways that familiar domesticated species in the right mix can allow a dizzying profusion of insects, flowers and birdlife to flourish as they used to until only seventy years ago.

279. Colin Thomas, 'Rural Society, Settlement, Economy and Landscapes', in Beverley Smith (ed.), *History of Merioneth II* (Cardiff: University of Wales Press, 2001), p. 207.

280. See *https://forestry.gov.scot/woodland-grazing-toolbox/grazing-management/grazing-regime/selecting-species-and-breed* (accessed 9 November 2023).

281. R. Elfyn Hughes et al., 'Studies in Sheep Population and Environment in the Mountains of North-West Wales I. The Status of the Sheep in the Mountains of North Wales Since Mediaeval Times', *Journal of Applied Ecology*, 10/1 (1973), 118, *https://doi.org/10.2307/2404720*; *https://farmwildlife.info/how-to-do-it/existing-wildlife-habitats/mountain-hill-and-moorland/* (accessed 14 January 2023).

282. See *https://statswales.gov.wales/Catalogue/Agriculture/Agricultural-Survey/Area-Survey-Results/total-livestock-in-wales-by-area* (accessed 9 November 2023).

283. See *https://www.bto.org/our-science/publications/conservation-advice-notes/managing-scrub-nightingales* (accessed 9 November 2023).

284. See *https://knepp.co.uk/wp-content/uploads/2022/01/Does-Rewilding-Benefit-Dung-Beetle-Biodiversity-Sarah-Brompton.pdf* (accessed 21 April 2023); it's in the nature of these things that you couldn't predict with certainty precisely what species would recolonise the land and which others that would in turn provide food and/or habitat for. But the increase in species richness is as near guaranteed under these conditions as anything could be.

Perllan

285. Also suggested inter alia by archaeological remains found at Peterstone, which according to Gwent Archaeological Trust 'as a surviving example of large-scale Roman reclamation, it is certainly unique in Wales, if not north-west Europe'. For such ditches to survive on a landscape scale, some maintenance and use is likely to have continued between the Romans' departure and later Norman works. See *http://www.ggat.org.uk/cadw/historic_landscape/Gwent%20Levels/English/GL_17.htm* (accessed 9

November 2023).

286. This is easily as long as the oldest Dutch polders, established in the twelfth century AD.

287. Paul F. Whitehead, 'Gwent Levels Traditional Orchard Invertebrate Study 2019–2021', Report for Gwent Wildlife Trust (2022).

288. Whitehead, 'Gwent Levels Traditional Orchard Invertebrate Study 2019–2021', 14.

289. Whitehead, *'Gwent Levels Traditional Orchard Invertebrate Study 2019–2021'*, 14.

290. Veteran tree at Porton Cottage with ceramic sherds dating to 1830 incorporated into rootplate, indicating planting around then, which is consistent with broader indications of resurgence of orchard planting on the levels around then. Whitehead, 'Gwent Levels Traditional Orchard Invertebrate Study 2019–2021', 7.

291. See *http://www.bernwodeplants.co.uk/oldesttree3.htm* (accessed 9 November 2023).

292. A feature of many Welsh, Irish and Cornish varieties. But whether this feature could be useful in fruit production is as yet unknown.

293. E.g. *Ptinella taylorae* and the *mycophilous cecidomyidd* fly.

294. As evidenced by countless estate and tithe maps noting orchard sites' land use as 'pasture'; the expert advice in this case being mid-twentieth-century edicts to grub up the trees to obtain greater productivity from pasture land.

295. Whitehead, 'Gwent Levels Traditional Orchard Invertebrate Study 2019–2021', 29.

296. From *County Observer and Mons Advertiser,* 13 February 1869.

297. A similar pattern can be seen at The Willows, where part of the current site under orchard was common land in the 1840s, but bounded to the south by an extensive orchard area, most of which is now lost. The habitat has shifted a little over time, but crucially, hasn't disappeared.

298. Lowri Watkins, 'Gwent Levels Historic Orchards: summary of mapping', Gwent Wildlife Trust.

299. From *Brecon County Times*, Friday, 14 August 1869.

300. The People's Trust for Endangered Species' 2013 report with NRW notes a 94 per cent reduction in orchard area in Wales between 1958 and 1994 and finds at the date of their survey a total of 653 hectares of traditional orchard. Cf. S. Oram, L. Alexander and E.

Sadler, 'Traditional Orchard Habitat Inventory of Wales', Natural
Resources Wales Evidence Report No. 18 (2014).

301. C. Graves, *Apples of Wales* (Llanrwst: Gwasg Carreg Gwalch,
2018), p. 51. It is worth noting that this is substantially larger than the
acreage in Scotland at this time.

302. Graves, *Apples of Wales*, p. 47.

303. See discussion of many other medieval poets referencing orchards
in the landscape in Graves, *Apples of Wales*, pp. 20–35.

304. See discussion and map in Graves, *Apples of Wales*, pp. 58–61.

305. This particular quote is from Annette Yates's *A Taste of Wales* (Ohio:
Lorenz Books, 2015), though similar dismissals are found widely in the
historic and culinary literature from the last few decades.

306. See my earlier book, *Apples of Wales*, for a discussion of this.

307. The varieties have been christened Tywysog Tredomen, Gellygen
Godidog, Trysor Tredomen and Tredomen Twins.

308. Due to a lack of regulation, in the UK, unlike in most European
countries, you can make a perry or cider stuffed full of sugar, flavourings
and other additives and still call it 'cider'. As a result, what passes for
cider or perry in most shops or supermarkets is a far cry in quality from
a drink like Andrew's.

309. One of those varieties of apple widely regarded as having the most
rounded and full flavour; a connoisseur's apple.

310. In Middle House Farm Phil was very proud of the doorway from
the living room to the kitchen. At some time in the past a barrel-shaped
bulge had been carved into the door frame to allow a large cask of cider
or perry to be carried through.

311. J. Thirsk, *Alternative Agriculture* (Oxford: Oxford University
Press, (1997), pp. 38–42.

312. Welsh cider and apple culture had become a thing out of mind
by the 2010s. When I and a lovely team of volunteers at the Botanic
Gardens of Wales were researching for the book *Apples of Wales* from
2010–17, I approached the now deceased foremost Welsh historian to
seek guidance in the research. His response to the question on the place
of apples and orchards in Welsh history was that he had never come
across a single reference to either. *Apples of Wales* demonstrates just how
much he and others had missed; but I see now that we were ourselves,
in a similar way, blind to pears while doing this work – assuming that
there could be no significant history of pear cultivation in Wales. Della

Hooke, *Trees in Anglo-Saxon England: Literature, Lore and Landscape* (Woodbridge: The Boydell Press, 2010), p. 168.

313. Strikingly, the pre-1000 AD Llandaff charters from south-east Wales record 27 pear trees as boundary features – as many as any region of England at the time.

314. Wade Muggleton, *The Worcester Black Pear* (The Three Counties Orchard Project, 2018), p. 7. See also the references to pears in the 1632/3 lists of John Jones, Gellilyfdy.

315. *Geiriadur Prifysgol Cymru*, 'perai'.

316. The orchard is present on the 1850 tithe map for the parish in question, when the field is noted as being, as now, 'orchard + pasture'. No ecological survey has ever been carried out here, but all the obvious indicators are present – and confirmed by the family.

317. *Nature*, 6 April 2023, 9.

318. D. Lefebvre et al., 'Assessing the carbon capture potential of a reforestation project', *Sci Rep*, 11/19907 (2021), *www.nature.com/articles/s41598-021-99395-6* (accessed 9 November 2023).

319. Precipitation levels seem to be one limiting growth factor, with its native range receiving 1.1 metres precipitation annually – comparable to levels in Cardiff or Swansea.

320. See *https://assets.publishing.service.gov.uk/government/uploads/system/uploads/attachment_data/file/1075311/sofies-biochar-network-project.pdf* (accessed 16 May 2023).

321. M. J. Smart and R. A. Winnall, 'The biodiversity of three traditional orchards within the Wyre Forest SSSI in Worcestershire: a survey by the Wyre Forest Study Group', English Nature *Research Reports,* 707 (2006).

322. See discussion of this in my first book, *Apples of Wales*, pp. 19–67.

323. Those 653 hectares are spread across 4,687 orchard sites, and only a little over a half of them were assessed in 2013 as being in good condition. Cf. Oram, Alexander and Sadler, 'Traditional Orchard Habitat Inventory of Wales'.

Epilogue

324. pH level of 4.8 to be precise – only slightly less sour than buttermilk.

325. Nitrogen, the other essential element for healthy plant growth, is in comparison easier to return to the soil than P and K thanks to the

ability of many leguminous plants (including beans, peas and many used as green manures) to fix nitrogen that exists abundantly in the air in the soil via their roots. The other elements, however, need to either be recycled – or mined in an extractive and fossil-fuel intensive process. Ultimately, within a multi-generational timescale all phosphorus needs to be recycled as minable reserves will peak and decline at some point between 2030 and 2250. The discrepancy is due in large part to the credibility different agencies accord to the Moroccan government's estimates of its reserves. If anywhere near the earlier date, this is a significant threat to current high-input systems of food production.

326. In this case Highland Cattle, though as Nathan says, they could very easily have gone with Welsh Blacks or another old, hardy breed.

327. As well as somewhere approaching the maximum nutritional yield this land could even theoretically produce – and certainly more than it would produce under conventional agriculture.

328. Again, *traduttore traditore*. Debates are conducted using terms within language, and those terms point to a myriad of connotations and reference points that inevitably differ significantly between languages. That is why a debate on secularism in English and laïcité in French will both start with different underlying assumptions and end in sometimes radically different places, even if ostensibly the very same question is asked. In the same way, to contend that Welsh culture is indigenous is at best problematic given the range of meanings of that word in English. To contend that it is not *brodorol* however would be nonsensical.

329. Clearly not exclusively, even within a Welsh context. Non-Welsh-speaking Welsh culture is an interesting phenomenon in its own right, influenced to varying degrees and in different ways both by wider anglophone culture, local tradition and the small, noisy and porous Welsh-language culture with which it has always shared a small country.

330. For a celebrated instance of the former, look no further than T. H. Parry-Williams's celebrated poem 'Hon', found everywhere from GCSE syllabuses to tea towels and which climaxes with the iconic line 'Ni allaf ddianc rhag hon' ('[Try as I might] ... from this [land] I cannot [in my spirit] escape').

331. D. Llywelyn, *Sacred Place, Chosen People* (Cardiff: University of Wales Press, 1999), p. 46.

332. Llywelyn, *Sacred Place, Chosen People*, p. x.

333. L. Jones, *Losing Eden: Why Our Minds Need the Wild* (London: Penguin, 2020), p. 197. NB that I am not suggesting that the Western act of listening to indigenous voices should include a Welsh voice. We are firmly on the Western side of that divide, and bear clear shared responsibility for Empire, among other misadventures. But we do occupy a particular and complex niche on that Western side, that allows certain insights into indigenous experiences in the global south, not least in the experience of minoritised language communities.

334. See, among others, discussion in Emyr Humphreys, *The Taliesin Tradition* (Bridgend: Seren Books, 1989) and Rebecca Thomas, *History and Identity in Early Medieval Wales* (Martlesham: Boydell and Brewer, 2022). A salient point in all these discussions is that until the early modern period, a cornerstone of that assertion was the irredentist memory of a claim to the whole island of Britain. This may still have salience within Welsh-speaking culture as evidenced by the angered response to changing the name of the Gorsedd from Gorsedd Beirdd Ynys Prydain (The Throne of the Bards of the Island of Britain) to Gorsedd Cymru (The Throne of Wales). The symbolism is not to be missed here.

335. 'Yma o Hyd' ('Still Here'). The 'here' in that phrase has a clear and unambiguous referent in the physical location of Wales.

336. The fact that the same argument can also be made of regions of England – Cumbria, Cornwall – distant from Westminster in more senses than one, detracts nothing from its salience. Note that this argument sits entirely comfortably with the argument advanced throughout *Welsh Food Stories* that a rounded understanding of Wales's food history can only be gained within the context of the relative stability and benign neglect that Wales has enjoyed for many centuries under Westminster rule. For Wales, do not see England; but do not see Ireland either.

337. See Mark Williams, 'Magic and Marvels', in G. Evans and H. Fulton (eds), *The Cambridge History of Welsh Literature* (Cambridge: Cambridge University Press, 2019), pp. 52–68, for an insightful discussion of this phenomenon.

338. A common definition of this as appears frequently in the associated literature runs: 'Indigenous People view both themselves and nature as part of an extended ecological family that shares ancestry and origins.' Taken from Johnson, *Pen and Plough: 20th Century Poets and Bards of*

Ceredigion (Llanrwst: Carreg Gwalch, 2016); Lyla June, *Architects of Abundance: Indigenous Regenerative Food and Land Management Systems and the Excavation of Hidden History* (Fairbanks: University of Alaska, 2022), p. 10.

339. Johnson, *Pen and Plough,* p. 42.

340. Some may raise eyebrows, but it is those who have only lived within one language and culture who are unable to see how very culturally mediated their own worldview is. This is not noted by way of anything but a desire to caution the reader to take stock before reacting to a world that may make them uncomfortable; they may well not understand all that is at play.

341. The imbalance of Welsh poetry until very recent times towards the male voice and perspective should, however, at this point be both noticed and bemoaned. Not that it has been monolithically so; see Gwerful Mechain, Ann Griffiths or Cranogwen for three pre-twentieth-century Welsh poetic female geniuses.

342. Tegwyn Pughe Jones, 'Ymddiheuriad', in Rhys Dafis (ed.), *Inc yr Awen a'r Cread* (Llandysul: Cyhoeddiadau Barddas, 2022), p. 139.

343. Although wild apples are counted as native to here – as are wild pears and sloes – the much larger domestic apples and pears originate in modern Kazakhstan while domesticated plums have come here via human trade routes from the Caucasus. Similarly, the ecospace that a hay meadow most closely resembles exists in the 'wild' is a continental steppe context. Nothing closely resembling either of these would exist in this landscape without human intervention.

344. In a truly rewilded landscape, many of these ecospaces might conceivably exist, but in almost all of Wales a wood-pasture structure would likely dominate from valley floor to mountaintop, with blurred rather than distinct ecospaces within that.

345. Such as chickens bred to the point where their bones cannot support their body weight, or cows destined from birth to suffer chronic and painful mastitis.

346. Is the theological category of original sin an appropriate lens through which to understand this? In my opinion, it undoubtedly is. 'Forgive them,' says Jesus, 'for they know not what they do' (Luke 23:34).

347. That this trend started under the British Empire and was accelerated by coal power is an important antecedent to its full twentieth-century

realisation.

348. I am indebted to Chris Smaje for this metaphor.

349. There is of course no one cut-off date at which this changes: it was a gradual process. But viewed from all sorts of angles, there were enormous and thoroughgoing changes in Welsh agriculture between roughly 1945 and 1965 that were driven by precisely the dynamics I am outlining here.

350. There are ostensibly serious suggestions at play, widely reported in the media, that would imply an ability to further transcend the basics of nutrient cycling by means of, among other things, lab-raised meats and precision fermentation. The desirability of these scenarios aside (given corporate capture of the technology), their relevance at scale is downplayed by basic energetics of their protein production as a function of solar energy conversion as compared to, say, soya. See C. Smaje, *Saying NO to a Farm-Free Future* (London: Chelsea Green, 2023) for a full discussion of this. Beyond this, the necessity of grain and veg production is in no way negated by a full-scale deployment of factory-raised meats, nor is the essential place of native breeds of livestock in semi- or fully rewilded landscapes. That picture, arguably, comes closer to 'something more akin to a traditional mixed-farming model' than it does to current fossil-fuel driven realities.

351. Food, Farming & Countryside Commission, 'Farming for Change' (2021). Available at *https://ffcc.co.uk/publications/farmingforchangereport* (accessed 9 November 2023).

352. It is probably worth stating at this point that suggesting a measure of desirability in some aspects of the status quo ante in land use as viewed from a vantage point *c.*1950 is in no way intended to imply the desirability of other aspects of the political economy in that period. Those should be debated on their own merits.

353. Ultimately, left unchecked by human intervention or predation, those herbivore populations will grow to levels where they graze the trees out of the landscape. One way of stopping that is by human management (e.g. targeted culling) of the herbivore population; in effect making their meat into a very, very low intervention farmed product.

354. The area necessary for this in northern Europe would likely be in the hundreds of square kilometres, with the Estonian island of Saaremaa, 1,000 square miles in size, supporting only two wolf packs.

This is the equivalent of an area one-eighth the size of Wales, or the whole of Carmarthenshire. Cf. W. Jędrzejewski et al., 'Territory Size of Wolves Canis Lupus: Linking Local (Białowieża Primeval Forest, Poland) and Holarctic-Scale Patterns', *Ecography*, 30/1 (2007), 66–76, *http://www.jstor.org/stable/30243198*; and also L. Plumer et al. 'Wolves Recolonizing Islands: Genetic Consequences and Implications for Conservation and Management', *PLOS ONE*, 11/7 (2016), *https://doi.org/10.1371/journal.pone.0158911* (accessed 27 May 2023).

355. As he went on to explain, 'historically, there were more active graziers on the mountain and more mixed farming, with heavier stock, whereas the ecology now is being governed by the sheep numbers to its detriment. My goal for Carningli is to see more natural regeneration and natural grazing. There is also now a significant issue with succession on Carningli, as is a problem with other Commons, putting the future of their sustainable management in question.'

356. Barnaby Caven, Bernhard Redl and T. Bechtold, 'An investigation into the possible antibacterial properties of wool fibers', *Textile Research Journal*, 89/4 (2018), *doi: 10.1177/0040517517750645*.

357. See *https://www.nffn.org.uk/new-report-finds-up-to-45-increase-in-commercial-return-for-nature-friendly-farms/* (accessed 9 November 2023).

358. Most of the above measures and outcomes could theoretically be worked into Welsh Government policy with current powers. But in truth, further powers are needed – particularly powers to tax the fossil-fuelled derived agricultural inputs marketed by shameless global corporations, thereby strongly disincentivising their use by farmers in Wales. Similarly, investment in land for non-productive purposes (e.g. only for the carbon credits or as an investment) should be highly taxed, thereby encouraging the maintenance and establishment of nature-friendly, land-based enterprises across the country at the expense of absentee landlords of any sort – the bane of Welsh history.

359. As some, from Stewart Brand to George Monbiot, are wont to do.

360. Some of this land – everything underneath what used to be roughly the 12m contour above old sea level – has now been rewilded in the sense that it is (summer-grazed) saltmarsh. One of the current hot land-use debates is around whether we should be using land like this, of which there are increasingly many thousands of acres, for rice cultivation. Feed people vs room for nature. *Plus ça change*, as the French still say.

361. See, for instance, discussion in Evelyne Leterme, *La biodiversité, amie du verger* (Arles: Rouergue, 2014).

362. These tree crops are many and varied, but a particularly important one these days is walnuts (and other heartnuts) that have provided an increasingly important part of the protein and calorific mix locally.

Acknowledgements

I am enormously indebted to a great number of people for this book. The book is in truth an extended essay and during most of its writing bore the tongue-in-cheek mock eighteenth-century title: 'An inquiry into Tir: namely the Cultural History of The Welsh Landscape, how it came to be and how understanding it could shape our Future'. That slightly rambling tone still befits the book in my opinion a little better than its current concise sobriquet: I have tried here to span a large number of disciplines – ecology, history, archaeology, literature, farming, folklore studies – to paint a picture of something which in part is incontrovertibly true when expressed in Welsh but can risk sounding painfully fanciful in English. And to the extent that I have at all succeeded, that has been due to the work of the experts in all these fields, whose insights, discoveries, knowledge and scholarship I have tried to build on. To the extent that I have failed, the responsibility lies entirely with me. I look forward to reading responses to the work: taking a broad view of Wales through the lenses of all these disciplines, what important strands have I neglected?

This book has almost entirely been written on evenings and weekends over the course of an intense eighteen months for our family. I have been blessed and aided enormously by the resources available online through the National Library of Wales (tithe maps, digitised newspapers and journals from 1800 to 2007, among other things) and most particularly by the staff and stellar resources at Carmarthen Library (special mention and thanks go to Catrin for sourcing many important volumes through inter-library loans). It is surely a mark of civilisation when an unqualified member of the public without access to university resources can attempt a project as stupidly ambitious as this with the aid of a public library.

So, to the current assiduous shapers, guardians and excavators of the Welsh landscape and its living cultures, so many of whom helped with the making of this work: *Diolch o galon.* Diolch yn arbennig i: David Austin a Rhiannon Comeau am eu manwl-gywirdeb; i Doug Lloyd a Sam Robinson am brynhawniau cyfoethog mewn caeau; i Alun am letygarwch yn nhraddodiad gorau ei fro; ac felly hefyd i deulu diwylliedig a hael yr Hengwrt; i Ray Woods am athrylith; i Meic B. am sgyrsiau difyr ar y mynydd, ac i Nigel Beidas am gyfoeth ei fro yntau; i Tegwen a Meinir am rannu atgofion; i Erwyd am sgyrsiau cyfoethog a llafnau pladur; i Dion am arweiniad i'r uchelfannau; i Andrew Jenkins am hawddgarwch; i deulu Maesydderwen am groesawu dieithryn; i Beccy a Linda am brynhawn cofiadwy o afaledig; i Nathan ac Alicia am domatos yn ffrwyth llafur ysbrydoledig; i Richard Edwards, Debbi Mercer a Stephen Jenkins am eu pellwelediad.

Many thanks too for help and advice from Steve Oram and Ainsleigh Rice who have done much in public service in their work for the conservation of fruit varieties that has yet to receive the general recognition it deserves. Diolch hefyd i Duncan Brown, Twm Elias, Christine a Wyn James, Gwyn a Joyce Morgan, Ruth Tudor, Bonni a Vivian, a Seimon Brooks am sgyrsiau difyr a defnyddiol dros ben wrth i mi geisio mynd â'r maen i'r wal. Diolch arbennig i Andrew Morton am anogaeth a phrawfddarllen diwyd; felly hefyd i Robyn Lovelock am ei haelioni ac i Hazel Thomas am sawl cymorth a chefnogaeth gyson. Yn fwy na hynny, diolch wir am bob cyfeillgarwch ac anogaeth.

Diolch i Mam yn arbennig am brawfddarllen yn ddwys ac ar fyr-rybudd, ac i Sarah yn arbennig iawn am hir-amynedd ac anogaeth ddiflino.

Finally, warm thanks indeed to a trio of wonderful editors for their wit, patience and well-honed skills in taking a rambling work and shaping it into a more rounded book by far: the indefatigable Amy Feldman, the gracious Abbie Headon and the warm and ever incisive Clare Grist Taylor. Sincere thanks to you all, as well as the wider wonderful team at Calon and UWP for bringing this into being.

I have tried in this book, as in *Welsh Food Stories* and indeed *Apples of Wales* to bring to an English-speaking audience a range of insights drawn from the extensive, endlessly rich written archive of work in Welsh, that encompasses everything from literature and theology to landscape studies, cultural studies, local history, political theory and more. These exist within a rich and textured cultural world with innumerable shared reference points, from music to events and proverbs, which together form a *diwylliant*. That *culture* knows of what part of earth it is formed, and has both the grave responsibility and privilege of handing on to coming generations 'yr haul i'w plant, o'u plyg'.

Bibliography

Adams, M., *The First Kingdom: Britain in the Age of Arthur* (London: Apollo, 2021)

Alexander, M., *Skomer Island* (Talybont: Y Lolfa, 2021)

ap Dafydd, Myrddin, *Llên Gwerin T. Llew Jones* (Llanrwst: Carreg Gwalch, 2010)

ap Gwilym, Gwynn, and Llwyd, Alan (eds), *Blodeugerdd Barddas o Farddoniaeth Gymraeg yr Ugeinfed Ganrif* (Abertawe: Barddas, 1987)

Austin, D., *Ystrad Fflur: Hanes a Thirwedd Mynachlog Gymreig* (Strata Florida: Ymddiriedolaeth Ystrad Fflur, 2022)

Barnwell, P. S., and Roberts, B. K. (eds), *Britons, Saxons and Scandinavians: The Historical Geography of Glanville R. J. Jones* (Turnhout: Brepols Publishers, 2011)

Benbough-Jackson, M., *Cardiganshire: The Concise History* (Cardiff: University of Wales Press, 2007)

Bevan, Gareth A. et al. (eds), *Ar Drywydd Enwau Lleoedd* (Talybont: Y Lolfa, 2021)

Bharatdwaj, K., *Physical Geography: Landscape Appreciations* (New Delhi: Discovery Publishing House, 2009)

Booth, T. et al., 'Tales from the Supplementary Information: Ancestry Change in Chalcolithic–Early Bronze Age Britain Was Gradual with Varied Kinship Organization', *Cambridge Archaeological Journal*, 31/3 (2021), 379–400, doi: 10.1017/S0959774321000019

Brace, Selina et al., 'Ancient genomes indicate population replacement in Early Neolithic Britain', *Nature Ecology and Evolution*, 3/5 (15 April 2019), 765–71

Brooks, S., *Hanes Cymry* (Caerdydd: University of Wales Press, 2021)

Brown, D., *Tro ar Fyd* (Llanrwst: Carreg Gwalch, 2020)

Caven, Barnaby, Redl, Bernhard, and Bechtold, T., 'An investigation into the possible antibacterial properties of wool fibers', *Textile Research Journal*, 89/4 (2018), doi: 10.1177/0040517517750645

Chambers, F. M. et al., 'Recent vegetation history of Drygarn Fawr (Elenydd SSSI), Cambrian Mountains, Wales: implications for conservation management of degraded blanket mires', *Biodiversity and Conservation*, 16 (2007), 2821–46, https://doi.org/10.1007/s10531-007-9169-3 (accessed 9 November 2023)

Clidro, Robin, *Welsh Poems: Sixth Century to 1600*, trans. Gwyn Williams (Berkeley: University of California Press, 1974)

Comeau, Rh., 'Crop processing and early medieval settlement: the evidence for Bayvil, Pembrokeshire', *Medieval Settlement Research*, 36 (2021), 61–7

Comeau, Rh., 'From Tref to Tithe: Identifying Settlement Patterns in a North Pembrokeshire Parish', *Landscape History*, 33/1 (2012), 29-44, *doi: 10.1080/01433768.2012.671033*

Comeau, Rh., 'Cytir and Crosses: the archaeological landscape of the parish of Dinas', *Archaeologia Cambrensis*, 158 (2009), 225–53

Comeau, Rh., *Land, People and Power in Early Medieval Wales: The cantref of Cemais in comparative perspective* (Oxford: BAR Publishing, 2020)

Comeau, Rh., and Seaman, A. (eds), *Living off the Land* (Oxford: Oxbow Books, 2019)

Comeau, Rh., and Silvester, B., 'Transhumant settlement in medieval Wales: the *hafod*', in Piers Dixon and Claudia Theune (eds), *Seasonal Settlement in the Medieval and Early Modern Countryside* (Leiden: Sidestone Press, 2021)

Condry, W., *The Natural History of Wales* (London: Collins, 1981)

Condry, W., *Woodlands* (London: Collins, 1974)

Conway, G., and Fuller, R., 'Multi-scale relationships between vegetation pattern and breeding birds in the upland margins (ffridd) of North Wales', *BTO Research Report No. 566* (2010)

Cummings, Vicki, and Whittle, Alasdair, *Places of Special Virtue: Megaliths in the Neolithic Landscapes of Wales* (Oxford: Oxbow Books, 2004), pp. 70–7, https://doi.org/10.2307/j.ctvh1djh5 (accessed 8 May 2023)

Dafis, Rhys (ed.), *Inc yr Awen a'r Cread* (Llandysul: Cyhoeddiadau Barddas, 2022)

Davies, Sir Leonard Twiston, and Edwards, Averyl, *Welsh Life in the Eighteenth Century* (London: Empire Press, 1939)

Davies, M., 'Rhosili Open Field and Related South Wales Field Patterns, *Agricultural History Review*, 4/2 (1956)

Davies, P., *Yr Efrydd o Lyn Cynon a Cherddi Eraill* (Llandybïe: Llyfrau'r Dryw, 1978)

Diserens, T. A. et al., 'A dispersing bear in Białowieża Forest raises important ecological and conservation management questions for the central European lowlands', *Global Ecology and Conservation*, 23 (2020), *https://www.sciencedirect.com/science/article/pii/S2351989420307319* (accessed 9 November 2023)

Dodgshon, R. A., 'Early Society and Economy', in J. L. Davies and D. P. Kirby (eds), *Cardiganshire County History, Volume 1* (Cardiff: University of Wales Press, 2001)

Driver, T., *The Hillforts of Cardigan Bay* (Hereford: Logaston Press, 2016)

Dunne, Terry, 'Transhumance and the Making of Ireland's Uplands', *Estudios Irlandeses*, 17 (2022), 219–22

Edwards, Huw M., *Dafydd ap Gwilym: Influences and Analogues* (Oxford: Clarendon, 1996)

Edwards, Hywel Teifi (ed.), *Cwm Cynon* (Llandysul: Gomer, 1997)

Evans, D. F. and Roberts, S. E., 'Y Bardd', *dafyddapgwilym.net* (accessed 12 January 2022)

Evans, G., and Fulton, H. (eds), *The Cambridge History of Welsh Literature* (Cambridge: Cambridge University Press, 2019)

Evans, H., *Cwm Eithin* (Lerpwl: Gwasg y Brython, 1943)

Fromentin, J. -M. et al. (eds), 'Summary for policymakers of the thematic assessment of the sustainable use of wild species of the Inter-governmental Science-Policy Platform on Biodiversity and Ecosystem Services', IPBES secretariat (2022), *www.zenodo.org/records/7411847* (accessed 9 November 2023)

Fuller, R. J. et al., 'Human activities and biodiversity opportunities in pre-industrial cultural landscapes: relevance to conservation', *Journal of Applied Ecology*, 54 (2017), 459–69, *https://doi.org/10.1111/1365-2664.12762* (accessed 9 November 2023)

Fulton, H., *Dafydd ap Gwilym and the European Context* (Cardiff: University of Wales Press, 1989)

Fychan, C., *Galwad y Blaidd* (Talybont: Y Lolfa, 2006)

Gate, N., and Macdonald, B., *Orchard: A Year in England's Eden* (London: William Collins, 2020)

Gerald of Wales, *The Journey Through Wales* (London: Penguin, 1978)

Glanffrwd, *Llanwynno* (Caerdydd: University of Wales Press, 1949)

Goulson, D., *Silent Earth: Averting the Insect Apocalypse* (London: Penguin, 2021)

Graves, C., *Welsh Food Stories* (Cardiff: Calon, 2022)

Graves, C., *Apples of Wales* (Llanrwst: Gwasg Carreg Gwalch, 2018)

Griffith, G. W. et al., 'The international conservation importance of Welsh "waxcap" grasslands', *Mycosphere,* 4 (2013), 969–84, *doi: 10.5943/ mycosphere/4/5/10*

Gruffydd, Llyr D., and Gwyndaf, R., *Llyfr Rhedyn ei Daid* (Caernarfon: Gwasg Dwyfor, 1987)

Hartnup, R., *Gold Under Bracken* (Talybont: Y Lolfa, 2011)

Hill, B., and Bradley, D., 'What Motivates Households with Very Small and Small Farms in Wales?', *EuroChoices,* 21 (2022), 58–65, *www.doi. org/10.1111/1746-692X.12344* (accessed 9 November 2023)

Hill, M. O., and Jones, E. W., 'Vegetation Changes Resulting from Afforestation of Rough Grazings in Caeo Forest, South Wales', *Journal of Ecology,* 66/2 (1978), 433–56, *https://doi.org/10.2307/2259145* (accessed 14 January 2023)

Hodder, K. H. et al., 'Can the mid-Holocene provide suitable models for rewilding the landscape in Britain?', *British Wildlife,* 20/5 (2009), 4–15

Hooke, Della, *Trees in Anglo-Saxon England: Literature, Lore and Landscape* (Woodbridge: The Boydell Press, 2010)

Howell, D. W., *The Rural Poor in Eighteenth-century Wales* (Cardiff: University of Wales Press, 2000)

Howell, D. W., *Land and People in Nineteenth-century Wales* (London: Routledge, 1977)

Hughes, R. Elfyn et al., 'Studies in Sheep Population and Environment in the Mountains of North-West Wales I. The Status of the Sheep in the Mountains of North Wales Since Mediaeval Times', *Journal of Applied Ecology,* 10/1 (1973), 113–32, *https://doi.org/10.2307/2404720* (accessed 14 January 2023)

Humphreys, E., *The Taliesin Tradition* (Bridgend: Seren, 1989)

Huws, John Owen, *Straeon Gwerin Ardal Eryri* (Llanrwst: Carreg Gwalch, 2008)

Ifans, D., and Ifans, Rh., *Y Mabinogion* (Llandysul: Gomer, 2007)

James, E. Wyn, and Jones, Tecwyn Vaughan (eds), *Gwerin Gwlad* (Llanrwst: Carreg Gwalch, 2008)

Jenkins, D., *Ar Lafar, Ar Goedd* (Aberystwyth: Cymdeithas Lyfrau Ceredigion, 2007)

Jenkins, G., *Crefftwyr Gwlad* (Llandysul: Gomer, 1971)

Jepson, P., and Blythe, C., *Rewilding: The Radical New Science of Ecological Recovery* (London: Icon, 2020)

Johnson, D., *Pen and Plough: 20th Century Poets and Bards of Ceredigion* (Llanrwst: Carreg Gwalch, 2016)

Johnston, D., *Iaith Oleulawn* (Cardiff: University of Wales Press, 2020)

Jones, E., *The War of the Little Englishman* (Talybont: Y Lolfa, 2007)

Jones, L., *Losing Eden: Why Our Minds Need the Wild* (London: Penguin, 2020)

June, L., *Architects of Abundance: Indigenous Regenerative Food and Land Management Systems and the Excavation of Hidden History* (Fairbanks: University of Alaska, 2022)

Kimmerer, R. W., *Braiding Sweetgrass* (London: Penguin, 2013)

La Trobe-Bateman, E., 'Snowdonia's early fieldscapes' (PhD thesis, University of Sheffield, 2020)

Leech, Alan, and Leech, Sally, *Struggle for Survival in the Cardiganshire Hills* (Talybont: Y Lolfa, 2009)

Lefebvre, D., et al., 'Assessing the carbon capture potential of a reforestation project', *Scientific Reports*, 11/19907 (2021), *https://doi. org/10.1038/s41598-021-99395-6* (accessed 9 November 2023)

Leterme, E., *La biodiversité, amie du verger* (Arles: Rouergue, 2014)

Lewis, Gwyneth and Williams, Rowan (eds), *The Book of Taliesin* (London: Penguin, 2019)

Lilley, M., *Hunters, Fishers and Foragers in Wales* (Oxford: Oxbow Books, 2015)

Linnard, W., *Welsh Woods and Forests* (Llandysul: Gomer, 2000)

Llwyd o'r Bryn, *Y Pethe* (Y Bala: Gwasg y Bala, 1955)

Llywelyn, D., *Sacred Place, Chosen People* (Cardiff: University of Wales Press, 1999)

Ludovic, O., 'The first aurochs genome reveals the breeding history of British and European cattle', *Genome Biology*, 16/225 (26 October 2015), *doi: 10.1186/s13059-015-0793-z*

Macdonald, B., *Cornerstones* (London: Bloomsbury, 2002)

Magan, M., *Thirty-Two Words for Field* (Dublin: Gill, 2020)

Mair, Bethan (ed.), *Hoff Gerddi Natur Cymru* (Llandysul: Gomer, 2011)

Mitchell, F., and Ryan, M., *Reading the Irish Landscape* (Dublin: Townhouse, 2001)

Monbiot, G., *Regenesis* (London: Penguin, 2022)

Monbiot, G., *Feral* (London: Penguin, 2014)

Moore, P. D., and Chater, E. H., 'The Changing Vegetation of West-Central Wales in the Light of Human History', *Journal of Ecology*, 57/2 (1969), 361–79

Moore-Colyer, R. J., 'Agriculture and Land Occupation', in G. H. Jenkins and I. G. Jones (eds), *Cardiganshire County History, vol. 3* (Cardiff: University of Wales Press, 1998)

Morgan, G., *Ceredigion: A Wealth of History* (Llandysul: Gomer, 2005)

Morris, J., *The Matter of Wales* (London: Penguin, 1984)

Mullard, J., *Pembrokeshire* (London: Collins, 2020)

Mullard, J., *Gower* (London: Collins, 2006)

Neil, S. et al., 'Land use and mobility during the Neolithic in Wales explored using isotope analysis of tooth enamel', *American Journal of Physical Anthropology*, 164/2 (2017), 371–93, *https://doi.org/10.1002/ajpa.23279* (accessed 9 November 2023)

Nunn, P., *The Edge of Memory: Ancient Stories, Oral Tradition and the Post-Glacial World* (London: Bloomsbury, 2018)

O'Brien, C., *Life in Ireland* (Newbridge: Merrion, 2021)

Oram, S., Alexander, L., and Sadler, E., 'Traditional Orchard Habitat Inventory of Wales', Natural Resources Wales Evidence Report No. 18 (2014)

'Our vanishing flora – how wild flowers are disappearing across Britain', Plantlife (2012)

Owen, Ann Parry (ed.), *Geirfâu'r Fflyd, 1632–1633: Casgliad John Jones, Gellilyfdy o eiriau'r cartref, creffiau, amaeth a byd natur* (Caerdydd: University of Wales Press, 2023)

Owen, D., *A Wilder Wales* (Cardigan: Parthian, 2017)

Parry, Rh., *Cerdded y Caeau* (Talybont: Y Lolfa, 2022)

Patterson, N. et al., 'Large-scale migration into Britain during the Middle to Late Bronze Age', *Nature*, 601 (2022), 588–94

Payne, Ff., *Cwysau* (Llandysul: Gomer, 1980)

Payne, Ff., *Yr Aradr Gymreig* (Caerdydd: University of Wales Press, 1975)

Payne, Ff., *Crwydro Sir Faesyfed* (Llandybïe: Llyfrau'r Dryw, 1968)

Pearce, F., *A Trillion Trees: How We Can Reforest Our World* (London: Granta, 2021)

Peate, I., *Diwylliant Gwerin Cymru* (Dinbych: Gwasg Gee, 1975)

Perrin, J., *Rivers of Wales* (Llanrwst: Carreg Gwalch, 2022)

Perrin, J., *Snowdon* (Llanrwst: Carreg Gwalch, 2018)

Perrin, J., *The Hills of Wales* (Llanrwst: Carreg Gwalch, 2016)

Proulx, A., *Fen, Bog and Swamp* (London: HarperCollins, 2022)

Pryce, H., *Writing Welsh History: From the Early Middle Ages to the Twenty-First Century* (Oxford: Oxford University Press, 2022)

Pryor, F., *Scenes from Prehistoric Life* (London: Head of Zeus, 2021)

Pryor, F., *The Making of the British Landscape* (London: Penguin, 2011)

Rackham, O., *Ancient Woodlands of South-east Wales* (Dorset: Little Toller, 2022)

Rackham, O., *The History of the Countryside* (London: Weidenfeld and Nicholson, 2020)

Rackham, O., *Woodlands* (London: William Collins, 2015)

Rédei, Tamás et al., 'Plantation forests cannot support the richness of forest specialist plants in the forest-steppe zone', *Forest Ecology and Management*, 461 (2020), 117964, *https://doi.org/10.1016/j.foreco.2020.117964* (accessed 9 November 2023)

Rees, E. A., *A Life of Guto'r Glyn* (Talybont: Y Lolfa, 2008)

Richards, G. M., '*ffridd/ffrith* as a Welsh place-name', *Studia Celtica* (1967), 2, 29–90

Richardson, F., 'The enclosure of the commons and wastes in Nantconwy, North Wales, 1540 to 1900', *Agricultural History Review*, 65/1 (2017)

Rieley, J. O. et al., 'The Ecological Role of Bryophytes in a North Wales Woodland', *Journal of Ecology*, 67/2 (1979), 497–527, *https://doi.org/10.2307/2259109* (accessed 14 January 2023)

Rose, Francis, 'Ancient British woodlands and their epiphytes', *British Wildlife*, 5 (1993), 83–93

Ross, A., *Folklore of Wales* (Stroud: The History Press, 2011)

Russell, M., and Laycock, S., *UnRoman Britain: Exposing the Great Myth of Britannia* (Cheltenham: The History Press, 2019)

Saladino, D., *Eating to Extinction* (London: Jonathan Cape, 2021)

Sandom, C. J. et al., 'High herbivore density associated with vegetation diversity in interglacial ecosystems', *Proc Natl Acad Sci U S A*, 111/11 (2014), 4162–7

Schama, S., *Landscape and Memory* (London: HarperCollins, 1995)

Schofield, L., *Wild Fell* (London: Penguin, 2022)

Shrubsole, G., *The Lost Rainforests of Britain* (London: William Collins, 2022)

Smaje, C., *Saying NO to a Farm-Free Future* (London: Chelsea Green, 2023)

Smaje, C., *A Small-Farm Future* (London: Chelsea Green, 2020)

Smart, M. J., and Winnall, R. A., 'The biodiversity of three traditional orchards within the Wyre Forest SSSI in Worcestershire: a survey by the Wyre Forest Study Group', *English Nature Research Reports*, 707 (2006)

Smil, V., *How the World Really Works* (London: Viking, 2022)

Smout, T. C., *People and Woods in Scotland: a History* (Edinburgh: Edinburgh University Press, 2012)

Stevens, M., *The Economy of Medieval Wales* (Cardiff: University of Wales Press, 2019)

Sylvester, D., 'The Common Fields of the Coastlands of Gwent', *Agricultural History Review*, 6/1 (1958)

Thirsk, J., *Alternative Agriculture* (Oxford: Oxford University Press, 1997)

Thirsk, J. (ed.), *The Agrarian History of England and Wales: Vol. 4* (Cambridge: Cambridge University Press, 1967)

Thirsk, J., and Piggot, S. (eds), *The Agrarian History of England and Wales: Vol. 1* (Cambridge: Cambridge University Press, 2011)

Thomas, D., *Cau'r Tiroedd Comin* (Lerpwl: Gwasg y Brython, 1952)

Thompson, T., 'Agriculture and Change in a Nineteenth Century Radnorshire Valley', *Radnorshire Society Transactions*, 69 (1999)

Tinsley-Marshall, P., Skilbeck, A., and Riggs, A., 'Monitoring of ecosystem function at landscape-scale demonstrates temporal difference in invertebrate abundance in Kent and South-East England', *www.kentwildlifetrust.org.uk/sites/default/files/2020-02/Bugs%20Matter%20report%20website%20version.pdf* (accessed 9 November 2023)

Tree, I., *Wilding* (London: Picador, 2018)

Vervust, S. et al., 'Optically stimulated luminescence profiling and dating of earthworks: The creation and development of prehistoric field boundaries at Bosigran, Cornwall', *Antiquity*, 94/374 (2020), 420–36, *doi: 10.15184/aqy.2019.138*

Warwick, H., *Linescapes* (London: Vintage, 2018)

Williams, Alun Llywelyn, *Crwydro Arfon* (Llandybïe: Llyfrau'r Dryw, 1959)

Williams-Davies, J., *Cider Making in Wales* (Cardiff: National Museum of Wales, 1984)

Wright, J., *A Natural History of the Hedgerow* (London: Profile, 2016)

Wynne-Jones, S., Strouts, G., and Holmes, G., 'Abandoning or Reimagining a Cultural Heartland? Understanding and Responding to Rewilding Conflicts in Wales – the Case of the Cambrian Wildwood', *Environmental Values*, 27/4 (2018)

Yeo, M. J. M., and Blackstock, T. H., 'A vegetation analysis of the pastoral landscapes of upland Wales, UK', *Journal of Vegetation Science*, 13 (2002), 803–16, *https://doi.org/10.1111/j.1654-1103.2002.tb02110.x* (accessed 9 November 2023)

Yunkaporta, Tyson, *Sand Talk: How Indigenous Thinking Can Save the World* (New York: HarperOne, 2020)

Zanette, Liana Y. and Clinchy, Michael, 'Ecology of fear', *Current Biology*, 29/9 (2019), pp. R309–R313